Cross-Cultural Approaches to Adoption

Adoption is currently subject to a great deal of media scrutiny. High-profile cases of international adoption via the internet and other unofficial routes have drawn attention to the relative ease with which children can be obtained on the global circuit, and have brought about legislation which regulates the exchange of children within and between countries. However, a scarcity of research into cross-cultural attitudes to child-rearing, and a wider lack of awareness of cultural difference in adoptive contexts, has meant that the assumptions underlying Western childcare policy are seldom examined or made explicit. The articles in *Cross-Cultural Approaches to Adoption* look at adoption practices from Africa, Oceania, Asia, South and Central America, including examples of societies in which children are routinely separated from their biological parents or passed through several foster families. Showing the range and flexibility of the child-rearing practices that approximate to the Western term 'adoption', they demonstrate the benefits of a cross-cultural appreciation of family life, and allow a broader understanding of the varied relationships that exist between children and adoptive parents.

Fiona Bowie is Senior Lecturer and Head of Anthropology at the University of Bristol. Her books include *The Anthropology of Religion: An Introduction*.

D1569304

European Association of Social Anthropologists

Series Facilitator: Sarah Pink, *University of Loughborough*

The European Association of Social Anthropologists (EASA) was inaugurated in January 1989, in response to a widely felt need for a professional association that would represent social anthropologists in Europe and foster co-operation and interchange in teaching and research. The Series brings together the work of the Association's members in a series of edited volumes which originate from and expand upon the biennial EASA Conference.

Titles in the series are:

Cross-Cultural Approaches to Adoption

Edited by Fiona Bowie

Routledge
Taylor & Francis Group

LONDON AND NEW YORK

First published 2004
by Routledge
2 Park Square, Milton Park, Abingdon,
Oxfordshire OX14 4RN

Simultaneously published in the USA and Canada
by Routledge
270 Madison Ave, New York, NY 10016

Routledge is an imprint of the Taylor & Francis Group

Typeset in Galliard by Keystroke, Jacaranda Lodge, Wolverhampton
Printed and bound in Great Britain by Biddles Ltd, King's Lynn

British Library Cataloguing in Publication Data
A catalogue record for this book is available from the British Library

Library of Congress Cataloging in Publication Data
A catalog record for this book has been requested

ISBN 0–415–30350–8 (hbk)
ISBN 0–415–30351–6 (pbk)

Jonathan Robert Telfer
8 December 1953–22 September 2002

This book is dedicated to the memory of Jon Telfer, one of the stalwart participants at a panel on Cross-cultural Approaches to Adoption at the meeting of the European Association of Social Anthropologists in Krakow, Poland, in July 2000, and contributor to this volume. He was active on the international conference circuit, contributing his own research on adoption issues, and doing creative and innovative work on, among other things, topics related to adoption and gender. As the adoptive father of two Korean daughters, Kristin and Mikella, Jon and his wife Julie had first-hand experience of cross-cultural issues in adoption. He was also a long-serving probation officer, both in front-line work and in staff development and training.

Of his own experience of parenthood, Jon wrote:

> After assuming the role of clients at the mercy of social workers and government policy (which changed us enormously, personally and professionally) we adopted our two daughters from Korea (which also changed us enormously, personally and professionally). . . . What followed was another extraordinary journey of cross-cultural transition by immersion learning – as we made tangible our commitment to our increasing cognizance of our inter-country, adoptive, parental duties and responsibilities.

Jon wrote about cross-cultural issues in adoption because they mattered to him, intellectually and personally, just as they touch the lives of millions of others. Our hope is that the varied perspectives and insights presented in this volume, drawing on data from many societies around the world, will also lead readers on their own cross-cultural journeys of understanding.

Contents

Illustrations

Figures

Tables

Contributors

Erdmute Alber is Junior Professor of Anthropology at the University of Bayreuth, Germany.

Astrid Anderson is a Postdoctoral Fellow at the University Museum of Cultural Heritage, University of Oslo, Norway.

Fiona Bowie is Senior Lecturer in Anthropology at the University of Bristol, UK.

Melissa Demian teaches Anthropology at Rutgers and New School University in the USA.

Claudia Fonseca is Professor of Anthropology at the Federal University of Rio Grande do Sul, Brazil.

Ernst Halbmayer is a member of the Commission for Social Anthropology of the Austrian Academy of Sciences and Lecturer at the University of Vienna.

Signe Howell is Professor of Anthropology at the University of Oslo, Norway.

Godula Kosack teaches Anthropology at the University of Marburg, Germany.

Esben Leifsen is a research fellow at the Department of Social Anthropology at the University of Oslo, currently writing a Ph.D. on abandonment and adoption in Ecuador.

Catrien Notermans is lecturer and senior researcher in the Department of Cultural Anthropology at the Radboud University Nijmegen, the Netherlands.

Inge Roesch-Rhomberg has taught at the universities of Heidelberg and the Free University, Berlin (Germany). She currently works as a freelance ethnographer and lives in Chile.

Peter Selman is Reader in Social Policy in the School of Geography, Politics and Sociology at the University of Newcastle, UK.

Aud Talle is Professor of Social Anthropology at the University of Oslo, Norway.

Jon Telfer taught Anthropology at the University of Adelaide and the University of South Australia.

Dietrich Treide is Emeritus Professor of Ethnology and former Head of the Institute for Ethnology at the University of Leipzig, Germany.

Huon Wardle lectures in Social Anthropology at the University of St Andrews, Scotland.

Barbara Yngvesson is Professor of Anthropology in the School of Social Science at Hampshire College, Amherst, Massachusetts, USA.

Preface

The chapters presented in this volume were, for the most part, first presented at a panel on Cross-cultural Approaches to Adoption at the 2000 meeting of the European Association of Social Anthropologists in Krakow, Poland. As an anthropologist and an adoptive parent I wanted to place the culturally rather unusual attitudes to adoption and the 'natural family' that dominate in Britain, and in Western countries more generally, in a broader context. I was aware of other anthropologists who had adopted children, domestically, transracially and often internationally. All were active in promoting the cultural heritage and identity of their adopted children. I was also aware from living in Cameroon, Africa, that other cultures do things very differently. Growing up with your biological parents is not necessarily all that common, and may not even be considered desirable. Who are considered family and kin is also culturally variable. The call for papers produced a fascinating spread of work and depth of expertise on a wide range of societies in different parts of the world. Almost all the data is based on original fieldwork and an understanding of the issues 'on the ground', as they are interpreted and lived by ordinary people. Global factors, such as Western attitudes to the nuclear family and the market created by international adoptions are seen to impinge on many societies, and there is always a process of change and transformation in ideal and practice. Although most chapters focus on the circulation of children, adults too may be adopted, and there are examples of such practices and the rationale for them in some of the contributions.

I would like to thank the EASA publications committee, the editors at Routledge, and all those who have contributed to making this book such a valuable addition to the field of adoption and of kinship studies.

Fiona Bowie
Bristol, January 2004

Glossary of anthropological terms

adrogation The term given in Roman law to the adoption of a person by his or her master.

affine *Consanguinial* (blood) relative of one's spouse; person in a 'marriageable' category. Relative through marriage.

agnate; agnatic Patrilateral kin, related on the father's side; descent traced through the patriline.

bilateral descent; double descent Group membership determined by relations traced through either or both parental lines.

brideprice; bridewealth Goods or money payable by a man or his kin to his wife or her kin on marriage (often a process over several episodes rather than a single event). The payment of brideprice is often seen to 'cement' a marital relationship, because if a woman leaves her husband some or all of the brideprice may need to be returned.

clan A *unilineal* descent group (tracing relations through either males or females but not both), often with a common name or purported ancestor. Clans may be exogamous.

complementary filiation In *unilineal* descent systems, the process by which links are created between a child and 'unrelated' descent group, i.e. that of the mother in a *patrilineal* descent system and of the father in a *matrilineal* descent system.

consanguine Biological ('blood') relative; relations assumed to be based on shared biological kinship; kin as opposed to *affines* (i.e. non-marriageable as opposed to marriageable).

cross-cousin Father's sister's child or mother's brother's child, i.e. children of opposite-sex siblings.

degrees of kinship The number of genealogical links between relatives.

Ego Point of reference in kinship diagram or description.

emic Insider viewpoint.

endogamy Marriage within one's group (however defined), as opposed to marriage outside one's group, *exogamy*.

ethnic group People sharing common attributes (such as language, culture, religion, territory, history). The term is to be understood in a relational rather than essentialist manner. It is commonly used to substitute for the older term 'tribe' in order to get away from notions of biological and cultural fixity.

ethnography The systematic description of a single (usually) contemporary culture, group or place, normally by means of *fieldwork*.

etic An outsider, usually 'academic' perspective.

exogamy Marriage outside one's group (however defined), as opposed to marriage within the group, *endogamy*.

fieldwork The process of extended participant observation in a place or with a group of people that constitutes the primary anthropological method of gathering data.

genetrix Biological mother of a child, as opposed to the social mother (*mater*).

genitor Biological father of a child, as opposed to the social father (*pater*).

levirate Rule requiring a widow to marry her dead husband's brother.

matricentric; matrifocal Kinship or social relationships centred or focused on the mother, or on women.

matrilineal Descent traced through women. There may be an eponymous (named) ancestor.

moitity The division of a society into two descent groups with complementary social and religious roles, which may act as *exogamous* exchange groups.

parallel-cousin Father's brother's child or mother's sister's child, i.e. children of same-sex siblings.

patricentric; patrifocal Kinship or social relations centred or focused on the father, or on men.

patrilineal Descent traced through men.

polyandry Marriage to more than one man. Less common than *polygyny*, marriage to more than one woman.

polygamy Marriage to more than one man or woman at the same time.

polygyny Marriage to more than one woman. Sometimes referred to as *polygamy*.

sororal marriage; sororate Marriage to deceased wife's sister, as opposed to the *levirate*, marriage to dead husband's brother.

unilineal descent Group membership determined by relations traced through a single parental line, *matrilineal* (through women), or *patrilineal* (through men).

uxorilocal residence; matrilocal residence   Residence with or near the wife's kin after marriage.

virilocal residence; patrilocal residence   Residence with or near the husband's kin after marriage.

Kinship abbreviations and symbols

Mother	M	Father	F
Brother	B	Sister	Z
Daughter	D	Son	S
Husband	H	Wife	W
Father's father (paternal grandfather)	FF	Mother's mother (maternal grandmother)	MM
Father's mother (paternal grandmother)	FM	Mother's father (maternal grandfather)	MF
Mother's brother's son/daughter (matrilateral cross-cousin)	MBS/D	Father's sister's son/daughter (patrilateral cross-cousin)	FZS/D
Mother's sister's son/daughter (matrilateral parallel-cousin)	MZS/D	Father's brother's son/daughter (patrilateral parallel-cousin)	FBS/D
elder	e	younger	y
Reference point	Ego	Deceased	▲
Female	○	Male	△
Marriage	=	Divorce	≠

Introduction

Chapter 1

Adoption and the circulation of children
A comparative perspective

Fiona Bowie

Adoption is one of Western society's best kept secrets. Many people in the United Kingdom have direct experience of adoption, or know someone who has, but it remains relatively invisible. The ideal of the nuclear family, in which natal and social parents are one and the same, is so strongly reinforced that instances of children raised by non-biogenetic parents are masked or denied.[1] Families may be regarded as 'making the best' of a situation, compensating for the inability of a biological mother to raise her child or children. Despite the numbers of children waiting in the care system for new homes, the United Kingdom struggles with an 'anti-adoption' culture, or at least a profound ambivalence towards adoption.[2]

It is so self-evident to most people in Euro-American society that children should be raised by their 'natural' parents that it might come as a surprise to learn that this is not always and everywhere the case. It is not only the lay public who are guilty of viewing others through the lens of their own culture. Many anthropological and sociological studies illustrate the tenuous relationship a presumed biological father or *genitor* may have with his children,[3] but an ethnocentric (and patriarchal) bias in kinship studies has ensured that 'anthropologists have not paid any attention to the possibility that various rights and duties, which are normally associated with motherhood in Western Society, may also be separated and assigned to different people' (Holy 1996: 34). In fact, to share or reassign maternal responsibilities emerges as a relatively common strategy in many societies, by no means always arising from necessity (poverty or redressing childlessness in others). In parts of South East Asia, for instance, it is the household and perpetuation of the House (its name, associations and relationships as well as physical presence) that forms the basis of social groups. Eating and living together constructs kinship relations in the way that real or imagined biological connections do in the West.[4] In many societies, from Latin America to Africa and Asia, the lineage or 'clan' may assume 'ownership' of children, and various strategies are employed to circulate or to keep children within a lineage. In other instances adoption and fosterage are used to form alliances between groups, and even enemies, as illustrated by Halbmayer's study of Carib-speaking groups in Amazonia (Chapter 10).

Adoption and fostering have a long history in Western Europe, and were not always considered as negatively as at present. Fostering was a common institution among the Celts of Britain and Ireland, particularly among wealthier families who exchanged children to foster political links.[5] The adoption of an heir, usually a son, to inherit an estate or to perform rituals on behalf of his adoptive father was recorded in classical Rome and Greece, and remained a common and acceptable reason for adoption in Europe well into the twentieth century. The land-owning classes would regularly put their babies out to wet nurses in Early Modern England,[6] and might not see them at all during what are now thought of as the crucial early years of bonding. Poorer children became indentured servants or farm workers, a practice that continued in some forms up until the 1950s with the sending of 'orphaned' children to the colonies, supposedly to a better life, but all too often to servitude.[7]

The importance given in parts of the Mediterranean to godparent-hood (*compadrazgo*), in which godparents of superior social status are selected to act as sponsors and extended kin to their godchildren, has been described by anthropologists as 'fictive kinship'. Those involved, however, do not differentiate in this way between biological and social or spiritual kin, and the distinction between 'real' (biological) and 'fictive' (spiritual) kin owes more to Western academic models based on the primacy of genetic kinship than they do to indigenous or emic categories of relationship.[8]

There are societies in which adoption is not only common, but an essential and often preferred means of raising children. Virtually all the contributors to this volume report that, whether or not it is immediately visible, the practice of circulating children to be raised by non-biogenetic parents is ubiquitous. Melissa Demian says of a Southern Massim society in Papua New Guinea that 'nearly every household in both of the Suau villages in which I have worked have adopted a person into or out of one of their generations' (Chapter 7), and Astrid Anderson writes of Wogeo Island, also in Papua New Guinea, that 'In some villages as many as half of the inhabitants are adopted' (Chapter 8). The picture is similar for Africa. Catrien Notermans in East Cameroon (Chapter 4) noted that around 30 per cent of children between ten and fourteen do not live with their biological parents, and that most children have spent at least some of their childhood in one or more different 'foster' homes. From her study of the Baatombu in Benin, Erdmute Alber (Chapter 3), reports that among more than 150 older people she spoke to only two had stayed their whole childhood with their biological parents. For the Baatombu, as for the inhabitants of Wogeo Island, adoption or fostering is a preferred means of raising chldren, certainly not a stigmatised second-best.

While adoption is often between specified categories of kin, this is not always the case. Huon Wardle in Jamaica (Chapter 13) and Claudia Fonseca in Brazil (Chapter 11) found that poor families might use unrelated foster parents or institutions to help bring up their children, and Dietrich Treide, in his study of adoption on Yap in Micronesia (Chapter 9), reports cases of the adoption of non-Yapese as a way of gaining rights to land, alongside familial adoption. Among the Yap, as in other societies, adults may also be adopted to look after elderly folk. While adoption is normally described as a form of filiation (creating parent–child links), Ernst Halbmayer describes cases of affinal adoption among Carib-speaking peoples in South America, a practice also reported from China.[9] As these examples illustrate, the interests of children or desires of adoptive parents are not the only motives for circulating people between families and social groups.

Terminology

In Western societies the term 'adoption' is conventionally used for the transference of full parental rights from birth to social parents, in contrast to fostering, in which only a partial transfer occurs. Even in Western societies this legal framework resembles a continuum rather than absolute contrast. At one end we have the, now rare, closed adoptions in which the birth parents are legally and socially (if not emotionally) erased from the record and the adoptee may not be aware that they are not the natural child of the adoptive parents. At the other end of the continuum are open adoptions in which the child retains one or more names, and maintains regular contact with birth relatives. Most Euro-American adoptions fall somewhere between these two extremes. Adoptive parents are discouraged from changing the 'given' or first name, by which the child was previously known, and are likely to have some type of direct or indirect contact with birth family members (often via an adoption agency or local authority 'post box'). The emotional bonds with foster children may be as strong as those with adopted children and, at least in the UK, potential adopters generally foster the children placed with them for months or years before an adoption order is granted by the courts, during which time their parental rights are limited, even though their emotional commitment is expected to be total.[10] When we come to apply these terms cross-culturally we encounter further difficulties. Not only are the legal frameworks and cultural understandings of parenthood different, but the terms 'parent' and 'child' themselves are not necessarily translatable, or may be have very different resonances (Goody 1976).

The current Western legal framework does not allow for the adoption of affines (potential spouses), of adults, or posthumous adoption, being concerned with the transference of children from birth families deemed unable to care for their offspring to foster or adoptive families, or institutional settings, in which that care can take place. Inheritance and the performance of religious duties, rights in land, absorption into a particular descent group, the formation of strategic alliances or the politics of marriage that dictate bringing 'ones own' (foster/adopted) children into the household, are all outside the purview of Western understandings. The terms 'adoption' and 'fostering' are necessarily used in different ways by different authors as they try to convey indigenous cultural practices using inadequate terminology. Rather than expend energy determining the most appropriate term, contributors have focused on trying to convey the variety of ways in which societies exchange, circulate, give and receive children (and sometimes adults), and the values attached to these movements.

Comparative issues

A cross-cultural approach to adoption throws new light on a number of interrelated issues pertinent to both kinship studies within anthropology and policy questions in the field of substitute childcare. These include:

- Definitions of 'the family'
- Biological versus social parenthood
- The desirability of substitute parenthood
- The formation of familial relationships
- Identity issues
- International adoption and the commodification of children.

I will deal with each of these briefly in turn.

Definitions of 'the family'

We often hear from conservative politicians and religious leaders that the (nuclear) family is the bedrock of society, while the demise of the extended family is bemoaned. In the face of historical and cultural evidence to the contrary, the family is presented as an enduring, if threatened, universal and divinely ordained institution. Consanguinity or biogenetic relations play a particularly salient part in Western notions of kinship. As David Schneider observed, the idiom of 'blood' or shared biogenetic inheritance is central to our notions of family and kin: 'The fact that the relationship of blood cannot be ended or altered and that it is a state of almost mystical commonality and identity is . . . quite explicit in American culture' (1968: 25).[11]

Anthropologists studying kinship relations in other societies moved from the fact that (at least until modern reproductive technology arrived) it takes a man and a woman to produce a child, to the assumption that this unit is the legitimate basis of subsequent relationships. In Western societies the genetrix and genitor (the biological mother and father) should also be married, and children that fall outside that legal relationship are regarded as illegitimate (although this is not in itself seen as a reason to surrender a child for adoption as was the case thirty or forty years ago). This cultural bias was transposed to other societies, where it was assumed that similar distinctions would also be made.[12] That this is not the case was evident from the ethnographic record. Evans-Pritchard's extensive work on the Nuer in East Africa included descriptions of woman–woman marriages, in which both the 'female husband' who was recognised as a child's pater or social father, and the biological father or genitor had recognised obligations and roles (1951). A similar form of woman–woman marriage was practised among the Bangwa in Cameroon (Brain 1972). The titled sister (or half-sister) of a chief or *fon*, known as the *mafwa*, could take wives of her own and become pater to the woman's children, thus avoiding status conflict inherent in her high social position as *mafwa* and loss of power and control as someone else's wife. Such cultural practices foreshadow some of the current debates surrounding the prospect of human cloning, and the already common reproductive technologies that enable us to separate the roles of genetic parent, carrying parent and social parent. We have not yet, however, reached the stage of acknowledging all those who contribute to a child as equally valid constitutive parts of who and what they are, or sought to maintain simultaneous relationships between all those constituent parts.

Societies vary from those in which kinship relations are even more atomised and individualistic than in Euro-American culture to those in which the lineage or descent group, rights over certain lands, or the possession of certain names, take precedence over any notion of the individual. In Wardle's description of Kingston, Jamaica (Chapter 13), the family is described as a 'dynamic equilibrium' with the emphasis on the dynamism, and 'the accumulation and dispersal of new family members through fostering/adoption' as one factor in a 'typical family flux'. Whereas Macfarlane (1980) sees English individualism as modelled on the triadic nuclear family, Wardle follows Gonzalez (1984) in understanding Creole kinship as composed of overlapping dyads – child–mother, child–auntie, child–grandmother, and so on – where the strongest child-focused relationships are almost invariably with women. In Aud Talle's description of the pastoral Maasai of East Africa (Chapter 5), by contrast, we see a society based on cattle-owning patrilineages and household groups. Children circulate not in the individualistic actor-oriented manner of the West Indies, but in order to ensure that the presence of children within households remains 'in balance'. Inge Roesch-Rhomberg (Chapter 6) describes a kinship structure in Korea rooted in patrilineal exogamous clans into which wives are incorporated. The clan takes precedence over individual needs, and adoption of an agnate of descending generational level is often necessary to perpetuate a patriline and ensure that ritual obligations are met. Adoption is lineage and not child-centred, often involves adults, including married couples, and may well be posthumous (the adoptive father having already died).

Some societies combine individualism with lineage-based concerns. In parts of West Africa the nuclear family as a concept has little resonance, even in populations who declare themselves Christian. Notermans (Chapter 4) gives an example from the Batouri area of East Cameroon, traditionally considered patrilineal, in which women usually submit to at least one formal marriage, but form only very weak alliances with their husbands. Instead they concentrate on building up 'their' families, by which they mean that of their matrilineage, through the maintenance of ties with matri-kin, including adopted matrilineal relatives – the only children they consider 'theirs'. Maternal grandmothers will resort to a number of measures to incorporate grandchildren into the matrilineage, including the creation of birth certificates that name a matrilineal relative as a child's father, irrespective of the identity of the actual *genitor*, or destruction of birth certificates that name a daughter's legitimate husband as the grandchild's father. Effort expended bringing up biological children who will be 'lost' to a husband's matriline, or looking after a husband's foster/adopted children, is considered 'time wasted', and on divorce a woman may seek financial compensation for this wasted time and effort. This and other examples of purportedly patrilineal, male-centred societies in Africa, indicate that by focusing on female strategies and the movement of children the importance of matrilines emerges as an alternative to or in addition to patrilines.

Biological versus social parenthood

In Western discourse the terms 'real' and 'natural' are often prefixed to 'parents' to refer to the birth parents of a child. The power of the blood relationship is sometimes seen as so strong that an attraction is inevitable, and potentially dangerous for the adoptive relationship (as Jon Telfer describes in Chapter 16). The pain of birth mothers who have given up children is often described in terms of having lost 'part of themselves', leaving a hole that can never be filled. One of the culturally created problems in Euro-American adoption is the 'either/or' premise on which it is based, combined with, and part of, our fixation on biological relatedness. The full force of the law is used to persuade adoptive parents that they do indeed become the legal mother and father of the child, and to ensure that adopted children are treated as if they had been born to their substitute family (Modell 1994).

The biological/social distinction is mirrored differently in other societies, not so much in terms of giving more weight to one end of the spectrum or another, but in removing the binary 'either/or' part of the equation. By using an additive rather than substitutive model of parenthood, it is possible to have both biological and social relatives in the frame simultaneously. Adoptive parenthood can be 'real' without replacing or denying biological parenthood, and without being threatened by it. The Baatombu in Northern Benin do not have terms for biological or social parents, and the term for 'giving birth' is used by both natal and adoptive parents when speaking about 'their child' (Alber, Chapter 3). The families studied by Claudia Fonseca (Chapter 11) in a poor neighbourhood of Porto Alegre in the south of Brazil combined a belief in the indissolubility of blood ties with the notion that 'mother is whoever brings you up'. New mothers do not cancel out old ones, and can indeed be multiplied. In one instance a woman left her two-week-old daughter in the care of a neighbour as she wanted to spend the weekend at the beach. The babysitter called her sister to wet-nurse the baby. Eight years later this triangular relationship between the three women still continued, and the child proclaimed proudly that she had three mothers, 'the mother who nursed me, the mother who raised me and the mother who gave birth to me'. The Mafa girl from Northern Cameroon given to Godula Kosack (Chapter 2) could similarly claim three mothers: her Mafa mother (who had died giving birth), the anthropologist who was given the child to take to Europe, and the adoptive mother in Switzerland who raised her.

Melissa Demian's work in Papua New Guinea (Chapter 7) also shows how narrowly conceived Euro-American notions of biological versus social parenthood are. In some cases an adoptee moves not just from one nuclear household to another but from one clan or lineage to another, with all that this implies for a shift in wider social relationships; in other cases the adoptee may be transferred to another household but remain in the same lineage. In Demian's fieldwork area of Suau, adoptees maintain obligations to both adoptive and natal parents, and adoptions are more likely where the distance between the two is not too great. The social parents do not replace the birth parents, but become another constituent in the complex of relationships that compose the individual child.

The desirability of substitute parenthood

In his study of adoption in Micronesia, Treide (Chapter 9) notes several characteristics that stand in contrast to Euro-American adoptions (quoting Brady 1976). These include the relative frequency (or visibility) of adoption, its place in systems of exchange, the reversibility of the relationship if obligations are not met, and the traditionally high regard for adopted children. Western adoptions are characterised as relatively rare (ideally if not in practice), held in low esteem (with adopted children often from 'the edge' of society), with asymmetric relationships between adopters and birth parents, and entailing disruption in the biography of adopted children. The title of David Kirk's (1984) classic *Shared Fate* sums up the place of adoption in Western societies. Adoption is the happy ending, at least for children in need of care and parents in need of children, born out of shared misfortune (abandonment, abuse and neglect on the one side and infertility and the wish to parent on the other). In fact, in the United Kingdom, most adoptions are of step children (until recently a biological mother also had to adopt her own children along with the step father). Around half of 'stranger' adoptions involve couples or individuals who already have biological children,[13] and altruism on the part of adoptive families is perhaps underplayed. Nevertheless, adoption is generally perceived as second-best, and all members of the 'adoption triad' are likely to experience a degree of stigmatisation. In societies in which adoption is part of a wider system of relationships, it may be the preferred means of bringing up children. The Baatombu of Benin seek to make the biological bond between child and parents as invisible as possible. Children are precious but are claimed by others, and it is the social rather than biological parents who are considered most suitable to educate and raise children (Alber, Chapter 3). Children are claimed before they are considered 'knowing' and it is not thought to harm them in any way to leave their natal families.[14] In many African societies, as elsewhere in the world, to refuse to give a child to someone who has a culturally validated right to ask for it is considered selfish and morally blameworthy. Children may be circulated between co-wives, as among the Maasai (Talle, Chapter 5), exchanged between brothers and sisters, or claimed by various categories of patrilineal or matrilineal kin, depending on the society in question. Relations may be asymmetric in terms of wealth, with children moving from poorer to wealthier homes, or between generations, with grandparents or adoptive grandparents claiming children of their sons or daughters; relations may be friendly, or hostile, as in parts of Lowland South America where the children of murdered enemies are commonly adopted (Halbmayer, Chapter 10). What we do not find, in most instances, is that adoption is regarded as undesirable, abnormal, second-best or stigmatised.

The formation of familial relationships

The process of becoming an adoptive family, and the effort involved, has received recent anthropological attention. Telfer (Chapter 16) describes the Quest undertaken by adoptive parents in their search for completeness, which does not end with the legal transfer of parental responsibility. Adoptive parents and their children know all too well that this is the beginning rather than the end of a lengthy journey. Relations have to be created in a process referred to by Signe Howell (Chapter 15) as 'kinning'. The circle of kin spreads outwards from parents and children to other relatives, and kinship is created and reinforced through family events, ritual occasions, visits and the construction of a common family history. This is the case for all children, although the position of adopted children in the wider family may be more tenuous than birth children, and require greater 'kinning' effort.

Researchers in other societies have also noted the work involved in creating an adoptive relationship and the often gradual process by which the family consolidate their status. Halbmayer (Chapter 10) shows how adoption among some Carib-speaking groups in Amazonia does not depend on a formal act of renunciation by birth parents, but a 'continuously ongoing transfer of rights' to the parents who feed and raise the child or children. As in other societies, this is an additive rather than a substitutive relationship, based on a notion of multiple parenthood. Demian (Chapter 7) also notes the importance of work in constructing the adoptive relationship: 'To work on behalf of an adoptee is a significant undertaking, because it is assumed the adoptee will stay with his or her adoptive parents until marriage.' The sign of a successful adoption is a contented and hard-working child. If the adoptee is not happy, there is always the option of returning to the natal parents. Treide (Chapter 9) records that in return for caring for an elderly person or couple, adopted adults in Micronesia can inherit land shares, but that if they fail to meet their obligations they may forfeit the rights acquired through their adopted status (as may birth children in comparable cases).

The individualism characteristic of Caribbean societies encourages children to forge their own relationships with a range of adult carers and potential carers in networks that may extend to the United States and United Kingdom (Wardle, Chapter 13). Fonseca (Chapter 11) notes the 'banality' and ease with which children in southern Brazil find substitute parents. Although not always able to exercise a high degree of agency, many West African children experience one or more moves between carers, often at their own instigation. Whether a relationship is temporary or permanent, and more closely resembles fostering or adoption, may only be determined in retrospect.

Identity issues

Western discourses of the individual, and of individual families, have an essentialising and reductive quality. Our identities and individuality are thought of as bounded but not static. We have a responsibility to ensure that our sense of self becomes rounded, completed, healthy and fixed. We should be comfortable with (or mildly guilty about) our 'race' (read skin-tone), 'culture' (often reduced to crude notions of racial essentialism), class, gender, and so on. This simplistic view of psychology and social relations can lead to various passionately held but partial views concerning such issues as transnational and interracial adoption,[15] relations between the various parties in the 'adoption triad' (birth mother, adopter and adoptee), the suitability of prospective adopters or adoptability of certain categories of children. With a slight shift of focus we can see identity as both more relational and more contextual. Marilyn Strathern argues that in Melanesia social persons are conceived 'as the plural and composite site of the relations that produced them' (1988: 13),[16] whereas Cohen (1994: 45) poses the rhetorical question 'is it really the case that identities can ever be complete or singular, or that they contain some internal essence which defines them for all time, for example as "white" or "black"?' If we see the person and the family as an interplay of history, memory, affective relations, rights and responsibilities, desires and fears, we might move past some of the polarised debates in Western discourses of adoption and identity, and view the individual as embedded in a much wider and more dynamic social framework.

Questions of secrecy or openness in adoption are often linked to identity, with the assumption that you can't know who you are or where you are going if you don't know where you come from.[17] This attitude could be a corrective to the years of secrecy and often shame surrounding adoption and the circumstances leading up to it in Euro-American cultures, rather than a universal assumption. Anderson (Chapter 8) reports that adoption in Wogeo, Papua New Guinea, is used precisely to disguise matrilineal origins, as they are linked to inheritable sorcery. Children are not necessarily told their matrilineal identity. Alber (Chapter 3) records that the Baatombu of Benin do not tell children, usually adopted as infants, who their birth parents are, although some may find out in later life. Birth mothers are expected to find opportunities to give tokens of affection to their children in secret, whereas birth fathers may be particularly unresponsive so as to emphasise the social distance between them and their biological children. Where adoption is ubiquitous, regarded as socially acceptable, even preferable to growing up with birth parents, there will be a different resonance to questions of secrecy and openness to those prevailing in the West.

International adoption and the commodification of children

The ways in which children move not just within but between societies receives attention in several chapters. Whereas in Micronesia international adoptions have made little impact on traditional practices (Treide, Chapter 9), this is not the case in parts of Latin America. Fonseca (Chapter 11) shows how Western standards and practices, combined with an international 'market' in adoptable children, has led to many parents who thought they were using orphanages as a form of temporary foster care losing their children to international adoption. Where cultural misunderstandings can be exploited, and there is money to be made, there will be people willing to take advantage of the situation. Esben Leifsen (Chapter 12), working in Ecuador, documents the willingness of a Spanish state-sponsored adoption agency (which has a monopoly on international adoptions in that part of Spain) to condone illegal means of obtaining children. The motivation may be to speed up an inherently corrupt process, in which children become the pawns of officials who use their position to extract payments, but can also come dangerously close to creating a market in babies whose parents have not given full or adequate consent. Indeed the means by which infants have to be legally and socially 'commodified', that is separated from their previous status before being given a new one, is not necessarily in the best interests of any of the parties involved. Adoption agencies may perpetuate the 'myth of the orphan' and present their services as a solution to Third World poverty, and adoptive parents, through ignorance or a willingness to collude, may fail to ask sufficiently searching questions concerning the adoption process.

While adoption in the West is gradually moving away from the notion of sealed records and a complete break with the past, in the international market the trend is still towards the freeing of infants for placement overseas by severing all links with their natal families (and countries). It is internationally adopted children and their parents who are beginning to question these practices. Barbara Yngvesson (Chapter 14) tells the story of two transnational adoptees brought up in Sweden who returned to Ethiopia to locate their birth families. They were able to integrate being both Swedish and Ethiopian in a way that may well resonate with other transnationally adopted people. As Yngvesson states:

> Rather than a cut-off from the past, adoption is increasingly bringing the past into the present in a multitude of ways, through roots trips to the birth country, reunions between adopters and their birth families, culture camps and language classes for adoptees, and other practices that acknowledge the birth 'identity' of the adopted child.

Yngvesson also looks at a highly regarded project in India that includes day care for children, domestic fostering and adoption, and international placements for children unlikely to find families at home, although these older, handicapped children, or groups of siblings, are not those most desired by the Swedish adoption agency underwriting the project. China has managed to avoid a free international market in children through close regulation of adoptions. The financial payments to orphanages and the exchange of Western expertise in developing foster homes as an alternative to institutionalisation have improved the lot of many thousands of Chinese children abandoned under the 'one child' (or 'one son') policy.

Opinions concerning the desirability of international adoptions are as polarised as those on domestic transracial placements, often focusing on similarly simplistic notions of cultural identity. The best interests of children, let alone of natal families, adopters or of the sending and receiving countries may be hard to determine, and each country and situation deserves individual consideration. Godula Kosack (Chapter 2) says of the Cameroonian girl whose adoption she mediated that she has become a 'real cosmopolitian' attached to her village people in Cameroon while at ease with her Swiss/French parentage. She may face racism, but that would be true of any African girl brought up in Switzerland, and nothing to do with her adoptive status. The personal, rather than academic, reflections offered by Godula Kosack also bring out vividly the interpersonal nature of the fieldwork relationship and the importance of context in considering issues related to transnational adoption. When Kosack returned to her 'daughter's' village, with the girl and her adoptive parents, three years later, she was thanked by local people for saving the child's life. It is worth noting that the other two Mafa children Kosack had been offered had, by that time, both died.

Conclusion

For the pastoral Maasai of East Africa a homestead with both cattle and children conjures up the image of a 'beautiful world'. Barrenness is feared and is a sign that something 'bad' has happened. 'The gift of a child, an act of sharing, is a sign of upholding a moral world in the face of God . . . Adoption within the patrilineal family (and occasionally the clan) can be seen as a way of bringing order out of chaos by rectifying a mistake made by "nature"' (Talle, Chapter 5). The ritual exchange of a heifer for a child can restore a household and its members. It is an act of completion, in much the same way as for the Australian adoptive families described by Telfer (Chapter 16). Not all mothers give up their children willingly – and several contributors to this volume instance how hard it can be. It is because a child is the most precious gift one can have that he or she has such value and the potential to build, restore, or even hide relationships between individuals, families, clans, strangers, allies and enemies. Decisions concerning the distribution of children among the Maasai are accepted if made by wise and respected elders – wisdom not always apparent in the politicised, polarised world of adoption in some Western countries.

Scientific advances in genetics and debates around the role of relatedness are having an interesting affect on the ways in which we think about kinship. As well as the dilemmas thrown up by the use of reproductive technologies, and the severance of the necessary ties between genetic inheritance, procreation and parenting, there are the discoveries based on the study of mitochondrial DNA (tracing female relatedness) and genes on the Y chromosome (tracing male relatedness).[18] The study of population genetics is thought to tell us 'who we really are' (Marks 2001) and who our kin are. For Euro-Americans, for whom biological relatedness and kinship are synonymous, this raises some novel insights. We might find that we share more genes in common, and therefore have a closer 'degree of relatedness' with someone from Polynesia than our similar-looking neighbour (Sykes 2002). Knowledge (for Westerners) creates kinship links, and is an important component of who we are and how we see ourselves. Discovery that one is heir to a titled family may effect a considerable social and financial transformation, but any genealogical knowledge has the potential to produce kin where none existed before, whether or not we choose to enter into a relationship with them. For adopted children such an emphasis on biological relatedness can pull in two directions. In learning more about the interrelations between peoples and societies, it becomes increasingly difficult to maintain racially based stereotypes, notions of 'good' and 'bad' blood, or to claim that we are not related at some degree of distance to any other human being (or higher primate). Even in transracial and international adoption genetics reassures us in a scientific, rather than emotional or religiously inspired fashion, that we are indeed all one family. On the other hand, knowing that one is not intimately or directly biologically related is still seen as a form of 'fictive kinship' that induces a degree of make-believe and insecurity into the adoptive relationship ('I will act as if you really were my mother, father, child').

There is no single message or right way of doing things, or any simplistic lessons that can be drawn from a cross-cultural approach to adoption, but it is worth remembering that for many societies relationality does not depend on biological filiation. The studies in this volume demonstrate the variety and complexity of child-rearing practices around the world, and the frequency and ease with which children often circulate. There are few instances in which substituting one set of parents or parent for another is thought to be harmful if the quality of the relationship is good. Such studies can help us place our supposedly normative Euro-American understandings of kinship in their place, as one form of cultural practice among many.

Notes

I would like to thank Oliver Davies, Vieda Skultans and Dimitrios Theodossopoulos for their comments on this chapter, and Diane Ford for her help in preparing the manuscript.

1 Cf. Sarah Franklin's (1997) account of attitudes towards assisted conception.
2 There are many examples of this in the adoption literature as well as in media reports and the anecdotal stories of people who have or have tried to adopt. Roger Fenton (2001) and Gerry Cooney (2003) for instance, revealed how poor agency responses in the UK are to potential adopters. Peter Selman (Chapter 17 in this volume) also illustrates the ambivalence of social policy makers in the UK towards adoption, and sets out some of the reasons for this.
3 See, for instance, Smith (1956) on matrifocal kinship relations in the Caribbean, and Wardle (Chapter 13 in this volume).
4 See Carsten (1995) and Carsten and Hugh-Jones (1995) on house relationships. Marshall (1977) shows how in parts of Micronesia kinship is acknowledged between people who do not share genetic substance. See also Treide (Chapter 9 in this volume).
5 See Nerys Patterson's study of early Irish kinship (1994).
6 Valerie Fildes's (1988) fascinating account of wet-nursing shows that it was commonly practised in much of the ancient world, and remains a widespread practice today.
7 Between the 1880s and 1950s over 150,000 children were sent from the UK to Canada, Australia and South Africa. As Cohen (1994: 52–3) points out, 'In retrospect what is significant about the child migrant scheme is that it combined elements of both legal and customary adoption in a way which ensured that the children had the worst of both worlds: apprentices who never grew up to be masters, migrants who found themselves in juvenile penal colonies rather than promised lands, adoptees who were made to lose one set of parents, but never gained another'.
8 For studies of godparenthood see, for instance, Pitt-Rivers (1968), Gudeman (1972), Esther Goody (1982). Mary Bouquet (1993) claimed that it was not just Western but specifically British models of kinship that have dominated and often distorted our understanding of alternative models of relatedness in other societies.
9 In one Yangtze village in the 1930s, 39 per cent of unmarried girls were adopted as affines (Fei 1939: 34, quoted in Goody 1969: 66). Ernst Halbmayer (Chapter 10 in this volume), points out that the Yukpa in Lowland South America favour affinal adoption so as not to reduce the pool of marriage partners in an area of low population density, endemic strife and few potential affines.

10 Cf. Modell (1994: 45–9) for the US situation regarding adoption and fostering.
11 See also Schneider (1984). Schneider's work has been extraordinarily influential in anthropological understandings of kinship, and led both to something of a crisis, in which kinship as a category of study was seen to dissolve altogether, and to a process of regeneration, in which our understandings of kinship began to focus less exclusively on biogenetic relatedness and more on the ways people form intimate familial relationships, including an examination of the influence of new reproductive technologies. This shift can be seen in the work of Jane Collier and Silvia Yanagisako (1987), Marilyn Strathern (1992), Yanagisako and Carol Delaney (1995) and Sarah Franklin and Susan McKinnon (2001), among others.
12 This assumption is apparent in some of the contributions to Radcliffe-Brown and Daryll Ford's (1950) volume on African kinship and marriage, as well as in many other works of the period.
13 Cooney (2003) found that around 51 per cent of applicants to a voluntary adoption agency in Wales did not have birth children, whereas in 49 per cent of cases one or both of the applicants already had birth children jointly or from previous relationships.
14 The idea that moving children between carers is detrimental to their well-being appears to be peculiarly Western. It may be that the trauma of abandonment and the abuse and neglect so often associated with Euro-American adoption has been conflated with the experience of changing carers, and that the 'primal wound' of separation from the birth mother (Verrier 1994) is as much a cultural and contextual as a universal psychological phenomenon.
15 See Richards (1994). Tizzard and Phoenix (1994:99) take issue 'with the tendency to reify racial identity as of unique importance to the individual' and the equating of 'positive black identity' with 'positive identity', stating that 'there is no convincing evidence that self-esteem and mental health are necessarily tied to attitudes to race, and the notion that there is a "black culture" which must be transmitted to transracially adopted children is unconvincing, given the plethora of contemporary black British lifestyles'.
16 See Anderson (Chapter 8) for an analysis of composite relationships in Papua New Guinea.
17 This is argued persuasively by Holly van Gulden (van Gulden and Bartels-Rabb 1995).
18 For a comprehensive survey of recent findings in population genetics see Oppenheimer (2003). Carsten (2004) explores the ways in which Schnieder's two categories 'nature' and 'law' or the biological and social, are often intertwined, and in cases of adoption and assisted reproduction necessarily so.

References

Bouquet, Mary (1993) *Reclaiming English Kinship*, Manchester: Manchester University Press.

Brady, Ivan (ed.) (1976) *Transactions in Kinship*, Honolulu: University of Hawaii Press.

Brain, Robert (1972) *Bangwa Kinship and Marriage*, London: Cambridge University Press.

Carsten, J. (1995) The substance of kinship and the heat of the hearth, *American Ethnologist* 22: 223–41.

Carsten, J. (2004) *After Kinship*, Cambridge: Cambridge University Press.

Carsten, J. and Hugh-Jones, S. (eds) (1995) *About the House*, Cambridge: Cambridge University Press.

Cohen, Phil (1994) Yesterday's words, tomorrow's world: from the racialisation of adoption to the politics of difference, in I. Gabor and J. Aldridge (eds) *In the Best Interests of the Child*, London: Free Association Press, pp. 43–76.

Collier, J. F. and Yanagisako, S. J. (eds) (1987) *Gender and Kinship*, Stanford: Stanford University Press.

Cooney, Gerry (2003) How the initial response of the adoption agency impacts and influences the decision to adopt, Masters dissertation, University of Cardiff.

Evans-Pritchard, E. E. (1951) *Kinship and Marriage among the Nuer*, London: Oxford University Press.

Fei, H. T. (1939) *Peasant Life in China*, London.

Fenton, Roger (2001) Initial agency responses to black prospective adopters: results of a small-scale study, *Adoption and Fostering* 25(1): 13–23.

Fildes, V. (1988) *Wet Nursing*, Oxford: Blackwell.

Franklin, Sarah (1997) *Embodied Progress*, London: Routledge.

Franklin, Sarah and McKinnon, Susan (eds) (2001) *Relative Values*, Durham, NC: Duke University Press

Gonzales, N. (1984) Rethinking the consanguinial household and matrifocality, *Ethnology* 23: 1–13.

Goody, E. N. (1982) *Parenthood and Social Reproduction*, Cambridge: Cambridge University Press.

Goody, Jack (1969) Adoption in cross-cultural perspective, *Comparative Studies in Society and History* 11: 55–78.

Goody, Jack (1976) *Production and Reproduction*, Cambridge: Cambridge University Press.

Gudeman, S. (1972) The compadrazgo as the reflection of the natural and spiritual person, *Proceedings of the Royal Anthropological Institute of Great Britain and Ireland for 1971*, London: RAI, pp. 45–71.

Holy, Ladislav (1996) *Anthropological Perspectives on Kinship*, London, Chicago: Pluto Press.

Kirk, H. David (1984) *Shared Fate* (revised edition), Port Angeles, WA; Brentwood Bay, BC: Ben Simon.

Macfarlane, A. (1980) *The Origins of English Individualism*, Oxford: Blackwell.

Marks, J. (2001) 'We're going to tell these people who they really are': science and relatedness, in Sarah Franklin and Susan McKinnon (eds) *Relative Values*, Durham, NC: Duke University Press, pp. 355–83.

Marshall, M. (1977) The nature of nurture, *American Ethnologist* 4: 643–62.

Modell, Judith (1994) *Kinship with Strangers*, Berkeley and Los Angeles: University of California Press.

Oppenheimer, S. (2003) *Out of Eden*, London: Constable and Robinson.

Patterson, N. (1994) *Cattle Lords and Clansmen*, Notre Dame, IN: University of Notre Dame Press.

Pitt-Rivers, J. (1968) Kinship: III. Pseudo-kinship, *International Encyclopedia of the Social Sciences* 8: 408–13, New York: Macmillan.

Radcliffe-Brown, A. R. and Ford, D. (eds) (1950) *African Systems of Kinship and Marriage*, London: Oxford University Press.

Richards, Barry (1994) What is identity? in I. Gabor and J. Aldridge (eds) *In the Best Interests of the Child*, London: Free Association Press, pp. 77–88.

Schneider, David M. (1968) *American Kinship*, Chicago and London: University of Chicago Press.

Schneider, David M. (1984) *A Critique of the Study of Kinship*, Ann Arbor: University of Michigan Press.

Smith, R. T. (1956) *The Negro Family in British Guiana*, London: Routledge & Kegan Paul.

Strathern, Marilyn (1988) *The Gender of the Gift*, Berkeley: University of California Press.

Strathern, Marilyn (1992) *Reproducing the Future*, Manchester: Manchester University Press.

Sykes, B. (2002) *The Seven Daughters of Eve*, New York: W. W. Norton.

Tizzard, Barbara and Phoenix, Ann (1994) Black identity and transracial adoption, in I. Gabor and J. Aldridge (eds) *In the Best Interests of the Child*, London: Free Association Press, pp. 89–102.

Van Gulden, H. and Bartels-Rabb, L. (1995) *Real Parents, Real Children*, New York: Crossroad.

Verrier, N. N. (1994) *The Primal Wound*, Baltimore: Gateway Press.

Yanagisako, S. J. and Delaney, C. (eds) (1995) *Naturalizing Power*, New York: Routledge.

Adopting a native child

An anthropologist's personal involvement in the field

Godula Kosack

EDITOR'S PREFACE TO CHAPTER 2

Godula Kosack's contribution, 'Adopting a native child: an anthropologist's personal involvement in the field', is rather different to the other chapters in this volume, giving a reflexive narrative account of her fieldwork in Northern Cameroon, and the circumstances that led to her mediating the adoption of a local child to Europe. She had not embarked upon fieldwork with any intention of adopting a native child, and had no desire to do so, but the events described unfolded as a consequence of chance remarks and the relationship that the Mafa villagers wanted to establish with her. One of their goals was undoubtedly to save a baby whose chances of survival were otherwise slim, but more germane was their wish to tie the anthropologist more firmly into their village kinship networks. Even when she made clear that she had no intention of raising the girl herself, the villagers continued to insist on her new status as a village mother – the mother of one of their children.

The chapter raises several important methodological and ethical questions. The most obvious is the reality of fieldwork as an inter-personal dialogue. However distanced or detached, abstracted or theoretical anthropological writing might be, the raw data is collected as the result of real people in relationships that are constantly nego-tiated and renegotiated, often in ways that defy expectations and any sense of scholarly authorial control. Within this observation are questions that have exercised anthropologists for decades, the relationship between participation and observation, objectivity and subjectivity, fieldnotes and text. Many anthropologists are proud to boast of their 'kinship status' in their adopted host society. It is often seen as a mark of acceptance and as a guarantee of sufficient insider status to lend authority to the anthropologist's subsequent writings. Few, however, illustrate what this means in practice, or use this data to advance our understanding of a so-called kinship-based society. The thick description of Kosack's narrative, on the other hand, allows us a privileged insight into the process of ethnography, the consequences of being absorbed into village kinship networks, and the transformative human potential of such relationships.

A second question is ethical rather than methodological, although the two are not unrelated. There are debates as to how far the fieldworker should become personally involved in the lives of others. When does participation become unwarranted interference? Laura Bohannon in her novelistic account of fieldwork among the Tiv in Northern Nigeria (published under the pseudonym, Elenore Smith Bowen) describes one such moment of crisis when her young friend was in desperate need of medical attention, attention her husband and family failed to provide. Such dilemmas are not uncommon, and everyone can reach a point when they act according to their conscience and the dictates of the circumstances, rather than according to some textbook notion of 'good fieldwork practice'.

Anthropologists working in simpler or less economically and technologically powerful societies are conscious of the power imbalances between them and their hosts, and may be wary of being seen as a neo-colonial official, missionary, government worker, spy or one of the other categories preserved for (often foreign) outsiders. The idea that we can insert ourselves into other's lives on our own terms is simply another conceit of power. The white anthropologist in rural Africa will always be an outsider who can provide valued resources, status and access to a wider world. Kosack demonstrates that it was in her dual role as adopted villager and European outsider that she was used and valued by the Mafa. It was precisely because she was an insider who could also remove a child from almost certain death in the village to the prosperity and security of Europe that she was seen as a suitable mother.

Some people will undoubtedly be unhappy at the notion of anthropologists, missionaries or other prospective parents removing children from their village, country and culture to bring them up in Europe or America. To say that this should not happen under any circumstances is yet another form of cultural hegemony that marginalises the individuals involved and the choices they make. While choice may be driven by poverty and disease, it may also represent the deepest and most positive aspirations of people to give a better life to their children. In the case described by Kosack, the Mafa child was fortunate to find parents who knew her home village, its language and customs, and who would continue to respect them. If we can generalise from one case to the much broader issue of intercountry adoption, Kosack's narrative would seem to point to the desirability of extended rather than reduced or substitutive kinship links. This remains a challenge to our notions of bounded nationality, cultural identity, parenthood and family, but a challenge that remains pertinent in a world of considerable population movement, with increasing gaps between those who enjoy the world's resources and those who are denied access to them. It could be, and often is, argued that the transnational adoption represents a form of cultural genocide, but equally the links of affection and family that are built between the richer and poorer nations can undermine the insecure borders of privilege the West is busy constructing around itself.

Reference

Bowen, Elenore Smith (1956) *Return to Laughter*, London: Victor Gollancz.

When I heard about the call for papers for a panel on cross-cultural approaches to adoption, I immediately thought of my personal experience. I once adopted an African child who afterwards was adopted by a Swiss–French couple. The child changed her national identity from Cameroonian to German to Swiss – a real case of cross-cultural adoption. Having learnt that participant observation obliges a researcher not to get emotionally or personally involved too deeply with the people with whom one is doing research, I was conscious of the fact that I had transgressed one of the golden rules of anthropological fieldwork. That is why I am glad to get a chance to present my case to the scientific community. I want to discuss the following questions. First, is it legitimate to transfer a child from the cultural background into which it is born into a completely strange one and do I not provoke a conflict of identity? Second, do I not disqualify myself as a researcher if I get personally involved with the people I am studying? Is this a form of "going native"? I want to say this much in advance: my story of adoption had an inner dynamic and I was not the only person to write this script. Furthermore, I do not claim to make any statements that could be generalized.

How did it all come about? In 1985 I settled in a Mafa village in North Cameroon with my family (husband and three children) for the first time, and at the invitation of the local population we constructed our own house. Since then I have spent about 30 months of fieldwork there. When in 1985 I went to say goodbye to the women I had been interviewing and chatting with, one of them disappeared into her house. Thinking that she had forgotten me, I was about to go, when my assistant asked me to stay. Pelhème returned with a large calabash of millet, a somewhat smaller one of peanuts, again a smaller one of sesame and on top of it a little hen. When asked why she was giving me all this, she replied, "This is what a mother gives to her daughter when she is going away." With this phrase I was adopted.

Henceforth, each of my stays was characterized by getting closer to the village people and in particular to the women. My "mother" assumed an important role in introducing me into the local customs and practices concerning women's lives. When in 1990 I spent seven months there with two of my daughters, my "mother" wanted to get me even more involved by offering me a Mafa child to adopt.

The first harbinger of this was a group of women, Pelhème among them, coming to ask me whether I could help a two-year-old child whose mother had died a few weeks before. The child was living with its mother's mother, who herself was struggling for her own and her children's survival, the youngest one being a baby. Before I had left for Cameroon, a German friend of mine, mother of four children, had asked me to keep in mind that if ever there was a child in need she would very much like to adopt it. I did not want to play with fate, yet I was thinking: if on the one side I am asked to mediate a child for adoption and on the other hand I am asked to help an orphan, I have to act. Before mentioning my idea I sent a letter to Germany asking my friend whether she still stood by her word. At the same time I asked my local confidants – the couple on whose ground we had constructed our house, key figures in the local community – whether they thought it a good idea to mediate the adoption of a Mafa child to Europe. Their answer was unreservedly positive, and before I had the answer from Germany they had spread the word that I, Godula, wanted to adopt a child – which was very much contrary to my intention.

The answer I received from Germany was: "We are sorry, our youngest child is chronically ill, and takes all our time and energy. We have no reserves left to adopt another child. But we stand by our word. Bring the child, we will find a solution together." The Mafa women, among them the child's grandmother, considered me as adoption-willing: there was no way back. I hated the idea of all the formalities with which I would have to comply. The first point to clarify was whether the paternal relatives would agree to giving "their" child away. For, although after its mother's death they had not once asked after the whereabouts and welfare of the child, under Mafa patriarchal law the child belongs to the patrilineage. The father was untraceable in the town of Garoua, and the father's father pronounced: "The child is to stay where it is, I don't want to get myself talked about." That was the end to the first chapter. Needless to say I felt relieved.

However, my "mother" and her friends did not give up. Once I had signalled my readiness to adopt a child, they were determined to find me one, despite the fact that I had made clear from the outset that I was only acting as a mediator and that I would pass the child on to other permanent adoptive parents. I had put the adoption chapter behind me, when two months later the women came to me with a new proposal. A young woman had died, leaving behind a two-week-old infant. It was looked after by the father's mother, who tried hard to get her breasts to produce milk again, fifteen years after she had nursed her last child. At the same time she visited other nursing mothers willing to give the baby the odd meal. Would I adopt it? I was asked. The way it was cared for, it had no chance of survival. I was not able to say: "Leave me in peace!" My confidant friend herself offered to go and regulate the affair with the child's paternal relatives. She returned with the answer: the child's father and its father's father are willing to give the child away, yet the grandmother has her doubts. They would come to a decision within a day. As I heard nothing the following day, it was clear the child would stay with its grandmother. Again I felt a burden lifting.

It was just after two more weeks that Pelhème returned to the subject. Last night, she explained, a young mother had died while giving birth to a premature baby. If I didn't adopt it, it was sure to die. This time, she added, I had a good chance of getting the child. There was a stepmother, who was herself nursing a child yet, since she had not loved her co-wife, she would not look after the baby satisfactorily. The child's father had already signalled his consent. I felt very uneasy at the thought that in addition to all the "normal" problems such an adoption implied, I would have to deal with a premature baby; my facilities in the bush-household were anything but luxurious. I had neither running water nor electricity, and only the use of a two flame gas cooker. How would I be able to deal with the baby's hygiene requirements? Yet, could I say: "No, I don't want to be bothered", when my closest friends and my adoptive mother wanted to entrust me with a child, the most precious and valuable thing thinkable? "What if the child dies under my care?" I asked. "Will people blame me and everyone participating in the transaction?" "No, there will be no resentment against you or anyone", was the answer. "Everyone knows, the child will die. It has only got a chance, if you take it." I gave in: "I'll take it, but only if everyone of the patrilineage agrees to it. I don't want to get attached to the child only in order to have it taken away again before I leave." "That is clear." Secretly I hoped that there would be no unanimous consent to giving the child up for adoption. When I heard nothing more that day I almost forgot about this request, only to be reminded of it early the next morning.

When I arrived at one of my assistant's houses for an appointment I saw my "mother" sitting there, holding a bundle on her lap and looking at me triumphantly. "Pelhème, you've got the child!" I exclaimed with such a mixture of emotions that I am still not able to analyse them all. She smiled and made me sit down next to her. I unravelled the rags. There was a tiny little something, thin arms, thin legs thrashing about helplessly, and its sex? Everything was so tiny and underdeveloped that I was not able to identify it at the first glance. "It's a girl", Pelhème explained without my having asked. I tried to think practically. What is the first step to take? When was the child's last meal? I had nothing in the house, neither a bottle nor infant milk powder. I would have to go to the nearest hospital (six kilometres away), have the child examined and buy the milk powder. I had heard of a woman in my neighbourhood who had delivered the same day as this child. Could she feed it until I had everything settled?

I will cut the tale short now. The baby weighed no more than 1070 grams (less than 3lbs), but apart from this was in good health. Needless to say it was very complicated to get the necessary papers to take her out of Cameroon. A legal adoption was, according to Cameroonian law, not possible, as the still valid French colonial law allowed only childless persons to adopt. The procedure to become the formal guardian would take longer than I was able to stay. By coincidence I heard that some years ago a Swiss family had adopted a child whose mother had died while giving birth. They became the legal parents by having their names put on the birth certificate. As I was known to the local authorities they agreed to that solution. Finally I had a birth certificate with me and the child's father registered as its parents. With this I flew to the capital Yaounde in order to have the child added to my passport by the German Embassy. In vain. According to German law only the biological mother can be registered on a birth certificate. So I invented a story that I had become pregnant by a man of "my" village in France and that I had delivered before the time in the bush although I had wanted to be back home for the birth. But the attachés of the Embassy did not believe me and refused to put the child's name on my passport. When they mentioned the term child-trafficking I got scared and gave up. I remember sitting in the airport lounge crying while waiting for my flight back to the north. I believed that I didn't have any chance whatsoever to take the child with me. I had looked after her for more than a month now and had got as attached to her as to any child born to me. It was only a few hours before my departure that I held a paper in my hands allowing me to leave the country with the child on the basis that her father wanted some medical treatment for her in Europe, as she was still in fragile health. In France and in Germany I successfully evaded the passport controls. I did not want to complicate matters, as the paper to take the child out of Cameroon was not a permit to take it into my own country.

The girl is now growing up in Switzerland. How did she find her adoptive parents? This was one of the miraculous things in this story. The village women kept asking me when I would have the child's name-giving ceremony, which is due when a child loses its umbilical cord. I had hesitated to announce the feast as long as I was unsure whether I could take the girl with me. I announced it the day I held the birth certificate in my hand with my name on it as the mother. It was a great party with a lot of millet beer and food for everyone. In the evening when I finally came to relax from the stress, my friend returned from a stay in the town with a message: a childless couple in Switzerland who had been here before me, friends of mine and of the village people, had heard about my having a child to adopt and were now asking whether they could become her parents. I had never thought of them in this context, and here they were, the ideal adoptive parents – people who knew the village and who would not try to make the child forget her origins.

What struck me about the story even when I was in the middle of it was the dynamic it had taken on the moment I had carefully asked one single person for her opinion as to whether she thought it a good idea to have a child adopted by a friend of mine. The message spread through the village: Godula wants to adopt a child. I was known as a person who showed an interest in the women's lives. They wanted me to become part of village society. And although I kept emphasizing that it was not me who would raise the child, they maintained that I was the mother and the others were the adoptive parents. Up to today this is the unanimous opinion of the child's relatives and of the village population. When three years later I went to visit the village with the child and her parents we had a ceremony both in the child's house of birth and in my house con-firming our relationships. I was addressed as the child's mother and I was thanked for having saved her life. I then passed the thanks on to the adoptive parents. The other two children who had been in question for adoption were by then no longer alive.

Later on I was asked by another Swiss woman whether I could mediate a child for her to adopt. Although I spread the word, nothing came of it. This proved to me the uniqueness of this story. The idea was not to have a local child grow up in Europe, but rather to tie me up in a family net. I am regarded as a daughter of the village in a double sense: first I am the daughter of a local woman. This too is a recognized relationship, and whenever she is making sacrifices which require her children's presence, it is important that I am there if at all possible. Second, I am the mother of a local child. The adoption of the child through me (I emphasize it was "through" and not "by" me) gave me a place in the system of descent. Whenever there are village rituals I find my place as the mother of their child. I am invited to participate in all ceremonies, my camera or camcorder with me.

To return to the questions I asked at the beginning: What happened to the child and her identity? When she was three her parents and I visited her village of origin together with her. We realized that she behaved like a child socialized in Europe. She made friends with the local children just as my children had made friends with them; she was the one who decided which games to play and how to proceed. She is now a teenager. She speaks French, German and Swiss German. She feels Swiss wholeheartedly. She has always known that she has relatives not only in Switzerland (from her father's side), or in France (from her mother's side) but also in Cameroon, and she knows that I also have played a part in her life story. When she is back in her village of origin, she is celebrated as the daughter who has come home, just like other people who have returned from the towns. She herself feels emotionally attached to the village people, and she was very upset when her biological father died a sudden death in a cholera epidemic. In short, she seems to be a real cosmopolitan. The only problem of identity I envisage she might ever have to face is being confronted with racism. But this has nothing to do with her being an adopted child.

And what about the value of my research? How far can or should a field researcher get involved with the population with whom she/he is working? I had been taught that participant observation meant participating in all kinds of activities but remaining emotionally uncommitted so as not to prejudice the results of one's findings. I was advised to carefully balance on the edge between objective observation and participation. Yet, I lost my innocence the day my house aid, the wife of my husband's assistant, was beaten by her husband. I took sides and discussed the matter openly. When interviewing women I always asked for their reactions to what they presented to me as cases of injustice in their lives. This made them reflect more upon their own attitudes. One day, my (male) friend criticized me; I'd make the women rebellious. Yet, nobody, neither women nor men, ever rejected my visits to their homes; nobody ever accused me of sowing seeds of disturbance. When I once went to say goodbye to my friends at the end of a stay, one of the women asked: "When will you come back? When you are here, we woman don't feel so meagre." I never hid my emotions. I expressed regret and sadness, I participated in their joy. When my husband left me, which disappointed not only the Mafa women, but also the men, my "mother" dried my tears with the hem of her skirt. Retrospectively I argue that this lack of objectivity did not prevent me from doing good ethnographic work. My experience is that it opens doors and that people make much more of an effort to explain to me their way of life, their thoughts and their emotions. If ever anybody raises the idea that they should try to get some financial benefit from allowing me to do my research, he is reproached with the remark: "No she is one of us and she is doing it for us and our children." The adoption story was a decisive step in the process of getting involved with the population. Instead of a research relationship I am enjoying a human relationship with the people of the village.

Part I

Africa

Chapter 3

"The real parents are the foster parents"
Social parenthood among the Baatombu in Northern Benin

Erdmute Alber

Introduction

In recent years, new kinship theories have revived the argument that kinship cannot be understood as biologically based social relations, but as social relations of belonging often expressed by metaphors coming from the biological arena.[1] As kinship relations that are not necessarily grounded upon biological relations, adoption and fosterage seem to be good examples to test the validity of that argument. One research possibility is to study the process of "kinning" (Howell 2003), which means to thematize the way in which a kinship relation is built up, which symbols and metaphors for this new relation of belonging are found and, finally, how an attempt is made to make adoptive relationships resemble biological ones. Studies of adoption in Europe and America have shown how much effort adoptive parents put into "naturalizing" relations with their adopted children.

This strong desire to naturalize adoptive relations can be interpreted as a consequence of the fact that adoption and fosterage in Euro-America[2] are seen as neither ordinary nor mainstream. The norms concerning good and "right" parenthood are oriented to the biological parents, who should ideally fulfill the roles of social and juridical parents as well. Another belief is that parental changes, for example from biological to foster parents, could damage a child's psychological health.

In contrast to these ideas and beliefs, this chapter talks about people who have a completely different vision of parenthood. Among the Baatombu in Northern Benin, West Africa, at least in rural situations, fosterage is not the exception but the norm. People think that biological parents are less able than foster parents to provide a good education for their children. The Baatombu therefore find it very reasonable to give their children to other persons to be fostered, without any negative connotations. To the contrary, people trying to prevent their biological children being taken by others are seen as bad.

Esther Goody's research on social parenthood in Ghana (1982) shows that West Africa is one of the regions of the world in which social parenthood and different forms of fosterage are particularly common. According to Hillary Page (1989), among some ethnic groups in the Ivory Coast around 50 percent of children between ten and thirteen do not grow up with their biological parents.[3] Even in this West African context, where fostering is a very common phenomenon, Baatombu norms and behavior appear extreme, going so far as to make invisible or even deny biological parenthood. People try to demonstrate that the foster parents are the real, potent and preferred parents. It is possible that such attitudes are more widespread, but that little research attention has been paid to the phenomenon.

Adoption and fosterage: terminological questions

Esther Goody makes a terminological distinction between different forms of social parenthood (1982: 7ff.) She argued that in order to carry the burden of social reproduction it can be rational for a society to share the tasks between different kinds of parents, the biological and the social. Goody outlined five different functions of parenthood, which in many societies are shared between biological and social parents: first bearing and begetting, second, status entitlements and rearing reciprocities, then nurturance, training and sponsorship. If other persons than the biological parents fulfill some of these functions, then she would call them "social parents".

Of all the possible social parents, she would call "adoptive parents" only those people who take all parental functions beside the first one, which cannot be transferred. As African children normally do not change their names even if they stay their whole childhood with social parents and merely visit the biological parents, she refers to them as foster rather than adopted children. This definition obviously leads to new termi-nological problems: "social parenthood" may be understood in a very broad sense, including all the persons who have "functions" in the daily life of children. Roost Vischer (1997) for example, following Goody, calls "social parenthood" the phenomenon that people other than the biolog-ical parents take temporary care of children, watch them in the absence of the parents or even educate them if they are playing with their children. Thus, the distinction between "parent" and "non-parent" can, following that definition, become very fluid. Even in Europe, in societies which emphasize biological parenthood, and in which parents have an educational monopoly over "their" children, other individuals such as babysitters, neighbors, teachers and grandparents have some limited responsibility for them.

The other problem of Goody's terminology is that, concentrating on the functionalist perspective, she is not able to answer the question how societies interpret the different forms of parenthood. One cannot differentiate between societies that transfer nearly all responsibilities to social parents and understand them as the real and important persons in children's lives, and those in which foster parents play a much more limited role. It is possible to identify some forms "between" adoption and fosterage in Goody's sense. Even among the Baatombu I have observed a whole spectrum of different forms of what she would call fostering, which can hardly be subsumed under a single term. As Baatombu foster children always retain the clan name of their biological father, I follow Goody in calling their practices "fosterage", although the emic meaning seems to me in most cases to be better understood as "adoption". Independently from the question of whether one should call these practices "fosterage" or "adoption" it should become clear from my "thick description" how and why Baatombu let their children "circulate".[4]

First I describe the traditional – that means in this context, the old and in many villages still current – practices of child fosterage. Second, I outline some underlying concepts and norms. Third, I show how these concepts and practices have undergone a process of transformation that has brought about changes in the modes of circulation of children without making these practices disappear.[5]

The Baatombu are part of the multi-ethnic Borgu region in north-eastern Benin and in north-western Nigeria. They share the land with other peasant groups, mainly Boko and Mokolle, with the pastoralist Fulani herders and with Muslim traders, called Dendi or Wangara. Today their major cash crop is cotton. Since about 1960, a strong migrational tendency can be observed towards the big cities in the south of Benin, mainly Cotonou, as well as a tendency to migrate within the Borgu towards the capital Parakou and other urban centers.[6]

Traditional forms of child fosterage in rural Baatombu areas

It is still common in Baatombu villages not to let children grow up with their biological parents. This practice has been widespread. Among more than 150 older people I have spoken to during my field trips, I have only spoken with two persons who told me that they stayed during their whole childhood with their biological parents. Usually aunts and uncles, or the classificatory grandparents, "demand a child to live with them", as the Baatombu say.

It is always a single individual of the same sex who takes the rights and duties of foster parenthood. The child normally moves into the household of the social mother or father aged about three to six. This age is preferred for child fosterage for two reasons, the child is not weaned until about three, and his or her younger biological brother or sister should already be born so that the mother will not stay without a child. It is maintained that the transfer of the child should happen at a young age, before the child would be "knowing", as the Baatombu say, a change which takes place at around six or seven. Among other things, this implies that events and changes that happen during this period cannot cause fundamental damage to the personality of the child or adult.[7]

The foster parent takes full responsibility, not only to rear the child but also to educate and teach all the gender-specific tasks and roles of a future member of the society. From the moment of transfer there are significant differences between the sexes. Women explained to me numerous practices that should help bind the girl to the social mother, such as special herbs that are put into the bath of the child, songs and conjurations, or small gifts that help to convince the child to follow the new mother. By contrast, men have a different emphasis. They very frequently stress the point that "their" boys follow them without manifesting opposition. They maintain that, except for the donation of new clothes when taking the boy from his biological mother, nothing special has to be done to facilitate the change. Significant gender differences accompany the entire process of social parenthood, which usually extends until marriage.

One effect of this gender-specific form of fosterage is that, in comparison to contemporary Euro-American society, the emotional impact of divorce on children is minimized. As in many societies in the West African–Sudan belt, marriage relations among the Baatombu are rather unstable. It is quite common for a woman to be married several times in her life. Giving away her biological children implies for a woman to be free to change the husband and to enter the new marriage without having to care for biological children from earlier marriages. Starting a new marriage with one or several fostered children should not, and normally does not, cause any problem for the new relationship. Husbands and wives deal independently with "their" social children, and in case of divorce each of them continues to take care of the children in his or her realm of responsibility. Thus, children are used to moving with their social parents, possibly several times during childhood. This is especially so for girls, for it is normally the woman who leaves the household.

The fact that husbands and wives deal independently with "their" social children leads to another important difference between the fosterage of girls by women and the fosterage of boys by men. Everybody takes on those children he or she has the right to claim. Women take children from their clan or their mothers' families, men from theirs. Married women live in the households of their husbands' families and have a precarious position there, especially when they are still young. They often have relations of rivalry or competition with other in-married women, and hierarchical relations with the women that belong to their husband's family. Their biological children – those whom one would call their own from a western perspective – belong to another patrilineal clan and tend to be fostered by others. In this situation, foster children strengthen the position of married women. They are from the same clan as their social mothers, they are also strangers, and they belong exclusively to them. This seems to be the most important reason as to why the fostering of girls in rural areas has not decreased to the same extent as the fostering of boys. It is a way to stabilize the precarious position of young women in the household they have married into.

When we talked about the difficulties for a woman living in her husband's household while she was young, an old woman said to me:

> If you are a married woman living at the husband's and you have your own family, then you will take your thing to hold it (foster it). Even if you have given birth to children with him, you'll do so. You'll take the child of your brother, the child of your sister to hold them.[8]

It is worth noting the instances where this woman used and did not use possessive pronouns. In saying "you will take your thing to hold it" she expressed with emphasis that the children of her family (here she used the French term *famille*, whereas the conversation has been in Baatonum, the local language) were her own, whereas she completely avoided expressing a sense of belonging regarding her biological children, whom she called "children you have given birth with him". "He" is, of course, the man she was married to at that time. As in the case of her biological children, she did not designate her husband with a possessive pronoun or any other mark of a relation of belonging. But in the case of her clan she used all the possible formulations of designating such a relation: "you'll *have your own* family", "you'll take *your* thing", "the child of *your* brother, of your sister".

Fostering children from her own clan – she called them her "own things" in this context – strengthened her position in a household where she continued to be a stranger, a person without the specific relations of belonging which are reserved to one's own family. She belonged, in a different sense, to the family of her husband, because they would call her "our woman" as the husband could say "my woman". But she could not do the same. However, "her children" whom she called here "her things"[9] were the biological children of her brothers or sisters. They belonged exclusively to her, whereas the children to whom she gave birth, which she could never call her "own", belonged first of all to the family of their father.

The social mother or father has various rights in his or her social children. There is the right to let the child work for her or him. This is especially important for elderly people who very often argue that they foster children in order to have somebody who takes water for them or carries things. In the case of women the fosterage of children is important for having little helpers for the numerous household tasks: cooking, making fire, carrying water, collecting wood, taking care of small children, being sent to neighbors with messages, and so on. Men need a boy to help them do agricultural work. However, child labor is always connected to the idea that a child should be trained to become a good farmer or a good housewife. A woman without a single foster child to send out and, most importantly, belonging in this context exclusively to her is a poor woman.

The fostering person does not only have rights, but duties as well. Possibly the most important (and the most expensive) duty is to give the child his or her first husband or wife. In the case of a girl this implies the payment of the dowry, for a boy, the payment of the brideprice. Marriage is not only considered the termination of childhood, but also the end of belonging to the social parents. The payment of brideprice or dowry sets the child free, and is considered compensation for the work the children have done for their social parents. There is an expression for this context. When talking about marriage French-speaking Baatombu very often use the word *libération* (liberation) which signifies in the urban context of

Benin the big and nowadays quite expensive feast at the end of an apprenticeship.[10] What is meant by using the term *libération* for a marriage is
that through the marriage a child is liberated from the dependence and
relation of belonging to his or her social father or mother. New forms of
belonging, especially the woman's belonging to the family of her husband
and the rights they have over her work and reproductive capacity, start
when fosterage ends.

There are certain rules about who has the right to demand a child.
The first child of a marriage should stay with a person from the clan of
the father, an aunt/uncle or a classificatory grandparent. The second child
belongs very explicitly to the person who reared the biological mother,
i.e. normally her social mother. This relation of belonging is said to be a
compensation for the labor and costs the woman had to rear the girl who
later on became the mother of the child. And, of course, it is said to be
a compensation for the labor the social mother has lost by "setting her
child free to marriage". If the second child is a boy and, therefore, the
mother of the woman is unable to foster him herself, she can give him to
one of her people, for example one of her sons.[11] The third child should
go to the family of the father, and the fourth child is the one the biological
parents have the right to keep for themselves. These rules do not fully
determine foster practices, especially because there are numerous persons
who can present themselves as relatives with a right to the child. Instead,
the rules serve to legitimize claims. The practices of child fosterage are
very flexible, leaving many spaces for individual preferences, personal
decisions and, of course, conflicts, which occur mainly when two people
present themselves as candidates for fosterage for the same child, or if a
family tries indirectly to refuse to give up a child.

Even if somebody tries to deny a particular request for fosterage, which
happens from time to time, there is a general consensus that people have
the right to "demand a child" and that biological parents do not
have the right to refuse such a demand and to keep the child with them.
Thus, in order to understand concrete negotiations surrounding the
transfer of a child it is necessary to outline general norms of behavior and
belonging.

Norms concerning childhood, parenthood and relations of belonging between children and adults

The practice of child fosterage is based upon the idea that biological
parents do not "own" their children and make decisions about their lives.

Rather, other people have these rights, to some extent. This concept appears in many practices. If, for instance, a visitor enters a Baatombu household and wants to be polite, he or she should address one of the children present in an "educational" way. Educating a child (for example, by telling him or her to greet in a correct way) shows interest and proves that the visitor takes some responsibility for the child. This, in a way, means to consider the child as one's own. When a child is born people congratulate the relatives, but rarely the biological parents, on the birth of "their" child. Parents express a general demeanor of shame in relation to their biological children in order to demonstrate that they don't consider them their own.

There are numerous taboos and rules of avoidance between biological parents[12] and children. They are forbidden to call the children by their first name. Instead, they have to use nicknames or paraphrases. Even in the first hours after birth I observed mothers expressing distance towards their new-born child in the presence of a watching crowd of friends and relatives. Possibly this social norm of demonstrating distance between parents and biological children is one of the reasons why, ideally, a Baatombu woman should deliver alone. Nobody should witness the very intimate moment of delivery, when the physical bond between mother and child through the umbilical cord is visible.

Another belief in Baatombu society is important to understand fosterage – that to change location and the persons to whom one relates does not do any damage to a child. Young children are thought unable to understand and "know" what is happening, and are seen to be able to adapt quite easily to new parents and circumstances. A person adopting puts new clothes on the child in order to demonstrate that it is now his or her task to care for him or her and to leave the "old clothes" behind. This is regarded as sufficient to convince a child to leave his or her home, biological mother and siblings and to follow the "new" father or mother. Women may also use some magical practices to bind the fostered child to them, but there are no special rites of passage to accentuate the moment of the fosterage. This is in stark contrast to the situation of marriage, which is structurally comparable to fosterage. In both cases the rights of belonging are transferred from one person to another; and in both cases the circulation of a person constitutes new family relations. One reason why fosterage is not more ritually marked may be the belief that early childhood is the time of not being "knowing" and that the things happening in this period do not affect the personality. Similarly with funerals and birth ceremonies; there is no traditional baptism or other name-giving ceremony in traditional Baatombu society, and children's funerals are very minor affairs, with hardly any ceremonial character, whereas the funerals of older persons are very large, elaborate and expensive affairs.

Many values of Baatombu society have changed in the urban environment. However, the conviction that children adapt easily if well treated, is shared within the urban context. As long as people are considered honest, there is no problem leaving one's child with them, even if they are completely unknown to the child. The conviction that children are not "knowing" until the age of about seven exists in the urban context as well as in the rural milieu.

The Baatombu believe that people are unable to act in a consistent and fair way with their biological children, and tend to be too lenient with them. They cannot therefore guarantee them a good education. This notion was expressed in a conversation I had with an old man. I asked him why Baatombu practice child fosterage. I was expecting answers such as "If you give your child to somebody, you will never forget this person", an argument that I had heard several times. I was taken by surprise when he explained to me that biological parents are not able to educate their children well.

> There are three things biological parents cannot teach their children, but they have to learn from others. Firstly, biological parents are not able to educate them in a rigid way. Secondly, children have to learn to express themselves in front of older people. And thirdly, they have to learn to respect the elders.
>
> (Interview in French, Cotonou, 21 March 1999)

This answer by the old man reveals much about Baatombu concepts of an ideal education. On the one hand, one has to respect the elders; on the other hand, in order to be a mature person one has to be able to express oneself even in the presence of older (or more powerful) people. This implies that a truly well-mannered person should have, at the same time, respect and *sekuru* – shame – if an older or more powerful person is present. Adequate shame, however, should not lead to an inability to express oneself. Biological parents are thought incapable of teaching both these sides of personhood – shame and self-confidence. The children should, therefore, learn these qualities from other adults.

To give a child away by no means indicates that Baatombu people do not consider children as valuable. To the contrary, as many people said to me, if one gives one's child away, one gives the most valued thing one could give, and this means that the person who takes a child will be forever grateful for having got the most precious gift one could possibly receive. The great value of children makes the gift of a child particularly precious. It is this great value attributed to children that qualifies them as ideal objects of exchange.

There are several modes of exchange in Baatombu society, and there are numerous rules concerning the right way to be generous and to participate in the exchange and redistribution of different gifts. In this context, it becomes evident that denying the "gift" of a child is an act of anti-social behavior that excludes people from the general comportment of social life based on different types of exchange. To demonstrate biological parenthood and to reclaim biological children as one's own is, therefore, an anti-social act in traditional Baatombu society, because in doing so one reclaims and monopolizes something as personal property and not exchangeable, which should belong to many people and not exclusively to the biological parents. Biological parenthood – despite of all these norms and practices that deny it – is seen as something especially valuable among the Baatombu. Possibly this is so exactly *because* one has to deny it in public. The issue of parental identity is symptomatic of this tension. It is part of the concept of fosterage that children are not told who their biological parents are. As they are fostered at quite a young age they do not remember them. Many people told me very emotional stories about how and when they came to learn the names and identities of their biological parents. I was told numerous stories about little gestures or little gifts offered secretly by biological parents to their children. Away from the watching public, hidden in their houses or when nobody is present, biological parents do take an interest in their children. They offer them food, give them presents of money or clothes, and take care of them from a distance. Such practices are not only shared knowledge, but are actually expected from biological parents, especially from the mother.

Men, representing much more than women the "official" side of behavior in Baatombu society, are frequently much more rigid than women. I was often told that the biological father, to demonstrate publicly that he respects the norms of distance between himself and his children, sends his biological child away if he or she comes and asks for something. The biological mothers, by contrast, often seek opportunities to meet their children secretly, in order to give them presents and to help them feel happy.

Thus, in Baatombu society there is a certain complementarity between biological and social parents. In public, the latter represent themselves as the real parents, but in secret the biological parents observe the child's well-being and try to influence it. At rites of passage, such as marriage or excision, both groups of parents have a function, albeit different ones. Baatombu people are proud of having biological children. But, in contrast to Western society, being a proud and satisfied father or mother does not involve co-residence. On the contrary, one can be very proud of one's child, telling how he or she lives with an important person or grows up in the house of a very good friend, in private. Showing pride in biological parenthood in public is not permitted as it would give the impression of disrespect, putting oneself on a status equal to one's own parents.

Many times I have been offered small children by my very good rural Baatombu friends. The idea of giving me one of their children, whom I could take to Germany, would have meant for them that I accept not only a very profound friendship but that I would make myself a real relative to them.

Transformations

The practice of child fosterage is undergoing a profound transformational process. This is due to general changes in society as well as to a process of change in values, norms and ideas concerning family and kinship. In cities in particular, "Western" ideas concerning the relationship between parents and children are becoming more popular. In rural areas many parents do not dare to deny the demand for a child, but increasingly they no longer conform to the traditional system of fosterage. This change has many causes. One of the most important is the growing importance of schooling, and the quite common practice of sending one's biological children to school while integrating foster children into agricultural work in case of the boys and household work among the girls. One new informal rule in the child transfer processes is that urban children are no longer fostered – and are not demanded – by rural people. The child transfer between cities and villages has become unidirectional: children are transferred from village to town but not vice versa.

If rural children move to towns the relation between their biological and social parents are negotiated in a new way. In some cases the social parents are only tutors who give them food and shelter without taking care of all their costs. In other cases, the social parents secure them a formal education – an apprenticeship or schooling – in compensation for their work in the household. These new forms of child fosterage tend to be much more temporary and, in a way, more functional, because they are no longer grounded upon the notion that children belong to people other than to those who have procreated and given birth to them. The "rural norm" of asking for a child just because one has the right to claim, and because the circulation of children is seen generally as an important measure to guarantee a good education for children, is practically non-existent in urban contexts.

At the beginning of this chapter I argued that the Baatombu present an extreme example of attitudes towards the circulation of children. In rural and "traditional" Baatombu areas even today, social parenthood is seen as the ideal, guaranteeing the foster children a "good" upbringing, which means mainly a good education. The empirical material shows that what in Europe is regarded as natural parental behavior – to stand by one's biological children, or to talk about them proudly in public – is seen as aberrant among the Baatombu, for whom appropriate behavior towards one's biological children is characterized by shame, distance and avoidance. The Baatombu case illustrates first, that there is no unique, "natural" or interculturally accepted notion of good parenthood. Even in the most "biological" moments of peoples lives, for example the moment of delivery, social behavior is highly dependent on social and society-specific norms. The Western preference for the biological parents to serve as the social parents cannot be generalized. Rather, from the per-spective of the Baatombu, it appears as one normative alternative among others. It would also appear that these alternatives do not automatically damage children's development.[13]

Second, the case of the Baatombu shows us that adoption and foster-age are not necessarily a minority phenomenon. This form of parenthood can become the norm. There is no connotation of shame or anti-social behavior for the Baatombu in giving one's children to other people in order to be fostered. To the contrary, this is seen as appropriate social behavior, because by so doing people are not claiming exclusive rights over their children. The Baatombu case invites us to re-think the moral connotations that giving up a child for adoption has in our own Euro-American society.

Third, I have shown that norms and behavior concerning parenthood are not only society-specific, but can be affected by general transforma-tions within a given society. Today we can observe a transformational process among the Baatombu, especially in urban settings. It is unclear whether we are observing a slow process, which will lead to the complete disappearance of traditional fosterage. My impression is that social parenthood will not disappear but will be slowly transformed into more temporary forms, strengthening the position of the biological parents. This cannot be seen independently from global influences, for example

Euro-American ideas of good parenthood which seem to have become the dominant discourse in many different societies. But I have shown very briefly that this process of transformation does not mean that local ideas of parenthood disappear completely. One important norm that seems to be resistant is the idea that parental change does not damage the child.

Finally, in this chapter I have shown that social behavior concerning parenthood derives from social norms. I have further mentioned that these norms are in a slow process of transformation, and that the actual practices of social parenthood in urban settings give more emphasis to the biological parents. These norms derive from a Euro-American discourse. Therefore the question arises as to why some norms and beliefs, for example the belief that foster practices do not damage children, remain, while others, for example the belief that children do not belong to their biological parents, disappear. The challenge of the Baatombu case study is to provoke such questions.

Notes

1 See Carsten (2000).

2 Using the term "Euro-America", I refer to Marilyn Strathern's way of using the term (Strathern 1996, 1998).

3 Among the literature concerning social parenthood in West Africa, see Allman (1997), Atto (1996), Bledsoe (1980), Bledsoe and Isingo-Abanike (1989), Isaac and Conrad (1982), Lallemand (1993 and 1994), Page (1989), Roost Visher (1997).

4 The circulation of children is a term Suzanne Lallemand uses for the phenomenon (1993, 1994). As in most of the French literature, Lallemand does not use Goody's distinction between adoption and fosterage.

5 I have done field research among the Baatombu in Northern Benin since 1992, about 24 months in all. I would like to thank the Deutsche Forschungsgemeinschaft, The Freie Universität Berlin and the Frobenius Institute, Frankfurt am Main for financial and institutional support.

6 For general anthropological and historical descriptions of the Borgu region and the multi-ethnic Baatombu society see Lombard (1965), Kuba (1996), Alber (2000).

7 This is quite different from the "Freudian" concept which tries to explain adult personality structures through traumatic experiences in the early childhood.

8 Recorded interview in Tɛbɔ, 24 March 1998, own translation from Baatonum.

9 The Baatombu do not seem to distinguish as sharply as Europeans between the ownership of things ("my car") and of people ("my child"). I found it remarkable that this woman – among others – used the term "thing" for children, when talking about relations of belonging between children and adults.

10 In Benin parents do not only have to pay for the apprenticeship of their

children, they have also to pay for the big feasts that put an end, officially, to the time of apprenticeship. Only after having paid all the requirements of that feast – beer, spirits, food, clothes and so on – is the apprentice liberated from the status of dependence on his or her master.

11 It is remarkable that adoption has the capacity of strengthening the clanship ties and therefore, patriliniarity, as well as cross-cut them. In the above-cited cases where women adopt "their" children to live with them in their husbands' households, adoption strengthens the relations of belonging within their own clans in opposition to a non-familiar environment, the families of their husbands. But it also happens frequently that children are adopted by members of their mothers' kingroup, by the adoptive mother of their mothers, or by their mothers' siblings. In these cases, belonging to a clan is crossed by belonging to the adoptive parents. Therefore the principle of patriliniarity is crossed by the bi-lineal concept of adoption. In another article I have outlined the tensions between the father's family and the mother's family in case of conflicts in Baatombu society. From the perspective of an actor within a conflict, various options exist to choose between the two (Alber and Sommer 1999).

12 I know that it is quite problematic to draw a dichotomous picture between biological and social parents. There is no Baatonum term for biological or social parents, only some expressions to make the distinction. Even the Baatonum term *mara*, conventionally translated as "giving birth" and designating the physical act, is used by men and women, and as well by adoptive parents if they speak about "their" child. But to simplify it, I use the term "biological parents" in an analytical sense, for the persons who bore and begot a child physically. With "social parents" I mean those persons who adopted a child in the sense described and take responsibility for them.

13 Esther Goody (1982: 86ff.) has done some research on this question as well. She compared the life careers of former foster children in Northern Ghana with people who had not been fostered as children. She showed that professional success does not depend upon whether or not one was fostered.

References

Alber, Erdmute 2000: *Im Gewand von Herrschaft*. Köln: Rüdiger Köppe Verlag.
Alber, Erdmute and Jörn Sommer 1999: Grenzen der Implementierung staatlichen Rechts im dörflichen Kontext. Eine Analyse der Rechtswirklichkeit in einem Baatombu-Dorf in Benin. *Afrika spectrum* 34 (1): 85–111.
Allman, Jean 1997: Fathering, Mothering and Making Sense of Ntamoba: Reflections on the Economy of Child-Rearing in Colonial Asante. *Africa* 67 (2): 296–322.
Atto, Ursula 1996: Verpflichtung, Belastung, Freude: Pflegekinder und ihr Verständnis der Hausarbeit. In: K. Beck and G. Spittler: *Arbeit in Afrika*, Hamburg: Lit Verlag, 225–242.
Bledsoe, Caroline 1980: The manipulation of Kpelle Social Fatherhood. *Ethnology* 19 (1): 29–47.
Bledsoe, Caroline and Uche Isingo-Abanike 1989: Strategies of Child-Fosterage

among Mende Grannies in Sierra Leone. In: Ron J. Lesthaeghe (ed.): *Reproduction and Social Organisation in Sub-Saharan Africa*, Berkeley/Los Angeles/London: University of California Press, 442–474.

Carsten, Janet 2000: Introduction: Cultures of Relatedness. In: Janet Carsten (ed.): *Cultures of Relatedness*, Cambridge: Cambridge University Press, 1–36.

Goody, Ester 1982: *Parenthood and Social Reproduction*, Cambridge: Cambridge University Press.

Howell, Signe, 2003: Kinning: The Creation of Life Trajectories in Transnational Adoptive Families. *Journal of the Royal Anthropological Institute* (incorporating *Man*) 9 (3): 465–484.

Isaac, Barry L. and Shelby R. Conrad 1982: Child Fosterage among the Mende of Upper Bambara Chiefdom, Sierra Leone: Rural–Urban and Occupational Comparisons. *Ethnology* 21: 243–258.

Kuba, Richard 1996: *Wasangari und Wangara*, Hamburg: Lit Verlag.

Lallemand, Suzanne 1993: *La circulation des enfants en société traditionelle*, Paris: L'Harmattan.

Lallemand, Suzanne 1994: *Adoption et Marriage*, Paris: L'Harmattan.

Lombard, Jacques 1965: *Structures de type "feodal" en Afrique Noire*, Paris: Mouton.

Page, Hillary 1989: Childrearing versus Childbearing: Coresidence of Mother and Child in Sub-Saharan Africa. In: Ron J. Lesthaeghe (ed.): *Reproduction and Social Organisation in Sub-Saharan Africa*, Berkeley/Los Angeles/ London: University of California Press, 401–441.

Roost Vischer, Lilo 1997: *Mütter zwischen Herd und Markt*, Basel: Verlag Wepf.

Strathern, Marilyn, 1996: Potential Property, Intellectual Rights and Property in Persons. *Social Anthropology* 4 (1): 17–33.

Strathern, Marilyn, 1998: Divisions of Interest and Languages of ownership. In: Chris Hann (ed.): *Property Relations*, Cambridge: Cambridge University Press.

Chapter 4

Fosterage and the politics of marriage and kinship in East Cameroon

Catrien Notermans

In some regions in Africa south of the Sahara, large numbers of children
live during long periods of time separated from their mother as foster
children in other households. In parts of West Africa, including East
Cameroon, the mobility of children is high; 30 per cent of the children
between ten and fourteen years of age do not live with their biological
mother (Page 1989). This high percentage of foster children indicates
that the upbringing of children is not only a task of the biological parents,
but is shared with many other educators. Though women in Africa are
children's most important educators, a gender approach has been lacking
in the anthropological inquiry of fosterage. Moreover, the importance of
kinship has also been neglected in recent anthropological theory.

This chapter argues that women use fosterage to construct their
matrilineage and to empower themselves within the domain of marriage.
I show how both the kinship system (a combination of patrilineal and
matrilineal descent) and the marriage system (characterised by formal
and informal polygyny, informal polyandry and flexibility of marriage)
contribute to the high frequency of child fosterage in Batouri, a small
town in East Cameroon. Ethnographic studies of the area typify Batouri
as a patrilineal, polygynous and male-dominated society. However, when
focusing on female strategies of fosterage, strong polyandrous and
matrilineal structures become visible. I will argue that the popularity of
fosterage has to be understood in the context of these matrilineages that
have often been neglected.

Theoretical approaches to fosterage

In the 1970s and 1980s anthropologists writing in English paid a lot of
attention to fosterage in order to explain its social functions in the local
context (Fiawoo 1978; Goody 1982; Oppong *et al.* 1978; Schildkrout

1973). These structural–functionalist studies mainly focused on the way fosterage as an institution was interrelated to other institutions. It was generally suggested that African parents care for other people's children as if they were their 'own' children (cf. Goody 1982). The outcome of equal treatment of biological and foster children would be that the children never know who their 'real' (biological) parents are. This harmonious representation of the African family, however, does not reflect the conflicts that may occur in foster situations. In East Cameroon, mothers often discriminate between children, although not primarily between biological and foster children but between foster children from their own lineage and foster children from their husband's lineage. It is this conflict in the conjugal domain and the wish of both spouses to foster equal numbers of children from their lineages 'to keep balance in marriage' that is inconsistent with common representations of fosterage, and that will be dealt with in this chapter.

Since the 1980s studies of fosterage and of kinship in general declined, partly due to the dissolution of the discrete domains of economics, politics, religion, and kinship which had defined anthropology (Carsten 2000:2). In the 1990s demographers picked up the anthropological interest in fosterage, but instead of focusing on kinship structures they looked at three other domains of social life in Africa: the relationship between fosterage and high fertility (Blanc and Lloyd 1994; Bledsoe 1990; Isiugo-Abanihe 1994; Oppong and Bleek 1982); the relationship between fosterage and high infant mortality (Bledsoe 1991; Bledsoe and Brandon 1992; Castle 1995); and the relationship between fosterage and schooling (Clévenot and Pilon 1996; Lloyd and Blanc 1995; Vimard and Guillaume 1991). An economic approach based on analyses of costs-and-benefits characterises these three domains of interest: women would send some of their children away because of high fertility and low incomes; foster children would fall ill or die more readily than birth children because of insufficient financial assistance; and children would be fostered out to attend school and to offer cheap domestic help to their foster parents. This emphasis on poverty and economic impulses of fosterage has to do with a rhetoric of dichotomies that typifies the demographic debate: the dichotomy between traditional and modern society, between rural and urban society, and between kinship structures and a cash economy.

However, to understand fosterage in a modern urban society, kinship has to be brought back into anthropological theory on fosterage. Kinship – a so-called 'traditional' aspect of society – is very alive in urban society and it structures fosterage, even when it is used for so-called 'modern' purposes like schooling. Categories like traditional and modern, rural and urban, are not as separated as they often seem to be in theoretical frameworks (Piot 1999). 'Modern' educational fosterage does not replace 'traditional' kinship fosterage; it is based on the structures of kinship fosterage and is therefore closely tied up with it. Though schooling may be an important factor in explaining high fosterage frequency in town, it cannot be seen as the only explicative one. Every foster situation is based on a combination of reasons and it is hardly possible to select one argument as the most relevant. I will focus on the kinship argument since it reveals more than the education argument, how women actively and strategically create kinship through fosterage.

Connected to this argument – to take kinship seriously when analysing urban fosterage – is my reaction to the economic approach to fosterage that prevails in demographic studies. The emphasis on poverty has resulted in interpreting fosterage as a custom of sending children out. However, fosterage in East Cameroon is basically not a matter of sending a child away but of asking for a child or claiming it. Even children from the villages who come to town and attend school, are often asked for by the foster parents who have other reasons than educational or economic ones to take the children into their household. These reasons have often to do with the construction of matrilineages and with a struggle for power balance in marriage.

European kinship theory has been dominated by a patriarchal paradigm, focusing on men as main actors in kinship affairs. This male European bias affected the understanding and interpretation of African data. The invisible, transitory or distant role of men as fathers in African kinship has been difficult to accept (Amadiume 1997). As a rule, matrilineality has not been recognised, as in the case of the Kako of Batouri (East Cameroon). Amadiume, who passionately throws into doubt certain established Eurocentric certainties about the origins and social character of kinship, states:

> By dismissing the link between gender and a particular type of descent, specifically the possibilities of authority and power for women in matriliny, I believe that European anthropologists were misled by their own ethnocentrism into insisting on a general theory of male dominance in all types of descent systems.
>
> (1997: 80)

The lack of a gender focus in anthropological studies on fosterage added to the tendency to neglect matrilineal descent as an important framework in which fosterage can be understood. Recently published studies on Cameroon confirm the complexity of the coexistence of different descent systems that call for a deconstruction of traditional typologies (Feldman-Savelsberg 1999; Gausset 1998). In conformity with these studies, I aim to reveal the dynamic conflict between different kinship principles that are constantly negotiated in everyday social practice. By focusing on women I want to point out that foster transactions enable them to construct and to strengthen matrilineal bonds; it yields them power and autonomy in a society where patrilineality operates simultaneously, and at certain moments in their life even undermines their freedom and power of decision.

New efforts have been made to revitalise the anthropological study of kinship (Bouquet 1993; Franklin and McKinnon 2000; Holy 1996; Schweitzer 2000). New directions in kinship studies no longer build on Eurocentric and static frameworks that are blind to the agency of women and children, but they are interested in the creation of kinship, applying a dynamic and actor-oriented approach. I want to join this kinship debate and to focus on the way women experience kinship, how they work with it and give meaning to it.

I will also draw on French theories of fosterage since any signs of 'kinship crisis' or gender neglect have been less obvious. Both former and recent studies characterise fosterage as an 'acte d'alliance' and as a strategy of female power in the kinship domain (Etienne 1979, 1987; Jonckers 1997; Lallemand 1988, 1993, 1994). Female anthropologists dominate French theory on fosterage and react to a main problem in French alliance theory – the construction of women as objects to be moved or owned by men. Etienne, pleading for the recognition of women's agency in fosterage, already stated in 1979 that it can be a strategy for women to reinforce their place in the conjugal household since 'the adopted child displays a wife's autonomy towards her in-laws and strengthens her matrilineal kinship ties' (1979: 89).

Another French anthropologist working on fosterage, Suzanne Lallemand (1988, 1993, 1994), also argues that fosterage has to be understood in relation to marriage structures since both can be closely interwoven. I will elaborate on the arguments of both French theorists and illustrate how female strategies of fosterage and marriage are interconnected in East Cameroon. I indicate that strategies of descent have also to be analysed to understand the gender negotiations within marriage and lineage that are essential to daily life experiences of women in Batouri.

Marriage and descent in East Cameroon

Batouri is a provincial town of 25,000 inhabitants in the savannah area of East Cameroon, 500 kilometres from the capital Yaoundé. Since 1992 I have been doing anthropological fieldwork in Batouri, first on polygyny and more recently on women's and children's experiences with fosterage.[1] Fieldwork focused on the district Mbondossi, a community of about 1,500 people from different ethnic backgrounds. Most people are Kako but also other ethnic groups from the Eastern province in Cameroon, such as the Yangélé and the Byemo, consider themselves natives of Batouri. For most people, urban life is linked to family life in the villages. This mainly happens through children who regularly move between kin in town and the surrounding villages.

Though people in Mbondossi occupy a low social and economic position, women enjoy respect and considerable independence in relation to men through monopolising the production, marketing and preparation of food. Women seldom look for waged work, as agriculture is time consuming and comparatively more rewarding. Women have free access to the fields outside the town that are abundantly available in this area. The main crops are cassava, maize and groundnuts. Since the soil is extremely fertile women produce a lot of food, much more than they need for their families, and sell the surplus in the local market. This food surplus is their wealth and their strength: the more (foster) children they can feed, the more powerful they are.

The men in the district do not assist in food production, as often happens in the villages. They are mostly trained to be bricklayers, carpenters or car mechanics and they are looking for a job to earn money to maintain their families. In spite of the troubles men have in finding work, women consider them the breadwinners and they hold them responsible for their wives' and children's financial support. Men, however, cannot meet this appeal to pay school fees, pay for medicine or pay for clothes and it often makes them desperate. Lack of solidarity generally characterises marital relationships since husband and wife both look after their own interests.

Marital conflicts are frequent in the district. Ethnic conflicts, however, are rare. Despite cultural diversity, people do not play off cultural differences but use Christianity to express their common identity. Christian missions started working in the area in the late 1930s. By the 1990s Christianity had become a popular religion with 85 per cent of the population belonging to one of the three most important churches in town, Catholic, Presbyterian or Adventist. Neither Christianity nor financial shortcomings, however, keep men from marrying several wives (Notermans 1999, 2002). A quarter of the households in Mbondossi are formally polygynous and almost all of these marriages include two co-wives.

People in the district declare that polygyny is more frequently practised than is revealed by official statistics, as monogamous marriages are often informally polygynous in practice. Men prefer to marry one woman officially and to combine this marriage with a number of mistresses since such an informal polygynous relationship is considered cheaper than assuming responsibility for several wives and their children. Women, for their part, also combine formal marriage with a number of informal conjugal relationships. They feel free to have different sexual relationships simultaneously and/or successively, and men take it for granted as women take polygyny for granted. In local language, extramarital relationships for both men and women are called *wanja*.

Women do not highly value marriage: they easily divorce or leave their husband for a while. Neither marriage nor husbands are in the centre of women's interest. Copet-Rougier argues that this attitude towards marriage arose in the 1970s when Kako women began to challenge male structures of dominance and gradually changed stable marriages into 'marriages of trial' (1985, 1987). This marital flexibility is possible due to the low brideprices, that nowadays are hardly even transferred. Amounts range from €50 to €125 and can be easily returned in case of divorce. Women's relatives rarely insist on receiving brideprice, to retain a claim on the children. This results in a high frequency of informal marital relationships, for men as well as for women. These relationships are said to be 'marriages' but have not been confirmed with a brideprice payment or a marriage certificate. If a *wanja* relationship has lasted for more than a year, people define it as 'marriage' since the exchange of food, money and sex is the core of both marital and *wanja*-relationships.

It is not shameful for women to give birth to children in different marriages. On the contrary, it seems to be their aim to bear children from different fathers. Even when women themselves do not strive for it intentionally, their mothers may urge them to have some children from informal relationships in order to claim the children for themselves. This attitude with respect to marriages and children has to be understood in relation to the descent system. Though Kako society, in anthropological literature, has always been characterised as polygynous and patrilineal (Copet-Rougier 1977, 1990), matrilineages do exist next to patrilineages. Women's contributions to their matrilineages are closely linked to polyandrous relationships that, due to gender-blindness, have also been overlooked in previous research in the area.

Main agents in matrilineages are not men but grandmothers, who often claim their daughters' children through preventing the children's fathers transferring brideprice or signing a birth certificate. As women do not easily enter into formal marriages, men often have to claim their children through signing birth certificates. Fathers offer little or no resistance to maternal grandmothers who make a claim, their decisions have to be respected. Grandmothers' claims also release fathers from paying for cloth and medicine and from paying fees in the future. Young fathers in particular often fail to provide financial support and easily give in when others are ready to accept responsibility. Fathers may refuse to recognise their children so as to avoid financial claims, since they also bear responsibility for children of their unmarried sisters.

In some cases grandmothers force the father to sign the birth certificate in order to make him pay for the baby's layette and initial medical care. However, in these instances grandmothers often do not allow the father to take the children with him, and keep them within the maternal household. Grandmothers may take possession of the birth certificates, and are able to tear them up when children have successfully survived their first years of life and medical costs become less of a risk. Having destroyed the original birth certificate, grandmothers are allowed to register the child again and to identify a male member of the matriliny as the child's father. Even when grandmothers allow the fathers to sign the birth certificates, they often make a second birth certificate in which a mother's brother, the mother's father or a deceased husband are recorded as the child's father. Such cases come into the open when the biological father who has financially supported his child for years refuses to give up his rights.

At the provincial department of the Ministry of Social Affairs in Batouri, people are received who feel powerless in the domains of kinship and marriage and ask for help. Most problems discussed at this ministry relate to the multiplicity of children's birth certificates and concern fathers who accuse their children's maternal family of having taken the children away. Concerning arguments about rights in children, women rarely ask a civil servant for help as they have a more powerful position in these affairs. All these gestures and problems concerning birth certificates that are negotiated, signed, changed, argued, destroyed or returned express people's flexible, changeable and multiple attitudes towards descent.

It is not easy to categorise these multiple and shifting attitudes towards descent in East Cameroon through standard anthropological frameworks that have been characterised by fixity, stability and timelessness. Kinship systems as described above require new frameworks that are open to the mobility and fluidity in people's lives. Theories of descent have played a vital part in anthropological history, though for the most part, they have only concentrated on unilineal descent as true descent (Parkin 1997: 143). This unilineal bias, emphasising patriliny in particular, has been so influential that up to now ethnographic studies have to re-examine and re-classify societies that previously have been characterised as unilineal. Recently published studies on Cameroon call for such a deconstruction and advance the existence of matrilineages in societies where previously only patrilineages had been identified (Feldman-Savelsberg 1999; Gausset 1998). In contrast to both Feldman-Savelsberg and Gausset who explain the descent systems in question as being double unilineal, this system does not apply to East Cameroon where children at birth are not recruited into both unilineal groups of descent. Though patrilineages and matri- lineages coexist, children can belong to either; group membership is not automatically given but has to be discussed and negotiated.

When taking women's different marital stages into account, matrilineal descent comes up as the dominating line of descent since mothers, either supported or forced by their own mother or brothers, mostly claim their children through preventing their child's father from transferring brideprice or signing a birth certificate. However, out of all relationships women enter into, they accept at least one as a formal marriage in which they move to their husband's place and give up rights to biological children in exchange for goods and money. Women enter into marriage mainly for financial benefit and social status and will resolutely bring their marriage to an end when reciprocity fails. When a husband does not compensate for his wife's suffering and reproduction of children, women speak about 'wasting their time'. They divorce and take the matter to court to claim damages for 'lost time'.

What in the 1970s was recognised as patrilineal descent in Batouri, is reduced in present-day urban society to brideprice payments and patrilocal residence for the duration of a marriage.[2] It is even questionable whether these customs prove the existence of extensive patrilineages as married men often place their legitimate children in the charge of sisters who are at a disadvantage in their conjugal household, barren or deprived of biological children through divorce. These patrilineal practices mean that a woman is in a less powerful position in the conjugal household than in informal marriages and in her own matrilineage. With fosterage women try to defend their position vis-à-vis their husband and co-wives, and to counterbalance the loss of biological children given to the husband's lineage with children from their own matrilineage. These children provide them with power and are asked for to keep balance in marriage.

Foster politics

Compared with the lack of solidarity and emotional support between husband and wife, there is an intimate and close relationship between sisters and brothers who easily exchange children during their life. It is in this kinship context that fosterage in East Cameroon should be understood. A combination of specific characteristics of the descent system and the marriage system, like brother–sister solidarity, formal polygyny, informal polygynous and polyandrous relationships, the high flexibility of marriages and almost non-existent brideprices, are related to the high frequency of fosterage in the area.[3]

A survey held in 1999 in the district Mbondossi revealed that 31 per cent of the children lived with foster parents. Surveys of schools showed even higher percentages, with 49 per cent of the primary school-children between nine and fifteen years old, and 94 per cent of secondary schoolchildren between thirteen and eighteen years old, living with foster parents. Even the children who actually stayed with their biological parents had already had the experience of living with a foster family. Primary schoolchildren, for example, had resided for long periods of time in an average number of two and a half households.

When leaving their mother's home, children always go to close relatives, such as their maternal grandmother, a sister or brother of their mother, a sister or a brother of their father, or to an older sibling. Though kinship networks are large and people in a polygynous society have numerous (half) sisters and (half) brothers, only full siblings are considered good and reliable foster parents. A mother's mother, mother's brother and father's sister are favourite and common foster parents. This solid relationship between sisters and brothers obviously points to the meaning matrilineal kinship has in structuring fosterage.

Before, during and after formal marriage, women maintain matrilineal ties through plural informal relationships and strong solidarity with mothers and brothers. Mothers claim their daughter's children, and sisters and brothers claim each other's children to strengthen their lineage. To illustrate this, I present the cases of Emilienne and Madeleine.

Emilienne and the plurality of husbands and children

Emilienne is fifty years old and living with two foster children She grew up with her mother and her mother's brother. She married but left her first husband more than twenty years ago. She 'tried' two other marriages but she finally came back to her mother's place. People told me that she had no biological children but cared for several foster children. I interpreted this as a biological infertility problem. Though I had close contact with her first foster daughter, it was only in the second period of fieldwork that I 'discovered' the existence of two biological children. Neither Emilienne nor her foster daughter had ever mentioned them as Emilienne lost these children when she divorced her first husband who claimed them and gave them to his sister. After her divorce Emilienne lived for a time in her mother's house in Mbondossi, together with her elder sister, who also had different husbands before returning to her mother's home. When Emilienne's oldest foster daughter left home to join her husband, Emilienne moved to a village sixteen kilometres from town to join her brother. Emilienne tells me:

> I have cared for four foster children. All of them are girls. I took the first one from my elder sister. Her first husband died but his family never claimed the children. My sister gave them to her mother and joined her brother. At his place, she had several other 'husbands' but the children she received from them, all belong to her since she consistently indicated her deceased husband as the biological father. I asked for one of these children when I left my husband. He claimed his two children and gave them to his older sister. I felt too lonely. I have got my first foster daughter when she was two years old and up till now she considers me her first mother. I have got my second foster daughter from my brother. She was two years old when her mother left her father. I asked my brother for the child since my first (foster) daughter was still too young to give me grandchildren. When she [the first (foster) daughter] gave birth to her first child at the age of 16, I did not want her to marry the man who made her pregnant. I even prevented him from signing the birth certificate. It would enable him to claim his child one day and to take her away. In order to keep the child in the family my elder sister [the biological mother of the foster daughter] declared her eldest son to be the father. That is what they wrote on the birth certificate. I brought this girl up as my own child. When her mother joined the father of her second

child, I told her to leave the girl with me. Two years ago, I also asked my eldest [biological] son for his child. He received the child in an informal marriage and his 'wife' left him to join another husband. Both of them agreed to give me the girl.

The case of Emilienne demonstrates the strategies women employ to construct a family of their own. Marriages are not considered definitive or long-term relationships, but temporary frameworks that provide them with respect, social status and financial support; but not with children. Therefore, Emilienne accepted formal marriage only once. To avoid lone-liness she puts a high value on foster children from matrilineal kin. In having 'own' children she is less successful than her elder sister, however, since she did not bear children from informal marriages and therefore depends totally on foster children. Therefore, both sisters join forces to defend matrilineal interests and independence from husbands. They do not value biological fatherhood but constantly negotiate matters of children with matrilineal kin. To acquire children for their lineage, they easily declare brothers, sons or deceased husbands to be the child's biological father. They do not construct lineages with husbands but with mothers, sisters and brothers. The next case of Madeleine will illustrate that women, even when being formally married, keep on belonging to their matrilineage and maintain it through fosterage.

Madeleine and the power balance in marriage

Madeleine is twenty-nine years old. Her mother died when she was nine. She grew up with the second wife of her father and at the age of seventeen she married her present husband. She gave birth to four boys, one of whom died. She actually cares for seven children – her three boys and four foster girls. When asking her about these foster children, Madeleine tells me:

Before I gave birth to my first child, my husband already asked his sister for a child. It was a child she gave birth to before marriage. The other foster children I care for are the children of two brothers-in-law who lost their wives. My husband asked for the girls when his brothers remarried and their new wives did not look after the chil-dren well. All three girls came to stay with us when they were very young. If they want, they can stay forever. They regularly visit their parents in the villages, during school holidays, but they always come back to stay with us. Since all the children I got are boys, I asked my brother to give me a girl. Since the other girls are from my husband's side, I wanted to have a girl of my own. I needed a child from my own side to keep balance in marriage. I do not like to work only for my husband's family. I also want my family to eat from the pot. My brother accepted and gave me a girl. He has two wives who do not like each other. He gave me the child to save it from their bad behaviour. The girl (four years old) keeps in close touch with her mother since she lives nearby. Now and then she even sleeps in her mother's house but she lives with us and will stay with us.

Such expressions as 'I wanted to have a girl of my own', 'to keep balance in marriage', and 'I want my family to eat from the pot', are important statements to explain the power aspect of marriage and fosterage in this area.

The foster transactions that took place in Madeleine's household are an example of exchange of children between sisters and brothers. Women consider the children that they solicit from their matrilineal kin, and especially from their brothers, to be their own children and they see the foster children that the husband added to the household as strangers, since they belong to his descent groups. The children that women classify as being their 'own' are either biological children born outside marriage – and fostered to their mother or brothers – or foster children from their brothers (who mostly also care for the children of their sisters). These children belong to her (lineage) and not to her husband's and will therefore stay with her, even when marriage ends.

An important reason why women, throughout the years that they are formally married, ask their brothers for foster children is that these foster children carry weight with them. Women need foster children, as they say, 'to keep balance in marriage'. When a husband solicits children from his family, his wife also solicits for children from her family to strengthen her position in the household. Though their interest is obviously not an economic one, the aspect of self-interest cannot be denied. Women themselves call it 'calculation'. If the husband cares for two children coming from his lineage, his wife will also ask for two children from her lineage; if he cares for three, she will also ask for three, and so on. Though husband and wife have to reach an agreement about fostering children, they both use it in their own interest and that of their lineage, and not in the interest of their common household. This rivalry for foster children often causes marital troubles and adds to the high rates of divorce in this area. When a husband disallows fosterage from his wife's side, his wife will probably not accept such a subordinate position in the conjugal household and will return to her matrilineal kin. To have a good marriage, women want to have their lineage present in it.

The case of Madeleine also illustrates that fosterage can be a strategy to keep the number of boys and girls in balance. Madeleine, who only had boys, did not ask for a 'child' but she asked for a 'girl'. Girls from the age of fifteen can provide their (foster) mother with grandchildren as long as they do not accept formal marriage. Women often stimulate their daughters to engage in short-term informal relationships, in order to confiscate the children that will be born from them. Through claiming foster girls, married women work on their matrilineage since these foster girls, and not their husband, can give them children who belong to themselves.

Conclusion

In this chapter, I bring kinship back to anthropological analysis of fosterage and elaborate on the fosterage–marriage connection as proposed in French theory on fosterage. To complement British structural–functionalist theory on fosterage, I focus on individual female strategies of fosterage and on the conflicts that may arise in foster practice. I use a dynamic actor-oriented approach of kinship to point out that women actively and constantly work with kinship and marriage to create their own family networks. My focus on the meaning of kinship in foster transactions is aimed at counterbalancing the emphasis on economic explanations of fosterage in current demographic theory. My approach reveals that common kinship frameworks, as developed in previous research in the area, cannot sufficiently explain the high rate of fosterage nor adequately capture the meanings fosterage has for the persons involved, and that matriliny and patriliny are options that women use for different goals at different stages of life.

This chapter reveals that there is no double descent system in the Batouri area of East Cameroon. Children do not automatically belong to the lineages of both their father and their mother, but rights to claim children are constantly negotiated. In both patrilineage and matrilineage, the exchange of children between sisters and brothers holds a prominent place. It is in this exchange that both matrilineal and patrilineal descent systems are combined. I also demonstrate that kinship, an apparently traditional feature of social life, is in fact a 'modernity' (Piot 1999). Plural marriages and matriliny have been intensified in processes of urbanisation and have given new impulses to the 'traditional' reciprocal relationship between sisters and brothers that engenders fosterage.

Notes

1   The research was funded by WOTRO (Netherlands Foundation for the Advancement of Tropical Research), and the Department of Anthropology and the Centre for Gender Studies at the University of Nijmegen.

2   I assume that discrepancies between data collected in the 1970s and the 1990s partly result from historical changes in the marriage and descent system in East Cameroon, and partly from changes in anthropological approaches, premises and concepts. Recent anthropological studies that challenge previous ethnocentric and androcentric biases in approaches to descent and no longer take marriage as women's central and most important trajectory, produce divergent results. Urbanisation and an increasing number of female-headed households in towns may affect attitudes to marriage and descent.

3   Besides marriage and kinship characteristics, high mortality rates in the area also influence the high frequency of fosterage. People often die in traffic accidents or of illnesses like tuberculosis and AIDS. Hospital reports in Batouri reveal that 50 per cent of the tested patients are HIV-positive. A person's health condition can be so weakened that they succumb to diarrhoea, malaria and other infections.

References

Amadiume, I. (1997) *Reinventing Africa*, London, New York: Zed Books.

Blanc, A. K. and Lloyd, C. B. (1994) 'Women's work, child-bearing, and child-rearing over the life cycle in Ghana', in A. Adepoju and C. Oppong (eds) *Gender, work, and population in Sub-Saharan Africa*, London: James Currey, pp. 112–131.

Bledsoe, C. (1990) 'The politics of children: Fosterage and the social management of fertility among the Mende of Sierra Leone', in W. P. Handwerker (ed.) *Births and power*, Boulder, San Francisco, London: Westview Press, pp. 81–100.

——(1991) 'The trickle-down model within households: Foster children and the phenomenon of scrounging', in J. Cleland and A. Hill (eds) *The health transition*, Canberra: Health Transition Centre, Australian National University, pp. 115–131.

Bledsoe, C. and Brandon A. (1992) 'Child fosterage and child mortality in Sub-Saharan Africa: Some preliminary questions and answers', in E. van de Walle, G. Pison and M. Sala-Diakanda (eds) *Mortality and society in Sub-Saharan Africa*, Oxford: Clarendon Press, pp. 279–302.

Bouquet, M. (1993) *Reclaiming English kinship*, Manchester, New York: Manchester University Press.

Carsten, J. (ed.) (2000) *Cultures of relatedness*, Cambridge: Cambridge University Press.

Castle, S. (1995) 'Child fostering and children's nutritional outcomes in rural Mali: The role of female status in directing child transfers', *Social Science and Medicine*, 40:679–694.

Clévenot, D. and Pilon, M. (1996) 'Femmes et scolarisation des enfants', *Séminaire internationale 'Femmes et Gestion des Ressources', IFORD, Yaoundé (Cameroun), 1996*, pp. 1–24.

Copet-Rougier, E. (1977) *Ngélébok*, Paris: Université de Paris X.

—— (1985) 'Contrôle masculin, exclusivité féminine dans une société patrilinéaire', in J.-C. Barbier (ed.) *Femmes du Cameroun*, Paris, Bondy: Karthala, Orstom, pp. 153–180.

—— (1987) '"L'antilope accouche toujours de l'éléphant" (devinette Mkako): étude de la transformation du mariage chez les Mkako du Cameroun', in D. Parkin and D. Nyamwaya (eds) *Transformations of African marriage*, Manchester: Manchester University Press, pp. 75–92.

—— (1990) 'Le clan, le lieu et l'alliance', in F. Héritier-Augé and E. Copet-Rougier (eds) *Les complexités de l'alliance*, vol. 1, Paris: Éditions des Archives Contemporaines, pp. 193–231.

Etienne, M. (1979) 'Maternité sociale, rapports d'adoption et pouvoir des femmes chez les Baoulé (Côte d'Ivoire)', *L'Homme*, 19:63–107.

—— (1987) 'Rapports de sexe et de classe et mobilité socio-économique chez les Baoulé (Côte d'Ivoire)', *Anthropologie et Sociétés*, 11 (1):73–93.

Feldman-Savelsberg, P. (1999) *Plundered kitchens, empty wombs*, Ann Arbor: University of Michigan Press.

Fiawoo, D. K. (1978) 'Some patterns of foster care in Ghana', in C. Oppong, G. Abada, M. Bekombo-Priso and J. Mogey (eds) *Marriage, fertility, and parenthood in West Africa*, Canberra: Australian National University, pp. 273–288.

Franklin, S. and McKinnon, S. (2000) 'New directions in kinship study', *Current Anthropology*, 41: 275–279.

Gausset, Q. (1998) 'Double unilineal descent and triple kinship terminology: The case of the Kwanja of Cameroon', *Journal of the Royal Anthropological Institute*, 4 (2): 309–323.

Goody, E. (1982) *Parenthood and social reproduction*, Cambridge: Cambridge University Press.

Holy, L. (1996) *Anthropological perspectives on kinship*, London, Chicago: Pluto Press.

Isiugo-Abanihe, U. (1994) 'Parenthood in Sub-Saharan Africa: Child fostering and its relationship with fertility', in T. Locoh and V. Hertric (eds) *The onset of fertility transition in Sub-Saharan Africa*, Liège: Derouaux Ordina, pp. 163–174.

Jonckers, D. (1997) 'Les enfants confiés', in M. Pilon, T. Locoh, E. Vignikin and P. Vimard (eds) *Ménages et familles en Afrique*, Paris: Centre français sur la population et le développement, pp. 193–208.

Lallemand, S. (1988) 'Adoption, fosterage et alliance', *Anthropologie et Sociétés*, 12: 25–40.

—— (1993) *La circulation des enfants en société traditionelle*, Paris: Editions L'Harmattan.

—— (1994) *Adoption et mariage*, Paris: Editions L'Harmattan.

Lloyd, C. B. and Blanc, A. K. (1995) *Children's schooling in Sub-Saharan Africa*, New York: Population Council.

Notermans, C. (1999) *Verhalen in veelvoud*, Nijmegen: Valkhof Pers.

—— (2002) 'True Christianity without dialogue: Women and the polygyny debate in Cameroon', *Anthropos*, 97 (2): 341–353.

Oppong, C., Abada, G., Bekombo-Priso, M. and Mogey, J. (eds) (1978) *Marriage, fertility, and parenthood in West Africa*, Canberra: Australian National University.

Oppong, C. and Bleek W. (1982) 'Economic models and having children: Some evidence from Kwahu, Ghana', *Africa*, 52: 15–33.

Page, H. (1989) 'Childrearing versus childbearing: Coresidence of mother and child in Sub-Saharan Africa', in R. Lesthaeghe (ed.) *Reproduction and social organisation in Sub-Saharan Africa*, Berkeley, Los Angeles, London: University of California Press, pp. 401–441.

Parkin, R. (1997) *Kinship*, Oxford: Blackwell Publishers.

Piot, C. (1999) *Remotely global*, Chicago: University of Chicago Press.

Schildkrout, E. (1973) 'The fostering of children in urban Ghana: Problems of ethnographic analysis in a multi-cultural context', *Urban Anthropology*, 2:48–73.

Schweitzer, P. P. (ed.) (2000) *Dividends of kinship*, London, New York: Routledge.

Vimard, P. and Guillaume, A. (1991) 'Mobilités familiales et spatiales des enfants en Côte-d'Ivoire', in A. Quesnel and P. Vimard (eds) *Migrations, changement social et développement*, Paris: Orstom, pp. 243–260.

Chapter 5

Adoption practices among the pastoral Maasai of East Africa

Enacting fertility

Aud Talle

This chapter concerns adoption among East African pastoralists and focuses on one particular form of adoption. Among pastoral peoples in this part of the world it is quite common for infertile or childless women to adopt children from co-wives, sisters-in-law or other close female relatives (Spencer 1988; Dahl 1990; Wagner-Glenn 1992). Although husbands and fathers may interfere in the decision-making, even initiate decisions on behalf of women, women are the major agents in these transactions. The prominent role of women in 'child exchanges' must be interpreted and located within wider cultural notions of femininity and gender, of procreation and prosperity in these societies. Cultural preferences and moral norms, however, must be given a *form*, and my argument in this chapter is that when women adopt children from each other, they evoke a meaningful image of the 'good life'.

My case refers to the pastoral Maasai, a population of some half a million people or less, surviving with their livestock herds in the savannah borderland between Kenya and Tanzania. The traditional habitat of the Maasai has shrunk dramatically during the last half a century or so mainly due to land encroachment by other ethnic groups and to the reallocation of common land into group and private ranches. The general position of the Maasai within the Kenyan as well as Tanzanian nation state is one of increasing poverty, economic and political marginalisation and the general insecurity of pastoral life (Talle 1988).[1]

Adoption, in contrast to fostering, normally refers to a formalised or legal transfer of rights and obligations in persons, resulting in a permanent alteration in social status (cf. Parkin 1997). With reference to the ethnography of East Africa, boundaries between the two, however, are sometimes fluid as one form may be transformed into another over time and, furthermore, do not only concern parent–child relations, but also relations between adults. During periods of drought and hunger, and during social unrest or upheavals, Maasai adults and children have for the purposes of survival been assimilated, temporarily or permanently, across ethnic boundaries in various adoption-like practices. Similarly, it has been common for neighbouring cultivators to be adopted into pastoral families, where they have acquired clan and age-set membership and taken up livestock keeping as a means of livelihood. Among the Maasai in Kenya, for instance, Kikuyu cultivators, living in the vicinity and often marrying into Maasai families, were fully integrated into the basic structures of Maasai sociality. Previous kinship ties were transferred to the host community when the adoptee was symbolically reborn by being shaved and anointed as a Maasai (Waller 1993: 231).

Adoption within the patrilineal or extended Maasai family, which is the concern of this chapter, is however of another moral order than the inter-ethnic adoption of adults and children. While the latter is chiefly legal and 'political' in nature, although not devoid of sentiments, the former is a bonding of a much more profound kind. It has its foundation in a deep-rooted worldview of commonality as a form of cultural and social practice and lived experience.

A morality of sharing

Livestock are the practical as well as ideological and emotional basis of the lifeworlds of East African pastoralists. Cattle, sheep and goats are the most commonly kept animals, but some groups such as the Somali, Rendille and Borana in Northeastern Kenya also keep large numbers of camels (Spencer 1973; Dahl 1979). Godfrey Lienhardt, doing fieldwork among the cattle-keeping Dinka in Southern Sudan in the late 1940s, has beautifully summarised the intimate relationship between human and livestock in these societies:

> The moral and the imaginative significance of cattle to the Dinka . . . complements their utilitarian importance. Their value is that of something to which men have assimilated themselves, dwelling upon them in reflection, *imitating them in stylized action*, and regarding them as interchangeable with human life in many social situations.
> (1961: 27, my emphasis)

The Maasai, as the Dinka, and the Nuer described by Evans-Pritchard (1940), along with many other similar groups, live by a deep-structured ethos of circulation and mutual sharing of livestock and livestock products. Livestock, in particular cattle, being divine gifts, belong to larger collectivities (families and lineages) than the individual. So also do children. Cattle and children are riches of the same sort, 'not made and "owned", but given into human care' (Lienhardt 1961: 22). The two are forms of property to which people hold shared rights. The collective rights to children, and the responsibility to care for them should need arise, find expressive form in, among other things, Maasai children addressing mother, stepmother, mother's sister and other close female relatives by the common term *yieyio* ('mother'). The same with the term *papa* ('father') being extended to a category of male relatives of the father's generation. In terms of address there is no difference between biological parent, adopting parent or step-parent. A child is a child, the Maasai often claim. Ideologically one may substitute for another.

In practical life, however, things may look different. Autobiographical accounts readily speak of the miserable fate of a motherless child left at the mercy of a capricious and sometimes abusive stepmother (Saitoti 1986). Jealousy and strife concerning distribution and inheritance of livestock within the polygynous Maasai family do not spare the children. Particularly boys, who are entitled to inherit the family's livestock herd, constitute a potential threat to the distribution of wealth.

The uneven distribution of resources inherent in the pastoral production system of the Maasai is regulated or 'equalised' (be equal, *aa-risio*; *erisioroto*) by the moral and social commitments of the 'blessed' ones (those who 'have') to dispose of their surpluses to less fortunate kin and age-mates. This redistribution is done through various institutionalised rituals of sharing and exchange. Adoption of children among Maasai women is one such ritual of sharing.

Within this deeply embedded morality of sharing and commitment towards each other, selfish or stingy persons (*epiak oleng*) are despised by fellow Maasai. As a consequence of their misdeeds they are particularly vulnerable to 'eyes' from other people, and even to divine wrath – forces which interfere in the world when humans fail to comply with moral commandments. Sooner or later they will meet problems.[2] The faith in a moral and righteous God and in ancestors (of living memory) who 'watch' the conduct of the living, has practical consequences in the lived experience of the Maasai.

The primacy of female procreation

'A woman is like Enkai [God] because she can bear children'. This quotation from a fertility song of the Arusha Maasai – neighbours and close affines of the pastoral Maasai in Tanzania – points to the divine quality of women's procreative capacity (Wagner-Glenn 1992: 130; also Spencer 1988). Among the Maasai fertile women epitomise the creation of life (*enkishon*). Their mythical originator Naiterukop, a creature or 'thing' (*entoki*) possessing both human and divine qualities, has a feminine singular relative prefix, *na-* (literally 'she who begins the world'). The feminine gender of the creator is not merely a semantic coincidence, but expresses a culturally constituted cognition of the female as 'an originating source' (Hillman 1992).

A woman who has not given birth to children is 'like a wilderness' (Ahr 1991: 98). She never matures fully and thus cannot be considered 'morally upright' or 'good' which means that she cannot be respected as an adult person (Wagner-Glenn 1992: 148). In their songs women say that people will not 'slaughter' animals for barren women, thus excluding them from crucial areas of sociality and from culturally constituted ties of sentiment and personhood. A woman without children is unable to act and engage fully in relations with other women or men. Infertility is a dreaded condition of which Maasai women are terribly mindful in religious as well as mundane practices. That barrenness is a personal tragedy for Maasai women is evidenced among other things by these women's sexual excesses on female fertility delegations, their intense and loud voices in collective prayers, and their eagerness to be the first in the row to receive the blessings at fertility ceremonies. Symptomatically, spirit possession appears to be particularly prevalent among childless Maasai women (Hodgson 1995; Hurskainen 1989).

Reliable figures on Maasai infertility are not available. Surveys on venereal diseases reckoned to cause female infertility during the colonial period showed that such diseases were rampant (Orr and Gilks 1931; McKay 1950).[3] Figures from pregnant Maasai women in Kenya between 1989–1992 indicate an average syphilis prevalence of 5 per cent, but with substantial annual variations, ranging from below 2 per cent (1990) to almost 13 per cent (1992) (Woodburn 2000). Gonorrhoea averaged about 11 per cent in both sexes for a number of consecutive years in the 1990s (Woodburn 2000). Contemporary medical sources claim that the high prevalence of primary infertility found among Maasai women is likely to be the result of untreated venereal infections (personal communication, Tanzania 1991–1994). The rapid spread of sexually transmitted diseases is attributed to an ineffective and inadequate medical system, but also to a comparatively high incidence of multi-partner sex in Maasai communities owing to high rates of polygyny and a system of morality that allows age-mates to have sex with each other's wives at their discretion (Talle 1994, 1995). Claims that female infertility is much higher among Maasai than other groups in the region remain relatively unsubstantiated.

Women's love for and nearness to children is ideologically so strong in Maasai consciousness that women are said to be ready to jeopardise the life and well-being of livestock – their means of existence and most precious property – to feed their children. In mythical times both men and women owned livestock, but through mismanagement, carelessness and favouritism towards their offspring, the women lost their animals to men (Talle 1988). Thus the story goes (as told to me by a male informant who had heard it from his father):

> A cow and a woman gave birth the same day. The cow left the calf to manage on its own until it could stand and walk by itself and she told the woman to do the same. The cow said, 'If you help your child it will take the same time for it to learn to walk as it took to develop in the womb and as it takes for you to nurse it'. But the woman did not listen to the advice of the cow. Instead she said to the cow, 'I want cud for my child because she is ill'. The cow answered 'When I am chewing come and take the cud'. The woman did and the child recovered. The woman said again, 'The child needs blood to regain its strength', and the cow answered, 'Tie my neck and remove the blood from my vein'. The woman continued, 'The child wants fat'. The cow told the woman to milk her and to shake the milk into butter, boil it and remove the fat. The woman asked for the fourth time, 'The child wants marrow', whereupon the cow replied, 'You want to kill me. Stop up my mouth and nostrils and I become a fool. Take the knife, search for my tail up to the top of my head and find the place where my death is. Our relationship will end there'.[4] Afterwards the cow recounted what she hated and what she loved most. A cow hates drought, darkness (because of predators and other dangers), forests (wild animals are not easily detected there) and women (they want to kill cows for food for their children); a cow loves rain, the moon (its brightness), plains (for the grass and the open land) and men who protect them.

In this myth men as a category are good for cattle and woman are bad. Men look after the livestock herds: they protect them against the dangerous wild animals, lead them to bushy places – where they can find young leaves and sprouts to eat – when pasture is scarce, and provide them with water during times of hardship. Women on the other hand do not care much about the herds: they are not able to protect them against danger or lead them to lush pastures. Women only care about children, Maasai say, and therefore they cannot fully possess animals. They may take the cud, draw blood and milk the cows, but they may not dispose of animals by killing them or selling them. Women's lack of full rights to animals is thus explained and interpreted with reference to gender specific properties, grounded in a reproductive and nurturing ability vested in the female gender. Hence, women who are fertile and give birth to children are a potential threat to the well-being and survival of the livestock herd. Ideologically a woman will always try to exploit a cow to feed her child. The fertile woman and the cow are images of each other – fundamentally alike in their capacity to procreate, but nevertheless forever in competition in their struggle to survive.

Children and livestock go together, singly they have minimal worth. The livestock herd, irrespective of its size, has no value in a childless homestead, and the opposite – a house filled with children, but emptied of livestock – is in a dire predicament. If a Maasai were to choose between livestock and children, however, most Maasai would prefer the latter (cf. Saitoti 1980) because children may generate livestock through sons' raiding during the period when they are young 'warriors' (*olmurrani*, pl. *ilmurran*, anglicised form *moran*) and through bridewealth at daughters' marriages. Although livestock may produce children by the acquisition of wives, the outcome is less certain, acknowledging the fact that female barrenness is widespread and child mortality high in their community.

The house: sanctuary procreation

The procreative power of women is practically and symbolically acted out in the house (*enkaji*), a physical structure and cultural domain imbued with feminine qualities. The Maasai house which is built, occupied and managed by married women, is the most important unit of social reproduction and holds a semi-autonomous position within the polygynous and patriarchal family. Every married Maasai woman has her own, separate house within the family compound and the wives of the same husband build their houses on alternate sides of the entrance leading into the homestead. The dual division of the family group into a right and a left side as you enter the homestead represent a structural dichotomy prevalent in Maasai cosmology and social organisation.

Women and house are so closely linked that semantically and conceptually they can substitute for one another. Maasai elders regularly refer to their wives by the term of the house. Both a metaphor and metonym for woman, the house embodies growth and fertility and, thus, is a place where 'peace' (*eserian*, also 'well-being' or 'prosperity', for example in greetings) reigns and no fighting or words of abuse are permitted. When husbands beat their wives, for instance, they would never do so inside a house, conscious of the fact that the act of beating would 'spoil' the house and invoke affliction.[5] The Maasai house is a sanctuary of pro-creation and prosperity: it is where children are conceived, born and nurtured. Important ceremonies in a child's life are also conducted in the house. The house is a centre of procreation, and in that capacity it is blessed space (Talle 1998).

The main assets of the 'house' as a social and productive unit are children and allocated livestock. It is through her prospective children that a woman is allocated livestock by her husband at marriage (*inkishu naasirakini esiankiki*, 'cattle smeared – pointed out – for the young bride'). These very first animals form the nucleus of the 'herd of the house' (*inkishu enkaji*) from which the woman feeds her family, distributes animals to sons (and sometimes to daughters) at birth and circumcision, and to other women when they marry into the family. Sons will add to the 'herd of the house' by animals they are given at ritual occasions when they grow up.

A house without children is no more a complete house than a house without livestock. As far as the Maasai are concerned the two assets are complementary – together they form a totality – and their respective growth is interdependent. A woman without children cannot ideally occupy a house by herself, irrespective of her number of animals. Therefore, for example, a newly wed woman will stay with an elder female in-law who has already given birth, and gradually build her own house in anticipation of her own children. The experiential relationship of woman–house–children is forcefully enacted when the Maasai bride arrives at her husband's homestead at the wedding ceremony. As she enters the homestead, she is immediately seated in the most intimate (female) part of the house and an infant child (of the family) is placed in her lap. The bride smeared in ochre-coloured animal fat and heavily clad in bead-ornaments holding on to the healthy (well-fed) child evoke a powerful vision of a 'beautiful' world. The wedding guests celebrating the occasion outside now and then peep into the house as if to inhale the sight of a potent icon. By a similar token, grandmothers who still own animals and keep a house of their own will always have a grandchild staying with them, 'to keep them company', Maasai say. A childless woman is likely to feel lonely, and will neither sleep properly nor feel hungry. How can she eat on her own? Only monsters do that, Maasai claimed, underscoring the 'unnatural' behaviour of such a person.

The first sign of pregnancy is a great relief to a young wife. Her relationships with her immediate kin change dramatically once she has given birth to her first child. According to one young woman, her husband became much less fierce and violent to her after she had children. This particular woman was strikingly beautiful and intelligent and had been forced into marriage while still a school-girl. The husband was very much aware of his wife's personal assets (which he guarded jealously), but also of the weak links she had to him and his family while still childless. After the birth of two boys, his disciplining of her however became more relaxed.

The barrenness of a married woman (*enkitok olupi*, the same expression is also used with reference to barren animals) is not socially confirmed until her age-mates – those who married at approximately the same time – have produced three or four children. By this time, the childless woman, often referred to as the 'unlucky' one (the one who has not been blessed by the God's providence) has most probably tried a number of medical and divinatory remedies in order to reproduce and, as noted above, has taken a very active part in common prayers. She may even have indulged in sexual excesses with men of younger age-groups than that of her husband endorsing the cultural doctrine that the sperm of the young, virile *morans* are 'hotter' and more fertile than those of older men. Except in cases of infertility, married women are normally prohibited from sexual intercourse with men of age-sets other than that of their husband.

Maasai see female childlessness as a sign of disorder and chaos. 'If women cannot produce offspring, what then are they good for?' Maasai men rhetorically ask. Husbands may even divorce a childless wife. Even women do not 'like' them, because they symbolise and remind women of their fragility. Both men and women, however, often pity such a hapless woman. In contrast, male barrenness is less visible socially and culturally as age-mates of the husband may, within given institutional and moral norms, impregnate his wives (Talle 1995). The fact that a man other than her husband has fathered a woman's child has peripheral meaning among the Maasai. Social fatherhood (*pater*) is of prime importance. This is not to say that biological origin lacks importance, it does, and contributes to a number of controversies in many Maasai families.

Childlessness in a woman is an indication that something 'bad' (*entorrono*) has happened – someone has been cursed (*adek*) or there has been a fight, or perhaps hard feelings exist between closely related people. The woman, however, is not personally blamed for her situation. The disorder in social relations reflected in female barrenness may be brought to 'peace' (*eserian*, balance, and coolness) by adoption. The gift of a child, an act of sharing, is a sign of upholding a moral world in the face of God. The return gift of the heifer has the potential of 'wiping out' (*aipok*, cleanse ritually) any sin. The heifer is the 'washer of sins', the Maasai say (*melang enkashe imbaa ekoriong* 'the arrows will not cross the heifer's back'), meaning that nobody will refuse a heifer as compensation.

The house without children constitutes an image of 'misfortune' and disorder within the homestead, even within the neighbourhood. The presence of such a house in any homestead creates an inauspicious atmosphere for prosperity and growth. A childless house is indeed a most unbecoming sight. One argument in this chapter is that the exchange of children from fertile to infertile women or between 'houses' – practical and emotional aspects aside – is not least a matter of morality and form. Adoption within the patrilineal family (and occasionally the clan) can be seen as a way of bringing order out of chaos by rectifying a mistake made by 'nature'. From this perspective it may appear that it is first and foremost the 'house' that needs a child, more than the woman as an individual.

Adoption practices

Adoption (*nongeeya*, name of the heifer in the herd that was given by the adopting mother, *ngishu oroto enkerai* meaning that a heifer has been exchanged for a child) is a commonplace practice among the Maasai, and most informants can recount cases they know of either from their own family or from neighbours. 'You find one in every family', was the common saying.

The procedure of adoption from one woman to another follows a general pattern. The childless woman approaches a pregnant relative, for instance a co-wife or sister-in-law (usually one with whom she has a friendly relationship), and asks to be given the child she is carrying. If the latter agrees (and her husband) and as soon as the child (if it is a girl, boys are normally not given away easily) is delivered, the adoptive mother takes over all the practical and social responsibilities connected with the birth. She provides the obligatory ram to be slaughtered for the woman in confinement to gain strength, but this time the fat is divided into two portions, one part to be left with the biological mother, the other part to be taken by the adoptive mother. This partition and drinking of fat from the same animal seals the close relationship between the two women. The fat from the ram is thought to produce milk in the mother, so also the adoptive mother. When the latter leaves with the child, she carries the fat in two containers, one of them being a small horn (*esekekua engarei* 'horn of the child', covered with leather at the pointed part, imitating a breast). This fat is set aside for the smearing and feeding of the newborn. Previously every family had such a horn, these days, however, they are less common. Traditionally, such horns were always used in connection with adoption. The adoptive mother fastens the baby onto her back, and with a special stick (*engundi*, of a certain bamboo tree which is 'holy' or blessed because it grows in evergreen places, tropes of fertility) she points to the animal she is giving the adoptive mother in appreciation of the child (*enkashe oengulak*, 'heifer of urine', the child has urinated on her).

The adoptive mother begins to suckle the child – sometimes alternately with the biological mother depending on circumstances – and after two months or so according to informants, the adoptive mother will begin to produce milk in spite of the fact that she has never been pregnant or given birth herself. As is the normal routine for newly delivered women, the adoptive mother remains secluded in her house during the first weeks, allowing the child to suckle without much disturbance. She eats well in order to produce sufficient milk, and she refrains from all heavy domestic work. The adoptive mother is referred to by the common term *entomononi* (a woman who has newly given birth, from *a-mon*, 'to pray', the implication being that she has prayed well to God who has granted her request for a child; cf. Mol 1978).

The transfer of a heifer to the biological mother confirms the formality of the adoption and seals the intimate social bond and tie of sentiment (*osotua*, 'umbilical cord') between the two women and that between the adoptive mother and the child. The legal and social relationship between the adoptive mother and the child is reconfirmed by her role at later ceremonies in the life of the child such as circumcision and marriage, and not least by inheritance of livestock. In social and practical terms then there is no difference between biological children and adopted ones.

Children are also adopted within families after they have been weaned by the women who delivered them. In some cases the mother of the child died and there was a childless woman in the family ready to take care of the newborn. It is also common that women who give birth to twins – a 'luck' beyond all expectations – may give one of them as a gift to a barren co-wife or sister-in-law. One large family had three different cases of adoption among their immediate kin. The first was a triplet girl who was given away to her grandmother (MoMo), the second an expectant woman who was ordered by her husband to give up her child to her barren step-daughter (the daughter of another wife), and the third was the case of a child born out of wedlock.[6] There are cases of women who delay conception after they marry, who may adopt a child and perhaps conceive later. One such case was loveable Lesenua. Being the eldest daughter (and child) in her family, she was given away – according to tradition – by the eldest brother of her father to a friend of his. She was taken out of school while still young, something her mother was very unhappy about because Lesenua was an intelligent child and clever in school. During the first years of marriage Lesenua remained childless. When a wife of her husband's brother passed away in childbirth at her fourth delivery, the baby girl was given to her. A few years later, however, Lesenua conceived, and gave birth to a son by Caeserian section. She now had two children, and when I once happened to refer to her as having 'one child', she immediately corrected me. 'I have two children', she stated firmly.

As a general rule, boys are not given away outside the immediate family. Within a patrilineal clan structure and a male age-set organisation boys are regarded as more important than girls for the building of the family and the livestock wealth. Where rules of patrilineal lineage and age-set exogamy prevail, girls tend to 'disappear' anyway, Maasai claim (Spencer 1988). In the majority of adoptions I recorded girls, not boys, had been given away. There are cases of adopted sons (some of them adopted at marriage) who, because of competition for livestock, have been chased away once they are grown-up by brothers born later.

Adoptees are not easily discernible by the naked eye in the Maasai homesteads; it is only upon inquiry that a child's biological descent is revealed. The fact that a child is adopted is not kept as a secret, it is just not mentioned. The children themselves are never told directly about their adoptive status, but they usually know anyway. A single child in a house may indicate a case of adoption. One particular grandmother who stayed in the same village as myself had adopted her daughter's daughter and was always busy nursing the child – appreciating her company immensely – and constantly referring to her as 'my child'. It was only when I questioned how she at her age could have such a young child, that she told me the full story. But she hastened to add that the child was her 'real' daughter and referred to the heifer gift she had given the mother in compensation for the child. When I visited the same community several years later I met the little girl, now married with two children, and my Maasai companion identified her as the daughter of her grandmother.

Women do not always give away their children willingly. Sometimes, in fact, they are ordered to do so by their husbands. Maasai husbands and fathers have the ultimate authority over children and wives, and they exert their will strongly in all family matters. As the foremost upholders – next to God – of a moral world of sharing, elder men are obligated to watch the balance of livestock and human resources within their families. If one woman does not have children and another has many, they must help each other. The family father who distributes his resources in a just way is respected and venerated by fellow Maasai – and is even well looked after by God, as it were. All Maasai subscribe to this ethos of sharing, and although they may suffer in silence, they comply without complaint. The main reason why women sometimes are reluctant to give away children, particularly if they have not chosen the adoptive mother themselves, is that they worry about how the child will be treated at the other place.

The Maasai live by a cultural model of balance and complementarity rather than of hierarchy. The dual division of their clans into moieties of 'red and black cattle', the senior and junior division of age-sets, the dual division of the extended family into a left and right-hand side, emphasise 'complementarity' as a cultural theme. A man I know was about to fetch his fourth wife, and when I asked a relative of his why he 'needed' another wife, he replied 'may be because of the balance'. Four wives means two on each side of the family gate, making the two sides of the family equal in terms of power, giving it a balanced and appealing form.

Stylised action

Adoption among Maasai women is a form of action and lived experience where both the woman giving and the one receiving the child perform and act in their cultural capacity as promoters and guardians of life and continuity. For instance when women give birth in their house other women in the homestead participate in the delivery by undressing (to release their bodies) and imitating the sounds and body movements of the woman delivering. Thus each delivery in the homestead is a common experience of women supporting each other.

As partners in *osotua* relations (named after the 'umbilical cord'), being the most generic symbol of bonding, women at adoption enact a longer life course ritual connecting the living to ancestors as well as to future generations. Within this cultural logic, childless women represent 'unfortunate' breaches – signs of collective immorality – in the reproductive cycles that tie Maasai to larger meaningful commonalties in time and space. To live a life without children makes no sense to the Maasai because it is children who remember you when you are dead and bring your name forward to future generations. Thus it is through children a person becomes 'immortal' and that continuity of life is ensured. To die without children is to die 'like a donkey' (*aye anaa osikiria*), which is a kind of curse (*oldeket*) as nobody will 'remember your name'.

To return to the earlier quote from Lienhardt, the adoption procedure is an imitation in 'stylized action'. Just as calves can be fostered by other cows in the herd (though not without difficulties), so children can be connected to women in the patrilineal family other than their biological mothers. As one herd, so also one family. The communal nursing of the child and the *osotua* bond through the heifer link woman experientially and bodily to each other in their capacity as mothers. Bond friendship and ties of sentiment emphasise the collective responsibility of women vis-à-vis children, as does the common effort at the time of delivery. Through the gift of the heifer and the 'image of the cow', biological and social motherhood are transcended.

Adoption among Maasai women then is not primarily a question of forming a family or satisfying 'individual needs' of children and adults (although of course it has practical as well as political and emotional dimensions), but is rather an act of staging and upholding a moral, 'beautiful' (*sidai* in terms of 'good') world where cattle breed calves and women nurse children. To adopt children is to get things 'right' morally and evoke a form of balance in the eyes of the spectator. A childless house is a potential site of disorder and as such may endanger the prosperity of the community. The adoption of a child, said one Maasai informant, cannot truly remove the sadness of the barren woman. It is an act mainly in 'front of the eyes' (*tedukuya inkonyek*). By keeping the woman 'there' (in her house of the family compound) with children at her side, things are brought into order. And the informant continued to elaborate 'A person cannot say: This woman does not have a child. Others will contest him: Whom do you think this child belongs to? It is hers. Can you not see? She is nursing the child right there in front of people'. The social order of the Maasai and their experience of reality must be brought out in a visible form – in an aesthetics of morality.

Notes

1   The material presented in this chapter is based upon long-term fieldwork in various Maasai locations in Kenya and Tanzania (Talle 1988, 1995). My thanks to Signe Howell for comments on the chapter and to participants at the session on cross-cultural adoption at the EASA conference in Cracow, 2000.

2   There are two types of mean people (*empiany*), there are those who try to exploit others, and those who are self-sufficient and unwilling to share with others. One example is the man who slaughtered in his bedroom in order to eat all the meat himself (Maasai men usually slaughter outside, close to the homestead in the open and share meat with all present).

3   In one survey in the Maasai district Narok the syphilis prevalence reached almost 20 per cent (McKay 1950).
4   The Maasai kill animals in two ways: at large ceremonies when many people are present the sacrificial animal is held down and strangled with a piece of skin; otherwise it is stabbed in the neck.
5   These days Maasai say, men are lacking respect and fight with their wives inside the house, even using their fists instead of the customary stick (a male attribute).
6   The husband worked as a night watchman in Nairobi and the wife had become pregnant while he was away, which the husband resented.

References

Ahr, C. 1991. *Fruchtbarkeit und 'Respekt'*, Göttingen: Edition Re.
Dahl, G. 1979. *Suffering Grass: Subsistence and Society of Waso Borana*, Stockholm Studies in Social Anthropology 8, Stockholm: University of Stockholm.
Dahl, G. 1990. 'Mats and milk pots: The domain of Borana women', in A. Jacobson-Widding and W. van Beek (eds) *The Creative Communion*, Stockholm: Almqvist & Wiksell, pp. 129–136.
Evans-Pritchard, E. E. 1940. *The Nuer*, Oxford: Oxford Oxford University Press.
Hillman, E. 1992. 'Maasai religion: celebrating life', unpublished manuscript.
Hodgson, D. L. 1995. 'The politics of gender, ethnicity and "development" images, interventions and the reconfiguration of Maasai identities in Tanzania, 1916–1993', unpublished Ph.D. dissertation, University of Michigan.
Hurskainen, A. 1989. 'The epidemiological aspect of spirit possession among the Maasai of Tanzania', in A. Jacobson-Widding and D. Westerlund (eds) *Culture, Experience and Pluralism*, Uppsala Studies in Cultural Anthropology 13, Uppsala: Acta Universitatis Upsaliensis.
Lienhardt, G. 1961. *Divinity and Experience: The Religion of the Dinka*, Oxford: Clarendon Press.
McKay, D. H. 1950. 'Venereal disease in Maasai. A field survey, June and July 1950', *East African Medical Journal*, 27: 451–457.
Mol, Fr. F. 1978. *Maa. A Dictionary of the Maasai Language and Folklore. English–Maasai*, Nairobi: Marketing and Publishing.
Orr, J. B. and Gilks, J. L. 1931. *The Physique and Health in Two African Tribes*, London: HMSO.
Parkin, R. 1997. *Kinship*, Oxford: Blackwell Publishers.
Saitoti, T. 1980. *Maasai* (with Carol Beckwith, photographs), London: Elm Tree Books, Los Angeles: University of California Press.
Saitoti, T. 1986. *The Worlds of a Maasai Warrior*, London: Andre Deutsch.
Spencer, P. 1973. *Nomads in Alliance*, London: Oxford University Press.
Spencer, P. 1988. *The Maasai of Matapato*, London: Manchester University Press for the International African Institute.
Talle, A. 1988. *Women at a Loss*, Stockholm Studies in Social Anthropology 19, Stockholm: University of Stockholm.

Talle, A. 1994. 'The making of female fertility: Anthropological perspective on a bodily issue', *Acta Obstetricion et Gynecologica Scandinavica*, 73: 280–283.

Talle, A. 1995. 'Desiring difference: Risk behaviour among young Maasai men', in K.-I. Klepp, P. Biswalo and A. Talle (eds) *Young People at Risk*, Oslo: Scandinavian University Press, pp. 69–85.

Talle, A. 1998. 'Male and female in Maasai life: Ageing and fertility', in M. I. Aguilar (ed.) *The Politics of Age and Gerontocracy in Africa*, Lawrenceville, NJ: Africa World Press.

Wagner-Glenn, D. 1992. *Searching for a Baby's Calabash*, Ludwigsburg: Philipp Verlag.

Waller, R. 1993. 'Acceptees and aliens: Kikuyu settlement in Maasailand', in T. Spear and R. Waller (eds) *Being Maasai*, London: James Currey, pp. 226–257.

Woodburn, F. 2000. 'Social, cultural and demographic factors of HIV transmission dynamics among the Maasai of Loliondo Game Controlled Area, Northern Tanzania', undergraduate thesis, School of Oriental and African Studies, London.

Part II

Asia and Oceania

Chapter 6

Korean institutionalised adoption

Inge Roesch-Rhomberg

Introduction

Since the 1970s, modern South Korea has been experiencing a revital-
isation of Neo-Confucian values on the one hand, and the assimilation
of Western legislative models into Korean 'customary law' on the other.
Agnatic adoption (i.e. adoption of relatives related through the father's
side) or what I call institutionalised adoption is just a part of a complex
whole relating to internalised values, the family and lineage system, ritual,
politics, status considerations, claims to inherited ancestral land and
tenancy rights. Some of the 1990 amendments to the South Korean
Civil Code of 1960 propose dramatic alterations with respect to agnatic
adoption. However, considering Korean attitudes towards law (Pak 1982:
14f.), it remains to be seen how Korean society will react. In theory,
the 1990 amendments have legally paved the way for a change of the
dominant kinship system characterised by a patrilineal ideology.

Modern medical technology will certainly influence Korean adoption
practices. A 'one-son only' family has developed in urban centres. Since
there has been a trend towards a lower birth-rate of females, medical
doctors are no longer allowed to give information on the sex of the future
baby. It would be interesting to know if assisted reproduction gives
preference to the genetic material of agnates.

Historically, Korea experienced a similar process during the Chosòn
period (1392–1910) when legislators tried to establish Neo-Confucian
ideology in a society with cognatic kinship structures, equal inheritance
rights for sons and daughters, uxorilocal residence patterns and a flexible
ritual succession system. Agnatic adoption was not emphasised. Deuchler
brilliantly analysed the transformation process which led to the present
patrilineal ideology (1992) and Peterson examined in detail the emergence of agnatic adoption within this system (1996). Opinions differed,

however, concerning the time span Chosòn society needed to develop its preferences for agnates (Pak 1982).

The aim of this chapter is to emphasise that although we attain fascinating insights into the processual character of adoption through socio-historical studies, the picture is one-sided insofar as it represents elite culture. I shall illustrate through my case studies from the field[1] that even within elite culture two types of customary adoption strategies should be distinguished. Peterson's historical analysis can be corroborated with respect to important primogeniture lines, but within minor kin groups some traditional practices remain, at least in the Korean country-side. The assumption of a 'trickle-down effect' postulated by Peterson seems too hastily expressed, as former commoners in all likelihood followed a different kinship pattern than the nobility and did not practise agnatic adoption (cf. T'aek-gyu Kim 1964, Yoon 1989, and my own field experience). Too much stress has been laid on the patrilineal ideal and it has been overlooked that Korea still has a bilateral type of mourning group, that wives marrying into a lineage are fully recognised after death as ancestors (Roesch-Rhomberg 1994a, b) and that marriage prohibitions were not restricted to the well known Korean exogamous rules (Kwang-kyu Yi 1985).

Background information

Two-layered laws on adoption

Korean institutionalised adoption is ideologically clearly distinguished from other forms of adoption and fosterage. Not only current practice, but also Korean law on adoption is two-layered. There is, first, the South Korean law on adoption and, second, a special Act covering exceptional cases of adoption, created for orphans and needy children.[2] Both types of adoption are equally termed *ipyang*, although there is ambiguity regarding the terminology to refer to an adoptee (Kwang-kyu Yi 1985: 254, Deuchler 1992: 196, Peterson 1996: 21ff., 187–9). Historically, the Great Code of Administration distinguished between the adoption of a child under the age of three, whose surname could be changed to the surname of the adopting parent, and adoption of a child after the age of three, whose surname could not be changed (ibid.). Reference terms in FWV were *yangja* and *suyangja* for an adopted son and *suyangttal* for a foster daughter. A son 'adopted out' was recorded as a *ch'ul-gye* (exit, lineage connection) in the genealogy, one 'adopted in' as *cha-gye* (son, lineage connection).

The ideal adoptee

Influenced by Neo-Confucian ideology and originally an elite custom, Korean institutionalised adoption describes the practice of adopting a ritual heir to succeed a sonless couple, to continue a primogeniture line of a clan, a lineage or a minor kin group.[3] An ideal adoptee has to be an agnate of the same generational level as an own son would have been, preferably a brother's son (*samch'on*), or an agnatic classificatory cousin's son (*och'on, yukch'on, . . .*).[4] Agnatic ascendants are excluded by law. Because of the hierarchy of lines within a Korean lineage, relative seniority between the adoptee and other classificatory descendants has to be observed. Adoptees are frequently adults, often already married with children of their own. Agnatic adoption in Korea is generally not intended for the welfare of children, it is 'parent-centred' (Peterson 1996). As I will show later, adoption in many cases is ancestor and lineage-oriented. Posthumous adoptions are frequent.

Values and rules behind the adoption system

Korean institutionalised adoption is rooted in a kinship system of exogamous clans (specified by the clan-origin name added to the Korean surname), whose lineages perpetuate their main lines by primogeniture succession and ancestral identity.[5] Wives are registered in their husband's family register and are equally cared for in death and ancestral rituals. Mourning obligations and status ascription have bilateral features (Deuchler 1992, 1998). Residence patterns after marriage are commonly viri- or neolocal (with paternal kin or in an independent household), although cases of uxorilocal marriages, where residence is with the maternal kin, also exist. The *terilsawi*, a son-in-law living at his wife's parents' place and commonly referred to as an adopted son-in-law, is often associated with a poor foster son. He normally keeps his own surname. However, the adoption of a daughter's son is still possible.[6] Succession and inheritance are separate issues, although they frequently overlap. Inheritance in Korea is not exclusively regulated by the primogeniture principle. A ritual heir usually inherits the main house and an extra portion of land set aside for ritual expenses. Central to ritual heirship[7] is the observance of mourning and ancestral rituals relating to ideas of an eternal relationship between the living and the dead – a heavy burden for an adoptee if he becomes heir of a main primogeniture line (Roesch-Rhomberg 1994a). Intensive negotiations between the parties involved precede an adoption. T'aek-gyu Kim noted that it was almost impossible for a poor household-head to obtain an adoptee (1964: 15). An adoption can be dissolved if the adoptee does not live up to the expectations of the adoptive parents.

In order to become legally binding an adoption has to be registered in the local family register. If a lineage council proposes an adoptee, the family court has to agree. An adopted child has the same duties and privileges as a natal[8] child. Legally, adopted children do not have any filial duties towards their natal parents, one of the points which have been criticised (Tai-yung Lee 1982: 106).

The South Korean Civil Code and its amendments

The enactments legislated in the Civil Code of 1960 (Lim 1972, Pak 1982, Bergmann and Ferid 1993) regarding family and succession recognised patrilineality, exogamous marriage rules, virilocal residence (with the husband's family), the household-head system, monogamy, agnatic adoption and, strangely, son-in-law adoption.[9] The Code provided for possibilities to legitimise illegitimate children via marriage. The amendments to this Code put into effect in 1990 repealed the following important traditional imperatives regarding adoption: the prohibition to adopt an eldest son except for a primogeniture line, the prohibition of succession if the adoptee has not the same clan/origin name as the adopting person, posthumous and adoption via testament, and the adoption of a son-in-law. Additionally, the idea of 'the equality of the sexes' was given more weight in 1990, especially through the formal abolition of the exclusive rights of the usually male household-head. (Although it had been recognised in the Korean Constitution it contradicted the Civil Code.) In the amendments the responsibility of both husband and wife for an adoptee was stressed, mutual consent to an adoption by both spouses was required and in case of the adoption of a couple, both the adoptee and his wife must agree. Also the place of residence should be arranged after mutual agreement (Bergmann and Ferid 1993). Confucian scholars, however, stood up for values embedded in Neo-Confucian ideology. I still remember the hotly debated issue in 1990 to skip the marriage rule which forbade members of the same surname and the same place of origin to marry, although membership has grown into millions in some clans. This prohibition only 'lost effect as of the beginning of 1999' (Chulwoo Lee 2000).

Korean women's associations have played an important role in criticising the family code and are presently asking for further reforms. According to a Korean newspaper, the Korean government has promised 'to scrap the household-head code that defines family members along the male line by 2007' (*Korean Herald*, 28 June 2002).

To summarise, I use the term 'institutionalised adoption' for agnatic adoptions considered part of 'customary law' by the South Korean Civil Code between 1960 and 1990. As I will show with my ethnographic examples, this type of adoption was in fact deeply rooted in the realm of social practices. Nonetheless, some customs reminiscent of Korea's 'cognatic' past, in which emphasis was placed on both maternal and paternal kinship links, have not yet completely disappeared, customs that might ease the modern process intended to reverse Chosòn ideology.

The setting

FWV1, a so-called clan-village,[10] was situated in Kyònggi province and historically belonged to a region in which during the Chosòn period it is presumed that the majority of the population were 'those who filled the middle and upper ranks of the Korean bureaucratic ladder' (Wagner 1972: 152). Of the 85 houses and households of my survey in 1989/90, X-*ssi* families occupied 29 houses. Some 26 houses belonged to a single lineage which experienced divisions into many sub-lineages in the course of village and lineage history. The majority of the X-*ssi* were owner-cultivators or tenants with cultivating rights assigned by the main lineage. When I started fieldwork, most of the households had recovered from poverty only recently – not unusual in the countryside. The lineage rituals had been discontinued due to poverty, and at the time of my fieldwork were only celebrated on a small scale. They were taken up again in the 1970s, a time during which the political and economic climate had changed. X-*ssi* village also attracted same-name newcomers. The remaining houses were occupied by different surname holders, some kindred-type groups, descendants of former commoners and a variety of families whom I call urban nomads, people who rented land and built temporary structures, but were not considered part of the village commune.

The genealogy of Clan-X

Figure 6.1 shows a simplified chart extracted from the Clan-X genealogy of 1981 and information obtained in FWV. Thirty-seven lineages (*kongp'a*) are officially recognised. They each relate to a scholar or scholar-official as focal ancestor and are named after his office title or pen name. Twenty-nine *kongp'a* genealogically branched off after the eleventh generation from lineage No.1 which had its primogeniture house (*chongga*) in FWV1. Before 1981, the focal ancestor (AI) – a famous scholar official of the fourteenth century – led the lineage genealogy. With the integration of different lineages into a coherent whole, this ancestor

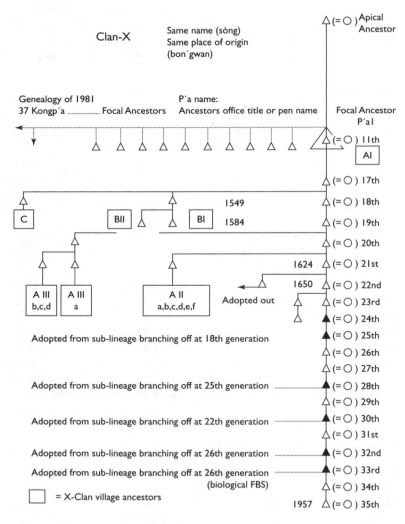

Figure 6.1 Segment of Clan-X genealogy.

– the most prominent scholarly figure of the clan – was presented as the eleventh direct lineal descendant of the main primogeniture line which comprised thirty-five generations from the apical ancestor onwards.[11] Figure 6.1 might also give you an idea of the scope of a Korean clan. AI refers to the main primogeniture line and its focal ancestor – the wives in brackets were, of course, all mentioned in the genealogy. AI, the 'lineage' (*munjung*) encompassed the ancestral lines of X-*ssi* owning houses in FWV1 (BI, BII, C, AII, AIII). AII and AIII to which most of the X-*ssi* villagers belonged, had formed informal sub-lineages (*p'a*). BI and BII refer to the ancestors of informal village lines belonging to an official sub-lineage B. C was the ancestor of only one household and refers to an official sub-lineage C. Although informal sub-lineages from the point of view of the Clan-X office in Seoul, representatives of the sub-lineages participated in the main lineage council acting for their member households. Within AII and AIII, a, b, c, d, e, f related to local X-*ssi* sub-groups (*dangnae*) owning houses in FWV.

Figure 6.1 also illustrates the generation system. X-*ssi* elders in FWV1 belonged to the 30th , 31st , 32nd and 33rd generations except for the closest agnates of the direct lineal heir who reached the 35th generation. Generation names, a syllable in each personal name, were prescribed. The enormous expansion of the lineages led to increasing age differences between classificatory lineage cousins. Lineage AI owned land around the graves on the hills surrounding FWV1 and FWV2, which had been allocated by the king during the middle of the sixteenth century to venerate the famous ancestor. Elaborate tombs, a ceremonial building for the ancestral tomb-site rituals, the primogeniture-house with its connected ancestral shrine and various other memorial monuments demonstrated the importance and status of AI, its focal ancestor and other prominent ancestors. The informal sub-lineages reproduced on a small scale the pattern of the main lineage. Ancestral land and the graves of their ascendants were part of the village area.

Adoptions in the X-*ssi* genealogy

The first adoption registered (Figure 6.1, AI) was an adoption 'out' – a younger son of the 21st generation descendant was given away during the middle of the seventeenth century. Of the six adoptions 'into' the main line between generation 24 and 33, the ideal of a younger brother's elder son adoption was realised in the 24th generation. The following four adopted sons came from distant sub-lineages as did the sixth recorded adoptee of the 33rd generation. However, the natal father of the last adoptee was by pedigree the younger brother of his adoptive father, the adoptee of generation 32. Village records and memorials in FWV1 showed that at least two of the adoptees of the main line had been influential leaders in the village history. It would take thorough historical studies to trace the exact connections between locality, pedigree and educational background.

Regarding the genealogical records of the sub-lineages AII, AIII, BI and BII, forty-five adoptions could be traced. From the thirty-five upward adoptions, thirteen were younger brother's sons. Of the ten adoptions by a younger line from an elder line, five were elder brother's younger sons adopted by a younger brother. The ideal adoptee, a 'brother's son', was therefore realised in 40 per cent of the total. Younger brothers, however, adopted more often a brother's son than elder brothers did. My record, of course, did not cover the bulk of adoptions mentioned in the official genealogy – only the ancestors of lineage members living in FWV were considered here. The regularity of adoptions between two minor lines could even be interpreted as an adoption exchange system.

By comparing the adoptions of the main line with the adoptions of minor lines, I was able to establish a pattern. The main primogeniture line adopted distant classificatory agnatic cousins, whereas the informal minor lines adopted closer ones. An informal interview in the Clan-X office in Seoul rendered additional insights:

> Adoptions into the primogeniture line (*chongga*) were a lineage concern and were decided in the lineage council. A candidate for adoption was thoroughly scrutinised. He had to be an educated man in a good position and be willing to attend to his ritual duties. The lineage council did not interfere in adoptions within minor lines or families. They were normally an internal family affair. Cases of son-in-law adoptions or daughter's son adoptions did exist and were not forbidden.
>
> (27 March 1991)

Another lineage rule was that the primogeniture descendant should reside in FWV1.

Case studies

It was not the goal of my fieldwork to collect data on adoption, the data I am presenting here are a by-product of 'traditional' ethnography.

Case One

During a walk I encountered a family hitherto unknown to me. They were celebrating a small ancestral ritual at a village grave. I watched the ceremony from a distance and after the family had started to tidy up the site around the grassy mound, I introduced myself and asked them who they were. It turned out that the family head had recently been adopted into a main line of an unofficial sub-lineage of AI. The family head was accompanied by his married son, his son's wife and his daughters. In order to comply with his duties as an adopted son, he and his family were visiting the grave of his adoptive father to greet him (bow to him), to celebrate a *chesa* (ancestral ritual) and to beautify the grave area.

When I checked his data with my notes, I found that he was a 32nd generation X-*ssi* member adopted into a main sub-line in FWV. He actually replaced six natural sons of a villager. Although they were all mentioned in the local lineage genealogy of 1978/9 compiled by a deceased scholar – a highly respected personality among the villagers – they were not named in the Clan-X genealogy of 1981. This adoption had already aroused my curiosity. Asking the elder who was responsible for the village entries of the new genealogy, I was told that the adoptive father was not really married, his sons were therefore illegitimate. After his death, the eldest son of his younger brother had to be adopted. (There might, of course, have been additional reasons unknown to me.) My annotations from the land register showed the natal father of the adoptee to be a comparatively large landowner in contrast to the adoptive father. The adoptee's younger brother inherited the land of his natal father. Economic reasons for the adoption could therefore be excluded.

The second occasion I saw this adopted family was at a *p'yebaek*, an important ritual segment of the marriage ceremony, in which bride and groom have to bow before the relatives of the groom. The groom in this case was a son of a former village head and incidentally also an adoptee. When bride and groom bowed to the elder relatives of the groom, they also bowed to the adopted descendants and their wives. During this ceremony, however, it became clear that the adoptee and his family were not very familiar with their local relatives. The distance was felt by everybody present. I was told that the adoptee continued to live in a nearby town and only followed his ritual duties in FWV.

Case Two

This adoptee was the informal leader in FWV1 during my fieldwork, a former politician and a lineage representative, who assisted the special committee established in Seoul in compiling the official Clan genealogy. He was a five degree classificatory nephew (*och'on*) to his adoptive father and the youngest son of his natal father. Obviously his education and status were more important than his relative age in order to qualify as an adoptee. Both he and Case One moved the genealogical ladder upwards into a direct line which branched off at generation 24 from a sub-lineage of the main lineage AI.

Adoptee two, a *yurim* (Confucian), was one of the most dynamic actors during many of the important ancestral rituals held in FWV (Roesch-Rhomberg 1994a). He stressed the importance of an adoptee's ritual duties during a conversation concerning some 'genealogical impossibilities in a genealogy', such as lines which suddenly came to an end and were continued later on by younger sons and descendants or sons who were older than their father. He commented: 'Nowadays, people do not adopt sons anymore, which was an absolute must in earlier times in order to have someone who celebrates the *chesa*. Obviously, the younger ones don't care about the rituals anymore' (15 March 1991).

Case Three

The former village head, a popular and respected villager, was a biological *och'on* (fifth degree) to his adoptive father, who himself had been adopted. In the adapted genealogical mode, however, he was a *kuch'on*, a nine degree agnatic relative to the adopting father. In addition, he had been adopted although his adoptive father did have a natural son. I don't know the circumstances, but the son might have died. Case Three moved into a direct line which branched off at generation 23. Cases One, Two and Three belonged to AII, generations 32, 31 and 32. All of them joined the annual main lineage ritual honouring ancestor AI.

Cases Four and Five

Cases Four and Five belonged to AIII, generation 30. Case Four was a *samch'on* (father's elder brother's younger son) moving in a downward direction into his father's younger brother's sonless house. He inherited the small portion of the land of his adoptive father and was caring for his old adoptive mother. Case Five moved into a distant house in the village, in downward direction, but into a straight line of five generations. The adoptee inherited the house and land of his adoptive father. Cases Four and Five were members of the local church. They celebrated the rituals for their sub-lineage ancestors in a slightly different fashion than their remote agnatic relatives mentioned above. Adoptee four had only ritual obligations towards his adoptive parents. I saw adoptee four at the main annual lineage ritual.

Additional notes

I did not come across any adoptions of children or even unmarried adults in FWV. When asked whom they would adopt, if need arose, X-*ssi* villagers replied: 'A *dangnae-adǔl*' (son of a minor kin group, comprising four to five generations of living members whose line might or might not ascend to a long line of ancestors). They rarely all lived together. In FWV1 some *dangnae* agnates shared ritual responsibilities. I observed a younger brother visiting an ancestral grave far away on the mountain as a substitute for his elder brother from town. After his return, three brothers and one son took turns in offering to their ancestors at closer graves.

One *terilsawi*, the husband of an X-daughter who kept his own family name, resided uxorilocally. Having only daughters, he told me that he valued his daughters as he would value a son – a statement which I heard quite often from Korean fathers. A female X-household-head referred to a young woman living in her house as a *suyang-ttal*, a foster daughter or adopted daughter. This so-called adopted daughter had another surname than the household-head and her deceased husband. The descendants of former commoners in FWV1 and FWV2 were all somehow related to each other through affinal (marriage) ties. I did not encounter adoptions within this group, who had only recently taken over the Sino-Korean kinship terminology.

Peterson (1996) on adoption: summary and comparison

Peterson's illuminating socio-historical study on Korean adoption can only be touched upon.[12] Peterson translated adoption applications and authorisations issued by the Ministry of Rites (for which royal permission was necessary), as well as genealogies and private documents. Agnatic adoptions were absent in the earliest genealogy of the fifteenth century (1996: 6f.). Drawing on Goody's (1973) 'strategies of heirship', Peterson showed that women gradually lost their rights, that rituals for the dead were no longer celebrated on a rotational basis, that polygyny was disapproved of and that sons of secondary wives or concubines were met with increasing prejudice. Primogeniture at the expense of younger sons became the rule for succession and agnatic adoption became a generally accepted norm. Some of the actual practices became even more rigid than the underlying code, which allowed for an heir 'by either wife or concubine' (p. 166). Peterson generalised an increasing preference to adopt more distant agnatic relatives in genealogies (pp. 173ff.) and postulated a 'filter-down-effect' with the conclusion: 'By the middle of the eighteenth century the ideal adoption, the adoption of an agnatic nephew, became the norm for all levels of society' (p. 190). However, his data are scarce in this respect. Anthropologists, by contrast, documented that former commoners did not adopt agnates, but sometimes son-in-laws (T'aek-gyu Kim 1964: 113ff., Yoon 1989). Uxorilocal marriages (to a matrilineal relative), followed by a few years of uxorilocal residence (with the wife's kin), were popular until the end of the twentieth century.

Comparing Peterson's generalisations with my own data from the field, his analysis matched my observations regarding the main primogeniture line, which adopted primarily from distant agnatic relatives. The genealogy of Clan-X also confirmed that agnatic adoptions began to appear in the middle of the seventeenth century. However, the assumed preference for distant agnates did not hold for actual practices within minor lines checked so far. Some 40 per cent were brother's son adoptions, followed by other close agnates.[13] Peterson did not relate his data to the necessity for elite lineages to renew their aristocratic status periodically. A constantly expanding lineage organisation made it more and more difficult to comply with the generation principle and upholding at the same time the status criteria for a main primogeniture descendant. Status was only partly hereditary, it had to be complemented by education. 'Blood ties, school ties and regional ties', the famous Korean pattern, played a role in adoptions. For minor lines, affiliation to a house in FWV was important.

Four of my cases from the 'ethnographic present' showed that there was a trend to continue long genealogical lines in favour of shorter ones. In other words, more upward adoptions in the sense of improving 'genealogical status' took place. Status within the lineage was attributed to a straight long line of direct ascendants. In my opinion, educated and wealthier men were interested in upgrading their relative genealogical position. The adopted agnates in FWV1 were of higher social standing than most of the other household-heads. It was difficult to compare economic resources before and after the adoption, but the life histories suggested that a prestigious person was preferred as adoptee. However, a long direct line in FWV1 also meant a modest house in FWV1 and portions of ancestral land to provide for the rituals. Adoptions had probably been necessary to keep the land of the main lineage AI, since absenteeism in landholding had not been possible before the 1980s. This has changed, however, and I witnessed the beginning of a dramatic restructuring in the village composition.

Case One indicated that the compilers of a genealogy were involved as agents in a posthumous adoption, when reality was transformed into the Neo-Confucian ideal. Although the 'image' of the genealogy was of concern, elements of power could not be ruled out. Regarding the 'ideal' of adoption, the requirements mentioned were met in FWV1, and ritual duties were observed irrespective of religious alignments. The only deviance – a younger son instead of an elder was adopted out – would, however, be in line with the new legal demands.

An interesting observation was made by the Janellis who noticed a double counting of people's pedigrees, namely actual blood ties besides the official genealogy (1982: 54). A preference of close biological to genealogical ties surfaced in one of my cases and in one genealogical example when two successive adoptions took place. Rather surprising was the large percentage of agnatic adoptions within the established houses in FWV1 – five in twenty-three, a relation which conformed to Peterson's presumptions (1996: 163). Regarding former commoners who did not practise agnatic adoption, a comprehensive kin-relationship study is, to my knowledge, lacking. Considering that many Koreans refer to 'little father' and 'little mother' for father's younger brother and father's elder brother's wife, an exchange of children/sons could have happened without formalities even in pre-Chosòn times.

Conclusion

Although it is generally acknowledged that the basic value behind the agnatic adoption system is the ideology of ancestral worship, the mingling of this value with Korean 'status criteria' should not be overlooked. Status played an important role in many adoptions.

Since the founding of the South Korean nation state in 1948 an equalisation policy has been fostered to erase the status boundaries between former commoners and the nobility. The 'trickle-down-effect' Peterson postulated for the eighteenth century certainly has become strong in postcolonial Korea, followed by a modern 'Yangbanisation process'.[14]

Despite the ground-breaking changes in the Korean family law of 1990, there is reason to believe that the Confucians indirectly scored a small victory by dropping the legal clause regarding 'son-in-law adoption', which could have been a relic of an earlier 'cognatic' system. This has been only vaguely described so far. It will be fascinating to observe the ongoing debates between the defenders of a vitalised Confucian ideology, Korean lawyers educated in Western law, Korean feminist voices and the process of its reception by the Korean people. 'Posthumous adoption', which has been described as 'irrational' by the modernists, was certainly 'rational' from the point of view of a lineage genealogist.

Notes

1   The data stem from my fieldwork between autumn 1989 and spring 1991 in a South Korean village, to which I refer as FWV (fieldwork village). Clan-X (X-*ssi*) dominated in FWV1, one of three villages that comprised the administrative unit FWV. Informal interviews in the Clan-X office in Seoul provided additional insights.
2   The Act for Special Cases of Adoption of December 31, 1976 (Bergmann and Ferid 1993: 21, *Minsapòp* 1999: 343–66) was created in order to promote and regulate the adoption of needy children under the age of eighteen. It replaced an earlier Act which provided for the adoption of Korean orphans by foreigners (ibid.). For details see Pechmann (1985). I personally have experienced a kind of taboo on the theme of adopting or fostering children of other families, probably due to the fact that many of them had been exploited as cheap labour (Kwang-kyu Yi 1985: 254, Yoon 1989: 19). The *Korean Herald* reported a slow increase of Koreans adopting abandoned children, whereby a 'girl preference' could be observed (17 May 2002).
3   An analysis of the Korean system in the light of recent discussions on 'lineage' is forthcoming by the author.
4   Kinship distance is measured in *ch'on*, there is one *ch'on* between parents and children of either sex and two *ch'on* between siblings of either sex (Kwang-kyu Lee and Harvey 1973). Classificatory cousins relate to each other as four *ch'on*, six *ch'on*, etc.
5   T'aek-gyu Kim 1964, Kwang-kyu Yi 1985, Janelli and Janelli 1982.
6   T'aek-gyu Kim 1964: 129, Kwang-kyu Yi 1985: 82 and 257f., Yoon 1989: 22.
7   An affinity to the concept of 'adrogation', in which the adoptee was his own master and not under another's power (Goody 1969), seems apparent. However, the separation between natal family and adoptive family was much weaker than it had been in ancient Rome.
8   The term 'natal' corresponds to the Korean use *saengbu* for 'natal father', meaning the biological and social father at the time of the birth of the child. Cf. Strathern for terminological issues (1992: 20, 177f.).
9   The assumption that son-in-law adoption and the household-head system were a Japanese invention (Pak 1982: 26f., Chulwoo Lee 2000) has yet to be thoroughly analysed. Deuchler pointed out that there was abundant Korean literature on historical household registers (personal communication).

10 The term 'clan-village' became widely used for what actually constituted a 'single lineage village' (Janelli and Janelli 1982); it defined a village with more than 50 per cent households of the same surname group (Man-gap Yi 1960).

11 With the exception of a genealogy of 1649, presumably a copy of a lost genealogy of 1513, and the village lineage genealogy of 1978/9, I could not compare the 1981 data with other editions. Genealogies present an ideal and have to be analysed within the context of their time (Barnes 1967, Shima 1998).

12 Limited space also prohibits discussion of Deuchler's classic (1992), which paved the way for Peterson's investigation, as did Wagner's (1972) pioneering work.

13 For similar observations, see 1964: 111f., Kwang-kyu Yi 1985: 256f., Janelli and Janelli 1982: 54, Joohee Kim 1981: 85f.

14 Kwang-kyu Yi, personal communication, own observation between 1986 and 1991.

Bibliography

Barnes, J. A. (1967) 'Genealogies', in E. L. Epstein (ed.) *The Craft of Social Anthropology*, London: Tavistock.

Bergmann, A. and Ferid, M. (eds) (1993) *Internationales Ehe- und Kindschaftsrecht: Korea (Republik Korea)*, Frankfurt am Main: Verlag für Standesamtwesen.

Deuchler, Martina (1992) *The Confucian Transformation of Korea*, Cambridge, MA: Harvard University Press.

—— (1998) 'Review' of M. A. Peterson, *Bulletin of the School of Oriental and African Studies* 61,2: 382–3.

Goody, Jack (1969) 'Adoption in Cross-cultural Perspective', *Comparative Studies in Society and History* 2: 55–78.

—— (1973) 'Strategies of Heirship', *Comparative Studies in Society and History* 15: 3–20.

Janelli, R. and Janelli, D. Y. (1982) *Ancestor Worship and Korean Society*, Stanford: Stanford University Press.

Kim, Joohee (1981) 'P'umassi: Patterns of Interpersonal Relationships in a Korean Village', unpublished Ph.D. thesis, Evanston, IL: Northwestern University.

Kim, Kwang-ok (1996) 'The Reproduction of Confucian Culture in Contemporary Korea', in Tu Wei-ming (ed.) *Confucian Tradition in East Asian Modernity*, Cambridge, MA: Harvard University Press.

Kim, T'aek-gyu (1964) *Tongjok purak-ùi saengwhal kujo yòn'gu*, Taegu: Chònggu.

Lee, Chulwoo (2000) 'The Socio-Legal Transformation of South Korean Society', unpublished paper presented to the International Conference on Critical Issues in Korean Studies, Manoa: University of Hawaii.

Lee, Kwang-kyu and Youngsook Kim Harvey (1973) 'Tecknonymy and Geonomy in Korean Kinship Terminology', *Ethnology* 12: 31–47.

Lee, Tai-yung (1982) 'The Legal Status of Korean Women', in S. Y. Chun (ed.) *Legal System of Korea*, Seoul: Si-sa-yong-o-sa Publishers.

Lim, Jung-Pyung (1972) 'Das gegenwärtige Familienrecht Südkoreas zwischen Deutscher Rechtsdogmatik und fernöstlicher Sozialdoktrin', Diss., Mainz: Johannes Gutenberg Universität.

Minsapòp (the Civil Proceedings Act) (1999) 'Special Act Relating to the Promotion and Procedure of Adoption', pp. 343–66.

Pak, Pyòng-ho (1982) 'Characteristics of Traditional Korean Law', in S. Y. Chun (ed.) *Legal System of Korea*, Seoul: Si-sa-yong-o-sa Publishers.

Pechmann, M. L. (1985) *Süd-Koreas 'ÜBRIGE' Kinder*, München.

Peterson, Mark A. (1996) *Korean Adoption and Inheritance*, Ithaca, NY: Cornell University.

Roesch-Rhomberg, Inge (1994a) 'Hierarchical Opposition and the Concept of "Ùm-yang" (Yin-yang)', *Anthropos* 89: 471–91.

—— (1994b) 'Ritual as Morality in Korea: The immortality of reciprocal relationships', unpublished paper presented at the third EASA conference, Oslo.

Shima Mutsuhiko (1998) 'Retrieving the Past with Genealogies', in M. Shima and L. Janelli (eds) *The Anthropology of Korea*, Osaka: National Museum of Ethnology.

Strathern, Marilyn (1992) *Reproducing the Future*, Manchester: Manchester University Press.

Wagner, Edward W. (1972) 'The Korean Chokpo as a Historical Source', in J. Palmer (ed.) *Studies in Asian Genealogy*, Ptovo, UT: Brigham Young University.

Yi, Kwang-kyu (1985) *Han'guk kajok-ùi kujo punsòk*, Seoul: Iljisa.

Yi, Man-gap (1960) *Han'guk nonch'on-ùi sahoe kujo*, Seoul: Han'guk yòngu tosò'gwan.

Yoon, Hyungsook (1989) 'Rethinking Traditional Marriage in Korea', *Korea Journal* 29,12: 17–27.

Chapter 7

Transactions in rights, transactions in children

A view of adoption from Papua New Guinea

Melissa Demian

Introduction

Much of the pioneering anthropological work on adoption sought to generate a comparison between different adoption regimes by framing them as transactions in rights between adults (Carroll 1970, Brady 1976, J. Goody 1969, E. Goody 1982). This was of course the anthropological strategy of the day; cross-cultural comparison was possible because kinship 'systems' could be broken down to common denominators such as rights, obligations, inheritance, corporate consolidation, and inter-group politics. It was perhaps felt that because of the tremendous disparities between Western-style[1] and 'customary' adoption, as well as the diversity of these forms of adoption themselves, the notion of adoption was only useful as a theoretical tool for the recognition of institutions in both the industrialised West and non-Western societies that dealt with transactions in 'rights to' children. 'Rights and duties' were the handles by which anthropological theorists transformed the parent–child relationship into a transactable object. The point was that rights and duties are conceptually and juridically separable from persons, and are not themselves persons, so that the discussion could be kept distinct from questions of slavery.[2] But rights-as-objects also enabled an interpretive step by means of which theorists could then proceed to 'property' or 'commodities'. Take, for example, a paradigmatic statement from Goodenough:

> People's labor, companionship, and allegiance are in effect commodities, and access to them, as to other valued commodities, is universally subject to social regulation. Although we do not ordinarily think of it in this way, the rights people have in regard to these things are a form of property. Adoption and fosterage are transactions in parenthood as a form of property.
>
> (1970: 398–9)

How did we get from rights to commodities? In seeking a way to concretise the relations between parents and children, and thus render the adoption transaction coherent across different social and cultural milieux, anthropologists in the 1970s chose an idiom which was accessible to the Euro-American economic imagination. If adoption could be conceived in terms of the market, then comparison was possible because market transactions, which deal in standardised and commensurate value, are by definition comparable. The value of 'rights in' adopted children and the means of transacting in them could be analysed by determining what these rights were commensurate with. Thus 'adoption' was established as a relational category instantiated by a particular type of transaction between adults. The transaction was not in children, but in rights to children. Almost the entire analysis of adoption in the 1970s concentrated on defining its jural status in a given society, and then using the metaphor of commodity relations to produce a comparative account of this status. The matter seemed to rest there, for almost no attention was paid by anthropologists to adoption until some twenty years later (Bodenhorn 1988, Carsten 1991, Gailey 1999, Modell 1994). But in the intervening period there had been a certain loss of faith in the possibility of comparing any modality of kinship with any other, and perhaps as a consequence studies of adoption never quite caught up with the 'new kinship', in that the transactions-in-rights model of adoption was not brought in for critique. In this chapter I hope to show that by re-asking what it is that the adoption transaction involves, we can integrate adoption with the wealth of work on personhood and relationality from which kinship studies have benefited in recent years.

I was compelled to ask this question in the course of my work on adoption in Suau, a Southern Massim society of Papua New Guinea. Nearly every household in both of the Suau villages in which I have worked have adopted a person into or out of one of their generations, and their reasons for doing so are limited only by the ingenuity of the families involved in the adoption process. As one might suppose, Suau adoptions do not occur under the particularistic conditions surrounding Euro-American adoption, but rather as a result of stress on other relationships – a dearth of girls or boys, improperly spaced children, troubled marriages, and outstanding debts. The fact that adopted children in Suau were sent along the same 'roads' of exchange as bridewealth pigs and the services of sorcerers suggested to me that an abstraction of this exchange in terms of rights might do a disservice to the actual process involved. But rather than reviving debates over whether the Euro-American institutions of adoption and fosterage can be used synonymously or even compared with those of other societies, my aim is to examine the ways in which new relationships such as the adoptive one are produced by Suau, and to ask how far the Euro-American model for adoption has infused discussions of the transfer of rights.

Appearance and disappearance

[I]n adoption, a child is moved from a birthmother to a social mother, who will become, and be recorded 'as if begetter.' The paradoxes entailed in thoroughly resting a contracted upon a blood bond, a legal upon a biological relationship, and 'culture' upon 'nature' are not academic for those whose actions the paradoxes frame – the person who raises as 'one's own' a child who is a stranger, the parent who forgets the child who is 'flesh and blood,' and the individual who constructs an identity out of having been chosen instead of born.

(Modell 1994: 5–6)

This passage, from the introduction of Modell's study of adoption in the United States, is dense with references to American understandings about the limitations to negotiating kinship. I will attempt to unpack them in order to generate a sense for the field of relationships being appealed to in this system, and how these relationships are made to appear and to vanish. There are three predominant ideas at work here. One is the infringement of 'culture' ('law', 'contract') upon a domain held inviolable in American kinship ideology ('blood', 'biology'). The 'as if begetter' aspect of statutory adoption points up the creation of a fictive 'genetic' relationship where none exists, by means of the concealment of knowledge. This is how the second principle comes into play: that one's identity, and more specifically one's sense of relatedness to others named as family, is bound up in knowing how one came to be related to them. What is an unproblematic relationship for those raised by their natal parents becomes problematised by the simultaneous privileging and denial by the courts of the 'bond of blood'. It is precisely the privileged status, the assumed primacy and immutability of blood which *necessitates* its denial; as Modell writes, the legal erasure of prior relationships is a response to 'the deeply held conviction that removing a child from its biological parent forever poses a threat that can be limited but not eliminated' (1994: 35). The 'threat' here is that of multiple versions of a relationship which ought to be unique, an aggregate of parenthood to which American courts find themselves unable to accede. Third and finally, the solution to the identity of a child truncated by the courts is to provide an alternative one which, in the language of late capitalism, has been 'chosen'.

Given these conditions for the contracting of an American adoption, it is certainly possible to envision it as a transaction in rights, and even to conceive of parental rights as commodities on a kind of kinship market.[3] Gailey (1999) offers an even more compelling picture of parents 'shopping' for the perfect baby through overseas adoption agencies. And as Modell (1998) points out in her essay on fosterage and the plural nature of family law in Hawaii, '[I]f children are to be distinguished from a commodity, the conditions under which they are distributed must be couched in the language of well-being' (1998: 160), which then has ramifications for legal judgements over the 'kind' of family into which it is acceptable to adopt a child. One has the sense here, that 'rights' are being used as proxies, substitutes for the person of the child so that transactions in *children* are not the subject of debate. And adoption can be legally distinguished from other transactions 'about' children (such as custody) in that rights are transferred in the form of knowledge about the child, that is, his or her name, location, and adoptive family. It is an extremely specific transaction. The sealing of birth records and restricted contact between natal parents and the children they have relinquished transforms the relationship between them into a *right to know* each other's identity. Control over this knowledge is what brings parenthood within the purview of the courts, and it can also thus be transferred between individuals as a 'bundle of rights'. Such legalistic sleight of hand ultimately produces the 'as if' of Euro-American adoptive kinship. Sealed records of a child's natal origin become elided with the origin itself, and 'biology' is thereby superseded by 'contract'.

What happens to the 'rights' model in adoption regimes where children themselves are sometimes quite explicitly objects of transaction? I will attempt to answer this question with an account of an adoption in Suau, followed by a brief discussion of adoption and fosterage practices in Massim societies more generally. I also hope to illustrate one of the most telling problems in any attempt to approach adoption ethnographically: it is frequently difficult to single out as 'an institution' because it often emerges from shifts in other, disparate relationships. To speak of adoption is to locate it in a social geography, that is, exploring the points at which it becomes a mapping-out of adjacent relationships. It was in this process that I came to question the usefulness of using rights to think about the adoption transaction, for rights, rather than pointing to the persons transacting in them, appear to have an *a priori* existence, abstracted from persons entirely. A right is not a relationship, but the index to a relationship. I do not argue that Suau do not use indices, but rather that they employ quite another kind, as I will try to demonstrate in the following example.

Eliciting the adoptive relationship

At a bridewealth repayment feast held during my stay in one Suau village,[4] a dramatic moment occurred. The family of the wife, discharging the debt of four pigs given to them by the family of the husband, Amos, brought their pigs to Amos's hamlet for presentation and distribution. As they arrived carrying their pigs, some of those assembled began spontaneously to weep. The first to start crying were the immediate family of Tabitha, a woman who had died four months previously, but soon all present joined in this sudden outpouring of grief. Then, as quickly as it had started, the crying stopped as the pigs were taken away to be killed. I asked people what had happened, but all Tabitha's widower Josiah could tell me was 'I'm thinking of my old lady' (*egu sinebada e nuatuhu*). Eventually it was explained to me that the bridewealth pigs should have gone to Tabitha, because she was the adoptive mother of Amos and she had provided his initial bridewealth payment to his wife's kin. Since she was dead, the reciprocating pigs were given instead to Amos's natal parents, but the pigs still reminded those present of Tabitha and the tragedy of the fact that she was not present to receive them herself.

It was a moment at which certain social transformations I had previously regarded as unconnected, that is, marriage, death and adoption, collided. Or rather, the registers of relatedness they had always shared were temporarily and dramatically made explicit. That I had not known Amos was an adoptee prior to this event was significant: his relationship to Tabitha and Josiah was subsumed by his relatively new status as a young husband and father, and so had 'disappeared' from everyday discourse. It was revealed again, temporarily, when his adoptive father wept at the memory-made-manifest of the pigs which ought to have gone to his dead wife. The relationships which were meant to have been redistributed in the course of her mortuary feast momentarily reverted to what I can only call a pre-funeral state. Time seemed to flow backwards; the display of uncontrolled weeping at the appearance of the bridewealth pigs was like a terrible replay of events culminating in the mortuary feast.[5] As soon as the pigs which at that moment were invested with memory of Tabitha were taken away and slaughtered, the mourners were transformed back into celebrants, released from the past and reinstated in the present.

Josiah did not eat the pig meat distributed at this feast, although he could have; he had not maintained any of the usual dietary restrictions following his wife's mortuary feast. In this instance, he said 'My feelings are bad' (*nuagu ya heyaya*) and could not bring himself to eat.

Roads or paths are an extremely common idiom throughout Papua New Guinea used to concretise the relationships between people that are made to appear as marriage payments, ceremonial exchanges, and other formal prestations. In the Suau context, roads (*dobila* or *'eda*) are used to denote relationships which typically require work on the part of third parties to help maintain them. For example, when I later spoke to Josiah about his adoption of Amos, he described Amos's marriage thus: 'We stayed together until Amos found his road, and so I carried his weight' (*'e miya gogo ya lau-eee Amos wa ena dobila ya loba'i, hinaga polohena e bahei*). 'Carrying his weight' refers to the pigs given by Josiah and Tabitha to the family of Amos's wife. A companion metaphor to that of roads, 'weight' describes the products of work done by interested kin on behalf of a person they are helping, in this case the pigs raised to give to Amos's wife's kin.[6] Josiah also spoke of the work Amos would ultimately do for him, that is, preparing his body for burial and mourning at his funeral when he died, as 'carrying my weight'. So the burden 'carried' by Josiah in the form of providing bridewealth for Amos would ultimately be taken up by Amos on the death of his adoptive father. Funeral work was not the only assistance Josiah expected from Amos, and Amos would not be the only one performing this work, but Josiah was laying out for me an ideal temporal sequence of work performed on another's behalf and eventually reciprocated. Because bridewealth was the final labour of parenthood by Josiah and Tabitha for Amos, funeral work would be the final labour of sonhood performed by Amos for Josiah. The relationship initiated by Josiah and Tabitha's agreement to take on the responsibility of raising him would be finished when Amos had discharged funeral duties for both of them, but especially for Josiah as the male parent. What made Tabitha and Josiah his parents in the first place was the work they had done on his account, culminating in their providing sufficient pigs to pay his bridewealth.

Adoption across the Massim

There are several words in various Suau dialects used more or less interchangeably to refer to adoption. They include *abiudo'i*, 'to take a different one', and *abihela'i*, 'to take and cause to grow'. Each of these terms suggests a particular aspect of the adoptive process: the latter emphasises the movement of a child from another household to one's own, and the former emphasises the nurturing work which makes this child indistinguishable from one's natal children. If there is an 'as if' in Suau adoption, it resides not in the body the child is born with ('biology'), but the body grown by his or her adoptive parents through their nurturance. They work for their adoptee 'as if' she or he were their own child, and by this same token the sign of a good or successful adoption is a contented and equally hard-working child. To work on behalf of an adoptee is a significant undertaking, because it is assumed the adoptee will stay with his or her adoptive parents until marriage. Sometimes, of course, the child does not: returning to the natal parents is always an option. The continuing contact anticipated between an adoptee and his or her natal parents means that the distance between potential adoptive and natal households, if very great, is sometimes cited as the reason why an adoption could not take place between them. Adoption is 'for life', but in no way do natal parents expect to 'lose' their child. Several people who had adopted out children maintained that they would be very unhappy if these children did not sometimes come to visit and help them. And as the adoptee grows older his or her obligations to both adoptive and natal parents increase accordingly. What is removed from natal parents is not their relationship with the child, but the work they must do to raise the child and the effect that not working, or working less, will have on the relationship.

'Work' (*paisoa*), along with 'help' (*sagu*), is in Suau one of the most popular devices for talking about the content of a relationship, and can refer not only to physical labour but to its products, such as the garden food and pigs used in all major transactions. It is therefore a useful rubric under which to discuss Suau adoptions, for instance in the statements made above by Josiah. I want to make explicit, therefore, the transactional aspects of a child's relationship to his or her parents which change as a result of adoption, and those that do not. All the obligations of parenthood are relocated to the persons of the adoptive parents, and with this the expectation that their efforts on the child's behalf will one day return to them. What usually does not change is the lineage identity of the child, and this, depending on which side of the family she or he was adopted from, may or may not be the same as the adoptive mother's lineage. Ideally, people say, a child is adopted from the wife's brother or the husband's sister, and in both of these cases the child may be said to have two lineage affiliations: the natal mother's and the adoptive mother's. And in cases where the child was adopted from the husband's sister, then one of these affiliations will be with the adopted father's lineage, creating a sort of *ad hoc* cognatic kinship. Several adopters confirmed that this was what happened, although they usually did not put it in such abstract terms. More often they might express the dual lineage identity of an adoptee in terms of their relationship to the land of their adopted lineage. 'She will share the land with her brothers', one man said of an adopted daughter. Another told me he hoped to be buried next to his adoptive father, rather than on land belonging to his own lineage.

Knowledge of relatedness in this kind of social environment is a necessarily mobile entity. The significance that people elicit from particular events appear and disappear with the events themselves, and although this significance is not in itself ephemeral, it is not invoked or built upon until the right set of circumstances emerges again. This means that people can draw relational knowledge from each other in two ways: by producing 'the same' relationships and by creating 'new' relationships to add to those pre-existing. The two strategies may happen separately or simultaneously, as in the case of adoption, which is a new relationship meant to do the same work as the natal one which preceded it. That the adoptive relationship occurs 'after' or 'on top of' the natal relationship (as opposed to 'in place of' in the West) provides, I think, a clue to its popularity among Suau people. In managing relationships by means of adoption, people are able to manage the flow of social time – they are creating an image not only of how things ought to be, but how they ought to have been. These ideas are related to a wider trend in Massim notions of exchange and its role in the transformation of relationships. Although adoption receives only passing attention in the Massim literature, what documentation there is demonstrates certain consistencies across the region. Adoption transactions and similar optative[7] parent–child relationships are ones which, regardless of whether or not they alter the bodily substance or lineage identity of children, serve as a means of generating 'more' relationships for the children and their parents, or to be precise, more productive relationships.

Kinship is embodied and reproduced by the work of nurturance in multiple registers of Massim social life.[8] It is work that can also be made commensurate with valuables for exchange in that these valuables are employed to alter or reverse the course of relationships created through nurturance, and may indeed be considered as constitutive of nurturance itself. Nurturing work, valuables, and children are variously conceived as versions of one another, which is why one can be substituted for the others.[9] It must be noted, however, that in much of the Massim literature the writers' emphasis is not on substance or identity but *rights* obtained through nurturing another's child. Adopted children on Kiriwina in the Trobriand Islands may return to their natal households at any time, since 'without exchange of a valuable, jural rights to the child are not transferred' (Weiner 1976: 124). On Fergusson, Chowning also identifies the giving of valuables in adoption as a transfer of rights in children (1983: 420). But the assumption that transactions involving children are necessarily transactions in rights requires further examination. The fact that a child's lineage affiliation can be changed by transmission of a valuable is an acknowledgement that the transaction has an effect on someone's person, but it is by no means obvious that the effect involved is a transference of rights. Luluaki (1990) suggests that a legalistic model is not always the most appropriate one to think with in Papua New Guinean family law. He has argued that confusing the identity of children with rights over children is inappropriate, since speaking of the movement of children from one family to another as having to do with rights is a misleading description of what is actually transferred. In the specific case of custody negotiations in East Sepik Province, Luluaki redirects the discussion away from rights and toward the identity of the child:

> What is of primary importance . . . is the question, to which group the child ultimately *belongs* rather than to which parent has the jural or socially recognised right to the immediate physical custody of their child following divorce. In this sense, then, it will be seen that the emphasis shifts from parental rights to group identity.
>
> (1990: 141–2, emphasis in original)

If we apply Luluaki's argument to adoption, then the 'adoption triad' of Euro-American literature (natal parents, adoptive parents, and adoptees) is an inadequate container for identity – the idea of a transaction between natal parents, adoptive parents, and adoptees fails to encompass the fact that in many parts of Papua New Guinea, an adoptee moves not from one nuclear household to another, but from one clan or lineage to another, with an accompanying shift in relationships around him or her. Or else, the adoptee may be transferred to another household but remain within the same lineage. In either case, the field of relations appealed to is far too broad to be encompassed by the provisions of statutory adoption law. A question of 'belonging' is not the same as a question of rights; the identity of a child is built upon previous belongings rather than replacing them. A child is composed of the work of numerous people, multiple entities, all of whom have an interest in his or her welfare, because it is simultaneously their own welfare they are safeguarding.

Rights, objects, and the mediation of law

I have already suggested that in Euro-American adoption 'the law' imposes itself on 'blood' by means of controlling the flow of knowledge about natal origins, and that such a 'chosen' relationship can supplant the 'real' one. Rights are the indices of the parent–child relationship in this system, precisely because one kind of parent must be replaced by another. In order to maintain the uniqueness of parenthood, rights in the person of the child are transferred from one adult or set of adults to another. Adults know they can claim a parental relationship to a child because a particular type of transaction has taken place. So too with Papua New Guineans; it is the content of the transaction which differs. Because the conditions for distinguishing between parents and non-parents are not solely couched in terms of 'blood', and because multiple parenthood is perfectly acceptable, the index of the parent–child relationship is the work performed by parents for their children and by children for their parents. Sometimes children themselves are indices of other relationships, if they have been given in adoption to extend or straighten those roads. Their identity as 'child of so-and-so' is not contingent upon who has the *right* to act as their parent, but on who *is* acting as their parent.

Perhaps another way to illustrate my point is with a 'backwards' reckoning of Suau adoption, starting from its termination, as sometimes occurs. Adopted children always have the option of returning to their natal parents. However, the natal parents of an adoptee who returns to them may be asked to pay compensation to the adopters for their nurturance of the child. Until that point, adoptive and natal parents will have presented a 'united front' in the decision to effect an adoption; uncovering the origin of a decision to adopt in or out is invariably difficult. The agency of an adoption must be seen to emanate from both sets of parents, because it is at least in part the similarity of their intentions which enables adopters to regard other people's children as their own. If an adoptee rejects his or her adoptive parents this image of similarity is split into one of differentiation. The fact that differentiation is made explicit and can be further acknowledged by means of compensation is consistent with the prevalent Melanesian notion of similarity as being assumed or innate, whereas difference must be enacted or elicited (Mosko 1983, Strathern 1988). Put another way: while presumably everyone knows that an adoptee is different from one's natal children,[10] the difference is ideally elided by identical behaviour toward natal and adoptive children. With the compensation paid by natal parents to adoptive parents for their work on the child's behalf, the image of sameness is dispelled.

It is important to note that demands by adopters for compensation are in fact the only circumstances under which adoptions will be brought to the village court, an arena for dispute settlement introduced by the Papua New Guinean government in 1973. But there is a whole field of claims which are not generally considered appropriate for resolution via the village court, most significantly those involving land and those involving children. Because village court disputes almost categorically end in compensation orders, and compensation itself is a display of difference between persons or groups, issues to do with ownership and identity are not generally introduced into this potentially fissive environment (Demian 2004). The only time adoption becomes a contested issue appropriate to the village court is when an adoptee returns for good to his or her natal parents; at this time the adoptive parents will demand compensation in the form of pigs, money, or both. Again, what they are being compensated for is their work; the adoptee's return to the natal parents is cast as an abdication of responsibility to the adopters and the toil and expense they went to in order to raise their child. Compensation for a 'runaway' adoptee is an attempt at maintenance of the positive relationship between adoptive and natal parents originally initiated by the adoption itself. The end of an adoption, which the demand for compensation in court effectively acknowledges, results in fewer (or less efficacious) relationships available to the parties involved, particularly the adoptee. There is another way to think about the distinction between the outcome of a village court hearing and an adoption. The former usually, though not always, culminates in a diversion or attenuation of the progress of a relationship through time; it is where a road is finished or is no longer usable. The latter, on the other hand, constitutes the extension of a relationship across another household; it is where a road begins or continues in a new direction.

If Suau adoption is not a transaction in parental rights, then what is it? The fact that one does not make claims of kinship through the village court, just as one does not make land claims, offers a clue to an alternative line of inquiry. Claims to land stewardship and claims to parenthood both involve an opening-out of available relationships to which people can appeal in order to legitimate their claims. Such strategies are of course the exact inverse of the circumscription of an adoptee's field of relations in the West, but more importantly, they point to some of the ways in which relationships are managed under these conditions of heightened social complexity. Conflicting claims in Suau are frequently resolved by the passage of wealth or feast events between the parties in conflict, which is said to 'straighten' (*hadudulai*) relations between them. That is to say, it objectifies the relations, makes visible and tangible the positive valence of their trajectory into the future. Just as Euro-Americans must transform relations into rights for the purpose of manipulating them in court, Suau must transform relations into objects to accomplish similar ends. That adopted children sometimes occupy the position of objects in the course of these transformations should not be construed as meaning that they somehow lack personhood or agency; nothing could be further from the truth. Rather, it is an illustration of the intersubjective capacity of social life in Suau, the fact that the value of relationships can be altered without being alienated from persons in the first place.

Notes

1 'Western' adoption is defined, for the purposes of this chapter, as adoption contracted through legal mechanisms and characterised by the concealment of the identities of the adoptee and his or her natal parents from each other. While the latter characteristic is starting to erode in the United States (Modell 2002) and Europe, and is by no means exclusive to 'the West' (Bargach 2002), it remains overwhelmingly the norm in 'stranger' or non-step parent adoptions contracted in Western countries.

2 Thanks are due to Susan Drucker-Brown for alerting me to this point.

3 The image has at times been quite literally true. Zelizer (1985) reports that as late as the 1930s, it was fairly common in the United States for the pool of children available for adoption to be spoken of as a 'market'.

4 Strictly speaking the village was not 'real' Suau because it is not located on the coast and speaks a more 'inland-sounding' dialect; it lies near the estuary of the Sagarai River and as such straddles both geographical (coast/inland) and linguistic boundaries between speakers of different Suau Cluster dialects.

5 It is a characteristic of Suau mortuary exchanges that they are said to facilitate 'forgetting' of the dead person and release the mourners from their state of bereavement so that the flow of normative, non-funereal relations can resume (cf. Battaglia 1992, Wagner 1989). In particular there is a specific stage of the mortuary process devoted to public weeping out of grief and respect for the dead, called *tantan* in the Suau hinterland and *doudou* on the coast.

6 'Weight' (*polohe*) can also mean 'responsibility' in the case of a mistake or wrongdoing for which someone must be made accountable (Demian 2003: 104).

7 The term is Lambert's (2000). I appreciate it for its applicability across the spectrum of adoptive and fostering arrangements, and into even less formal relations between adults and children. Rather more than the 'choice' to be related to someone, the notion of 'opting into' a kinship relation implies its own inversion of 'opting out', which is what some Suau children do if they are unhappy with their adoptive families, and which is what any adult who adopts or fosters a child does. By opting to act as parent, they also opt out of the other available kinds of relationship they could have with the child,

a process Strathern has described as 'the suppression of multiple possibilities in favour of one' (1988: 277) in order to elicit the appearance of agency.

8 See, for example, the role of nurturance between cross-cousins reimagined as standing in a 'father' and 'child' relationship to one another on Sabarl Island (Battaglia 1990).

9 Chowning (1983) notes that both adopters and custody claimants on Fergusson Island can expect the valuables they give in exchange for a child to be reciprocated at the child's marriage or funeral. Adoption here is aligned, by means of exchange homologies, with the negotiation of custody. Other adoption-type relationships in the Massim, such as the 'simple' and 'complex' fostering arrangements described by Young (1971) for Goodenough Island, are characterised by nurturance rather than the exchange of valuables, although it is to be noted that the work done by the nurturer is often repaid later in some way by the child. For Suau, it is not even necessarily the nurturers who are compensated; one woman of my acquaintance adopted the daughter of a woman who was her own adoptive sister. She explained that she took the girl 'as payment for the breast' (*susu maisana*) that they had shared as infants.

10 I knew of only one instance where an adoptee did not know she was adopted until she was around seventeen or eighteen, but her circumstances were unusual in that she had been adopted by an affine on Dobu Island quite some distance from Suau. She nevertheless returned to her natal parents when she left school.

References

Bargach, J. (2002) *Orphans of Islam*, Lanham, MD: Rowman & Littlefield.

Battaglia, D. (1990) *On the Bones of the Serpent*, Chicago: University of Chicago Press.

—— (1992) 'The body in the gift: memory and forgetting in Sabarl mortuary exchange', *American Ethnologist* 19: 3–18.

Bodenhorn, B. (1988) 'Whales, souls, children, and other things that are "good to share": core metaphors in a contemporary whaling society', *Cambridge Anthropology* 13: 1–19.

Brady, I. (1976) 'Problems of description and explanation in the study of adoption', in I. Brady (ed.) *Transactions in Kinship: Adoption and Fosterage in Oceania*, Honolulu: University of Hawaii Press.

Carroll, V. (ed.) (1970) *Adoption in Eastern Oceania*, Honolulu: University of Hawaii Press.

Carsten, J. (1991) 'Children in between: fostering and the process of kinship on Pulau Langkawi, Malaysia', *Man* (N.S.) 26: 425–43.

Chowning, A. (1983) 'Wealth and exchange among the Molima of Fergusson Island', in J. W. Leach and E. Leach (eds) *The Kula*, Cambridge: Cambridge University Press.

Demian, M. (2003) 'Custom in the courtroom, law in the village: legal transformations in Papua New Guinea', *Journal of the Royal Anthropological Institute* (N.S.) 9: 97–115.

—— (2004) 'Disputing damage versus disputing ownership in Suau', in L. Kalinoe and J. Leach (eds) *Rationales of Ownership*, Oxford: Sean Kingston Publishing.

Gailey, C. W. (1999) 'Seeking "Baby Right": race, class, and gender in US international adoption', in A.-L. Rygvold, M. Dalen and B. Sætersdal (eds) *Mine, Yours, Ours and Theirs*, Oslo: University of Oslo Press.

Goodenough, W. H. (1970) 'Transactions in parenthood', in V. Carroll (ed.) *Adoption in Eastern Oceania*, Honolulu: University of Hawaii Press.

Goody, E. (1982) *Parenthood and Social Reproduction*, Cambridge: Cambridge University Press.

Goody, J. (1969) 'Adoption in cross-cultural perspective', *Comparative Studies in Society and History* 11: 55–78.

Lambert, H. (2000) 'Sentiment and substance in North Indian forms of relatedness', in J. Carsten (ed.) *Cultures of Relatedness*, Cambridge: Cambridge University Press.

Luluaki, J. (1990) 'Customary family law in Yangoru: implications of legal pluralism in a Papua New Guinean Society', unpublished Ph.D. dissertation, University of Cambridge.

Modell, J. S. (1994) *Kinship with Strangers*, Berkeley: University of California Press.

—— (1998) 'Rights to the children: foster care and social reproduction in Hawaii', in S. Franklin and H. Ragoné (eds) *Reproducing Reproduction*, Philadelphia: University of Pennsylvania Press.

—— (2002) *A Sealed and Secret Kinship*, Oxford and New York: Berghahn.

Mosko, M. (1983) 'Conception, de-conception and social structure in Bush Mekeo culture', *Mankind* 14: 24–32.

Strathern, M. (1988) *The Gender of the Gift*, Berkeley: University of California Press.

Wagner, R. (1989) 'Conclusion: the exchange context of the Kula', in F. H. Damon and R. Wagner (eds) *Death Rituals and Life in the Societies of the Kula Ring*, DeKalb: Northern Illinois University Press.

Weiner, A. B. (1976) *Women of Value, Men of Renown*, Austin: University of Texas Press.

Young, M. (1971) *Fighting with Food*, Cambridge: Cambridge University Press.

Zelizer, V. A. (1985) *Pricing the Priceless Child*, Princeton: Princeton University Press.

Chapter 8

Adoption and belonging in Wogeo, Papua New Guinea

Astrid Anderson

As is the case in many places in Oceania (cf. Brady 1976; Carroll 1970), adoption is common on Wogeo Island in Papua New Guinea.[1] In some villages as many as half of the inhabitants are adopted. Ian Hogbin (1935/36), who conducted anthropological research on the island in 1934 and 1948, accounted for the numerous adoptions by a high degree of infertility and the fact that many young girls had children before marriage. In the 1990s it was still the case that many couples were infertile and many girls had children without being married, but my contention is that adoption in Wogeo is not necessarily, and not even primarily, about childlessness or fatherlessness. Single women and couples with biological children also adopt, and the explanations for these adoptions need to be sought elsewhere. As much as providing children to infertile couples, and parents to children without fathers, adoption is a way of creating continuity and of commemorating historical events. Adoption can secure alliances and ease conflict-ridden relationships; it is a means of concealing a person's matrilineal identity and of manipulating kinship relations in order to gain power and influence.

In Wogeo adoptions are said to follow many 'pathways' (*jala*). In this sense 'pathway' is a metaphor for relations but refers also to actual movements in the landscape. Taking as a point of departure the relational and contextual emphasis that Marilyn Strathern (1988) and others have elicited as characteristic of socialities in the region, I show how people's places in the Wogeo geographical and social landscape are created in various ways, and not necessarily with filiation based on birth as the ideal model of continuity.

Following the trend from kinship studies elsewhere in the region, Hogbin moved from describing Wogeo social organisation in terms of patrilineal clans or descent groups (1935, 1939) to seeing cumulative filiation and kindred as the key organising features (1978). A closer look at relations of adoption supports Hogbin's conclusion that models of descent-based groups and alliance do not give a satisfactory image of Wogeo social organisation. Still, descent is important when it comes to locality and belonging in Wogeo. Filiation, descent, alliances and the history of places can all be seen as 'arguments' that are used to determine a person's place in the world, and adoptions place people in the landscape accordingly (see also Anderson 1996, 2003b). One aspect of descent is particularly important when it comes to adoption: a man cannot adopt his sister's child. I shall discuss why this taboo is made explicit but still broken and how adoption in relation to matrilineal identity is said to be a way to 'hide'. My conclusion is that relations of adoption in Wogeo do not primarily imitate other more 'authentic' relations, but are themselves essential to the constitution of the social landscape.

Differences between adoption in Norway and Wogeo

In Norway, as in much of the rest of Europe and the USA, adoption is primarily motivated by childlessness and a wish to create a family; kinship and family are central values in shaping men and women as social beings (Howell 2001: 73). As in so-called 'house-based societies', adoptees create continuity by carrying on the family name, property and history (cf. Carsten and Hugh-Jones 1995; Lévi-Strauss 1983). Here there is an important similarity between adoption in Norway and in Wogeo, where adoptions also secure the continuation of names and history, but it is the names and histories of places rather than families that are perpetuated.

Most adopted children in Norway are adopted from overseas and the birth parents and adoptive parents have usually no knowledge of each other. The relations into which a child is born are replaced with a new set of relations and the birth parents loose all rights in the child. When a Wogeo child is adopted, the relations that produced it are not replaced by a new set of relations. Rather we can say that adoption adds relations that become part of the constitution of the child as a social person. Adoption does not necessarily imply a total transfer of care for the child but is always about creating a proper belonging for the child by giving him or her name and rights that are spoken of as belonging to a place. Adoption is as much about where children should belong as about who should raise and nurture them.

Contrary to Hogbin's account (1935/36: 23), people told me that the adoptive mother ideally should take the child just after birth and go through the same ritual cleansings as the birth mother (cf. Hogbin

1970: 91–92). Adoptions should not be spoken of and children should not know that they are adopted. According to people's recollections, people were more successful in keeping adoptions hidden in the past. It is possible that Hogbin was unaware of many adoptions and therefore emphasised childlessness and fatherlessness as motivating factors. These days people know about most adoptions, but in many cases it is still not proper to talk about them, a matter discussed towards the end of the chapter.

Marilyn Strathern has argued that in Melanesia, social persons are conceived 'as the plural and composite site of the relationships that produced them' (1988: 13). A child is the product of the relationships that produced it and becomes an objectification of the relation between a man and a woman. From this perspective we can say that when a child is adopted he or she becomes an objectification also of the relationship between the biological parents and the adoptive parents and between the adoptive parents themselves (cf. Leifsen, Chapter 12). All these relations become parts of the composite person and show which place is the right one for him or her: 'a white stone belongs in a white place, a black stone in a black place,' they say in Wogeo.

A landscape of people, places and history

Wogeo is a volcanic island of about thirty kilometres in circumference, situated seventy kilometres off the coast of East Sepik Province. Around one thousand Austronesian-speaking people live in the twenty villages that are scattered along the coastline. The villages are of varying sizes, from four to twenty households. Suitable gardening land near the villages is a limited resource and questions concerning land rights are central in the life of the islanders. A household typically consists of a married couple, children, and often elderly parents and unmarried siblings. Other relatives can stay in a household for months at a time. It is common for children to be sent to live with relatives in other villages in order to get to know places other than their own. At a death close relatives from other places usually stay in the village of the deceased for several months. Married couples often stay for an extended period with the parents of a spouse from a different village, and conflicts can lead people to take up residence elsewhere.

In spite of this mobility, belonging to a place is of crucial importance. What always remains the same, no matter where people reside, is where people 'have their names'. Names belong to places and when a person is given a name, he or she is also given a 'platial' identity and rights to cultivate certain plots of land. Since the island is relatively small, it is usually not a problem to cultivate the land one is entitled to, even if living elsewhere, and many people are entitled to cultivate land in several villages. There are a limited number of names in Wogeo and a person can only be given a name that is free.[2] The names can be said to constitute a social landscape that is always larger than the people living. Names are embedded in the geographical landscape like a map of relations into which people are placed. The names and the land rights are associated with the houses in the villages in a particular manner – more specifically, with the sixteen rafters (*ro*) in the ceilings of the house. 'The rafter is the root, and the land grows from it,' one of Hogbin's informants said (1939: 163). When someone is given name and land rights, it is such a rafter he or she is given.

Wogeos often state that a *ro* should be passed on from father to son but this is an ideal representation of continuity and does not necessarily point to actual paths of inheritance. A 'patrilineage' does not designate a principle of continuity and there is no term for such lines of succession. In the village where I worked, there were only two out of about ten principal holders of land rights who had inherited from their biological fathers, and two of these ten were women. Patrifiliation – the relation between father and child – is only one among many paths a person can follow to receive the right to a *ro*.

'Adoptions have many pathways'

Paths are common metaphors for history, continuity and relations in Oceania.[3] In Wogeo, following pathways are first and foremost about repetition, to follow pathways that others have walked before you. As Parmentier commented on Belau:

> [P]aths are . . . established linkages, relationships, and associations among persons, groups, and political units which were created by some precedent-setting action in the past, and which imply the possibility, as well as the obligation, for following the path in exchange, marriage, cooperation, and competition.
>
> (1987: 109)

A pathway is created by people's movement in the landscape, between places and people belonging to places, and these movements become a part of the history of the places. History and mythology in Wogeo is closely connected to the landscape, in particular to conspicuous formations in the landscape. Whereas places evoke histories about certain people and events, pathways remind people of relations between people and places. The more a pathway is followed, the clearer the path is and the stronger the relation.

Such pathways can be referred to in order to decide which place people should have in the social and geographical landscape, to which place they should belong and from which *ro* they should cultivate land. If a person initiates a relation with someone from another place, the pathway they follow to each other's places becomes a conduit for future movement, and to follow this pathway is to continue the relation.

An emphasis on the relational and situational have long been central in anthropological studies of kinship and group formation in Papua New Guinea (e.g. Strathern 1988; Wagner 1974). It might appear as though the model of the Wogeo social landscape that I have presented implies clear-cut criteria for group formation since people are seen to find their place within a pre-structured universe of names and places. This is not the case. The names and the places appear as structured and continuous, but people's places within this 'map' of names, places and pathways are not given from the outset since each person can follow several different pathways into different places. A child is the product of the relations that produced it which are again products of other relations: the child is 'a plural and composite site' of relations going back in time (cf. Strathern 1988; see also Roalkvam 1997). It is the stories of these relations that are drawn upon when the name and belonging of a child is decided. Patrifiliation is one such story and this is a 'path' that often is preferred but other paths can be just as good and proper. The stories about the relations that have produced a child are not only about genealogies and alliance but also relations between places.

Examples of adoption

To illustrate the salience of places and pathways in constituting a person's identity in Wogeo I shall present some examples of adoption. A story tells how a *ro* was given to two men who came to Dab village from a district to the east. The two later left Dab, and similar stories about *ro* given to them can be found in several villages (Anderson 2003a: 56). Eventually they ended up in Bajor on the other side of the island. The recent history of this *ro* has been as follows (Figure 8.1): Bo from Dab had the right to the *ro*. He was married to Olala from Bajor. Bo died while their son Gimoro was still a child and Olala moved back to Bajor with him. Kintabi then acquired the right to the *ro* by following a path from a village to the

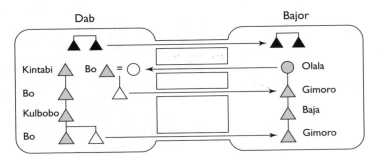

Figure 8.1 A Wogeo pathway of adoption: Dab and Bajor.

east. He named one of his sons Bo. Bo's son's son, Gimoro, was given in adoption to Baja, the son of the previous Gimoro, in Bajor. Gimoro's older biological brother was given the name Bo, like two of his predecessors, and now has the right to the *ro*. Gimoro in Bajor holds partial rights in the *ro*.

This adoption was about maintaining and recreating the relation between the people belonging to the places and thereby 'following history'. The pathway between Dab and Bajor is a strong and clear pathway that is also walked upon when people from the two places need each other's support and help.

It is necessary to distinguish between adoption and fosterage in Wogeo. The Wogeo term for adoption (*oala*) was translated by one man as 'to take something out of a bundle and add it to another'. For fosterage the term for 'look after' is used. Adoption is different from fosterage in that adoptions are always about transfer of names, belonging and rights. If a couple cannot provide a suitable name and place for a child, they can still take care of that child, but this is spoken of as 'looking after' the child. Adoption, on the other hand, does not necessarily involve transfer of care or residence from one set of parents to another – it is the name and rights that are crucial, not necessarily nurture and residence. In some cases the adopted child has as much contact with its biological as with its adoptive parents, whereas in others she or he relates only to the adoptive parents.

A young man provides an interesting example (Figure 8.2).[4] During my fieldwork this man lived in three different villages. In 1993 he was ill and lived in Moaroka with his birth mother. It was not until I learnt that the name he used at that time was from Joboe that I realised that he was adopted, and had his house in Joboe. His brothers by birth said that

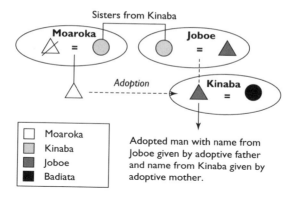

Figure 8.2 An adaptive pathway: sisters from Kinaba. Shading indicates village of belonging and the encompassing circles actual residence. Dotted lines indicate relations of adoption.

only his real mother could provide proper care when he was that sick. But when the illness worsened and he had to go to the health centre on the neighbouring island, it was his adoptive parents who accompanied him. When I returned five years later the man was well again, but now lived in Kinaba and used a different name. His adoptive mother, who was the sister of his birth mother and came from Kinaba, had given him this name. He said that he was tired of Joboe and now belonged to Kinaba. His wife was from Badiata, and they had gardens on land belonging to all of these four villages.

If someone asks to adopt a child and can point to what one man called a 'logical reason' for the adoption and has a name to offer the child, it is difficult for the birth parents to refuse. One young woman had a daughter out of wedlock. The father of the child came from Koil Island and did not want anything to do with the two of them. A young couple wanted to adopt the baby. They had already given the child a name from their place and told me they wanted a playmate for their daughter by birth. The potential adoptive mother was, like the biological father, from Koil and her movement from Koil to Wogeo constituted a pathway for the adoption to follow. The birth mother was very attached to her daughter and when I tried to discuss the adoption with her she became quiet and uneasy. Eventually she said that the couple might give her daughter a name and that she could play with their daughter, but there was no way was she going to let her live with anyone else. It is unlikely that the couple would force her to give up her daughter but it is difficult, particularly for young single mothers, to refuse someone with a 'logical reason' to adopt a child if there are no other and more obvious pathways for the child to follow. Power and position are important in this respect, something another young woman's story exemplifies.

This woman married the adoptive brother of an older woman with an important position in Wogeo (Figure 8.3). The young woman already had a daughter with another man when she married, and the older woman adopted this girl. This adoption followed a pathway not only because of the marriage of the girl's birth mother with the adoptive mother's brother, but also because the birth mother had been fostered by the adoptive parents of the adoptive father. When the young woman's husband went to work on the mainland, she went to stay in her natal village with a baby girl they had together. She also brought with her the older daughter so that she could help her look after her sister. After some time she gave birth to a son and the oldest daughter was sent back to her adoptive parents. The girl missed her mother and was quite miserable. After a while her birth mother and her newborn son got seriously ill and came to stay with the older woman so that she could look after them. She soon got better but the little boy died. She kept on staying in the village and her oldest daughter was happy to have her mother nearby. The girl was, however, not allowed to call her 'mother' or to spend much time with her.

When I returned to Wogeo five years later, the husband had found a new woman on the mainland. His wife had a new partner and had given birth to twins two years earlier. Both of them were adopted into different families since people thought that there was still a chance that her husband would return. But he did not return, and when I arrived the woman had just given birth to yet another son. She moved to another village with her new partner to avoid the now quite strained relationship with her

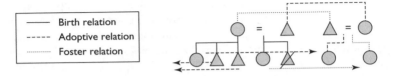

Figure 8.3 An example of adoption and fosterage. The younger woman of the story is the one to the left in the senior generation in the chart. The children she had outside of marriage are drawn directly underneath her and the two from the marriage beneath the sign indicating marriage. The arrows indicate adoption and fosterage. The youngest son is not included in the diagram.

former husband's sister. Her oldest daughter moved with her because her adoptive mother had tired of the girl's refusal to accept her as her mother. The younger daughter, however, remained with her father's sister, who hoped that eventually the child's father would return.

The situation was thus that the younger woman took care of her oldest daughter who had been given away in adoption to her former sister-in-law, whereas her younger daughter who was still regarded as her own daughter was taken care of by the former sister-in-law. In addition her twin sons lived in two different villages and did not know their birth mother at all. What the woman who had given up so many of her children felt about the situation she would not tell me. As a young woman without many allies and close relatives she did not have much to say and wished to avoid conflict.

Even if adoption is common it does not imply that people find it easy to give away their children. It happens, although not often, that adoptive children are treated less well than biological children and that children move back to their birth parents because they are unhappy staying with their adoptive parents – something that is in stark contrast to the ideal representation of adoption on the island: 'We love all children the same – mine, yours or your cousin's – that is why adoption is not a problem in Wogeo,' a woman who had adopted away five of her six children said. At a church gathering some children performed a play about an adopted child who eventually died from negligence. The audience applauded and those sitting close to me commented how important the moral message of the play was and how you would never find anyone in Wogeo treating an adopted child differently from other children. I shall not discuss this any further but suffice to note that adoptions are not emotionally uncomplicated even if Wogeos 'love all children the same'.

Adoption and rights

A man who controls large land areas in Dab has eight sons and not enough *ro* to offer them. He has solved this by having three of his sons adopted, although all of them still live with him: 'He loves them too much,' people said. The man's sister and brother-in-law have adopted one of the boys (Figure 8.4) but the adoption is not explained by the siblingship. The man's wife comes from Moaroka, and the brother-in-law (who has his name in Badiata) has inherited rights in a *ro* in Moaroka from his mother's adoptive brother. It is these rights he has given the boy, together with the name of his mother's adoptive brother.

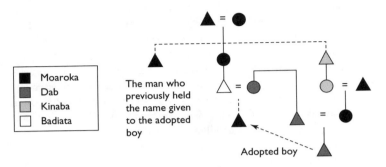

Figure 8.4 Adoption from Dab to Moaroka: naming and land rights. The shading indicates village of belonging, the dotted lines adoptive relations and arrow direction of adoption.

In Figure 8.4 I have indicated the villages of belonging from this example, and it is apparent that there is no unbroken continuity in where the people involved belong over generations. But if we instead follow the movement of the people in question, from Moaroka to Dab and back again, it is here that continuity is created: this is the path that the adoption follows. The boy thus has a 'logical reason' to take the place of the man in Moaroka who previously had his name.

A person can also be adopted as a sibling in Wogeo. The man from the example above had adopted a younger man as a brother because the younger man, according to 'history', had rights in one of the *ro* under his control. The situation was, then, that he had adopted away three of his sons because he did not have enough ro, but had himself adopted a brother in order to give him one of the *ro* under his control.

Adoption can be a way of easing conflict-ridden relationships. A woman in Dab had been adopted in this manner. Her birth father from another district was for a long time involved in a conflict with a man in Dab. Eventually a headman suggested that the man should send his child to Dab as soon as it was born. The two parties agreed and the baby girl came to Dab. I knew that the woman had been adopted but she refused to discuss the adoption and got upset when the topic was brought up: she had only one father and he was from Dab. In spite of this, she maintained relations with her birth relatives and had adopted a girl from one of her sisters. The two men were long dead, but people said that relations between the two parties had been good since the adoption. As one man stated: 'If you have something of my body, the two of us cannot be cross.'

Kinship, descent and adoption

There are not many limitations on who can adopt whom as long as the adoptive parents can show a pathway for the adoption to follow. With only around a thousand inhabitants on the island it is not difficult to find such pathways or histories. There is, however, one relation that is tabooed when it comes to adoption: a person cannot call his or her mother's brother 'father'. This touches perhaps the most important reason for why adoption is such a powerful political tool in Wogeo.

All Wogeos belong to one of several named matrilineages. Those who belong to the same matrilineage are spoken of as being of 'one body' or 'one blood'. In the Wogeo tongue a matrilineage is called *tina* ('mother'). Contrary to belonging to places, belonging to matrilineages is unchangeable and given at birth but they are seldom spoken of in public: they are 'something to hide'. Hogbin did not write about the matrilineages, probably because they were hidden more successfully in the 1930s than in the 1990s. I did not become aware of them until my eighth month on the island.[5] The main reason for this secrecy is the alleged ownership of *iaboua* – sorcery used to kill people. Some lineages are said to use *iaboua* more often than others and if one person uses the magic, the whole matrilineage shares the responsibility. People said that through time attempts had been made to eradicate lineages with a reputation for using *iaboua* too often and without good reasons; by the means of magic and remedies for sterilising women or by straightforward killings. Which lineages are dangerous depends on who one is talking to, and since all the lineages potentially can come into focus, nobody likes to draw attention to their matrilineal identity.

Both adoptions and matrilineal identity are kept outside common discourse and in this way it is possible to hide the matrilineal identity of an adopted child – 'adoption is a way to hide', one man said. Even though it appears impossible to keep kinship relations hidden on such a small island, it is possible to create sufficient uncertainty of an adopted person's (or any person's) matrilineal belonging for a person not to be immediately associated with his or her matrilineage if conflicts arise. When so many people are adopted over generations without this being a topic of everyday conversation, it is difficult to keep in mind the whole picture. People know their own and their closest family's matrilineal identity and the older and most powerful men probably have such knowledge of most people, but my impression was that people in general were unsure about this when moving beyond their own village or district.

Members of a matrilineage seldom arrange to meet on the grounds of their shared identity. The most usual reason is conflicts involving their lineage, but then normally involve only the senior men and the people directly involved. They try to keep a low profile and other people do not interrupt. One of my friends once went to such a meeting on the other side of the island. I asked her husband why she went, but he said that he had not asked her – it was none of his business. We can say that the matrilineages are embodied parts of every 'plural and composite person' that rarely are made evident or manifested as a social group.

If the distribution of names in the landscape constitutes a sort of timeless map that always is larger than the people actually living, in a sense the matrilineages become the opposite. In contrast to clans that can continue to exist without living members in terms of their names, positions and associated knowledge (Harrison 1990), Wogeo matrilineages disappear with their members. Trusted allies of other lineages can guard the knowledge belonging to a family if the eligible heir is too young, but they should not put the knowledge to use unless granted permission. If the matrilineage dies out, the knowledge is buried with the last surviving member in the shape of a plant (*Cordyline*) associated with knowledge and power.

The matrilineages also own the named houses on the island. Such houses exist independent of the built structures and share some common traits with Houses in 'House based societies' (Carsten and Hugh-Jones 1995) in that they are associated with names, knowledge, qualities and valuables. In this context the *ro* in the ceiling of the house are not parts of the house: they are associated with the place and are the same in all the houses in a village. The rights to a *ro* should not be given on the basis of people's matrilineal identity. Still I have heard people claim rights to land with reference to the house of their matrilineage and here lies a great potential for conflict.

Since a daughter usually moves out of a house when she marries, a house seldom contains people of the same matrilineage over more than a generation. Even though it is desirable for a matrilineage to fill their house with their own, the houses usually contain people who live there due to their platial belonging. It is disadvantageous for the people living in a house because of their affiliation to the place if the matrilineage gets too much power in the place, and here is a reason for the explicit taboo on a man adopting his sister's children. If a man adopts a child from his own matrilineage, the rights to the land remains within the lineage over two and even three generations. If a man who lives in the house of his own matrilineage adopts from his own matrilineage, the influence of his lineage in questions concerning the place increases and the balance between the matrilineal families and the people of the place is disturbed. I know of several such adoptions but these are never discussed openly. Powerful matrilineal families easily become the object of suspicion and gossip, particularly concerning the use of *iaboua*, something that makes it difficult and undesirable to openly maintain such a position over time.

Consensus and belonging

As Wogeos create and maintain social relations, they move along pathways between places that become conduits for 'the best way to go' (Tilley 1994). People's histories in the shape of these movements show people their proper places. The matrilineages are enduring categories in the social universe but are seldom visualised and not localised as social groups. They do, however, play a significant part in deciding where people should belong. During my last fieldwork I learnt of more and more adoptions that were about sending people to places in which their matrilineages claim to have rights. At times it seemed as though the complex web of pathways and histories leading people to their places, often spoken of in terms of patrifiliation, was a sort of smokescreen for the fact that it all was about matrilineages. But here I should take care not to construct a system where there is none. Wogeo social organisation cannot be adequately described through models of descent groups that possess rights to land and form alliances with other groups. If we again look at one of the examples of adoption presented above (Figure 8.4) it should be easy to see if matrilineal descent creates continuity over generations in terms of platial belonging. In Figure 8.5 I have replaced the shading indicating

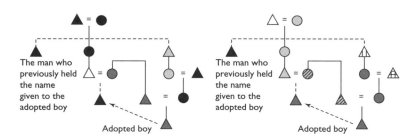

Figure 8.5 Adoption from Dab to Moaroka: pathways in the landscape of matrilineal continuity. The shading indicates village of belonging in the figure to the left (as in Figure 8.4); in the figure to the right shading indicates matrilineal belonging.

village of belonging with shading indicating matrilineal belonging. It becomes apparent that matrilineal descent does not create any continuity in terms of platial belonging and does in this case not provide a better explanation for the adoption than the movement between places.

Rather than focusing on either matrilineal descent or platial belonging as more 'real' or 'authentic' than the other I shall elaborate upon the reality that is continuously created and recreated in social life. As products of the relationships that produced them, all Wogeos belong both to places and matrilineages. To understand the processes of establishing people's social identities it is more beneficial to see 'place' and 'mother' as parts of each and every person rather than as groups in relation to each other. To maintain a balance between these, often contradictory, forms of belonging is a huge and endless work. Since everyone belongs to a place and usually emphasises principles of patrifilial inheritance, it does not benefit anyone if the matrilineages become too powerful. On the other hand, people wish to maintain a certain degree of control over the house of their matrilineage and the place to which it belongs. But even if matrilineal belonging can be the incentive for following certain pathways, this was seldom emphasised when explaining a person's place in a village. Adoption is an important means of keeping the balance between the two sides, both by keeping the matrilineages in their houses and by maintaining and strengthening the continuity and history of the people belonging to the places.

A person's platial belonging can easily become the topic for gossip and discussions. I seldom got the same version of a person's kinship history from different people. Even if the person in question was not adopted, usually at least one of the parents or grandparents was. There was general agreement about only a few people and these were all highly respected individuals who had managed to avoid becoming the objects of gossip and criticism. The various notions of how continuity is created – patrifiliation, matrilineality, alliances, histories and pathways – can be seen as arguments that are used to define a person's place in the social and geographical landscape. When rights to a *ro* are transferred it is said that at least three or more men from different places should agree that the person has followed a proper history for that ro. Such an agreement is, however, fragile and the problem is to maintain a general consensus about a certain history over time. Only in that manner can a secure position in the village be preserved, and gossip concerning sorcery and matrilineal identity avoided. Successful adoptions are important in securing such positions.

Adoptions distribute people in the landscape according to the histories that are infused in it. This does not mean that adoption is about such a distribution alone. People adopt for many reasons and none of these, such as the continuation of descent lines, can be given more salience than others. Adoption is also about other forms – about continuity, about place and land rights or, as in Norway, about wanting a child. Adoptions in Wogeo have in common with Norwegian adoptions that they create relations that are modelled upon relations between parents and birth children. The most conspicuous difference is that, rather than being substitutes for other, more 'authentic', kinship relations, relations of adoption in Wogeo are sought because in their own capacity they are important constituents of the social landscape. Relations of adoption must therefore have a central place in the analyses of Wogeo social organisation as something more than an add-on to a focus on kinship and family life.

Notes

1 Wogeo (Vokeo) belongs to the Schouten Islands, East Sepik Province. Research in Wogeo was carried out in 1993–1994, 1998 and 1999. The chapter is based on a paper first given at a seminar at the Department of Social Anthropology, University of Oslo, Spring 1999. A Norwegian version of the text has been published in the journal of the Norwegian Anthropological Association (*Norsk Antropologisk Tidsskrift* 12(3): 175–188, 2001). Acknowledgements for valuable comments should be given to the participants in the seminar, to two anonymous reviewers for *Norsk Antropologisk Tidsskrift* and to Signe Howell, the journal's editor.
2 Cf. Lindstrom (1984: 293).
3 See e.g. Hoëm and Roalkvam (2003), Hviding (1996), Keesing (1993), Roalkvam (1997), Tilley (1994).
4 I mostly avoid using personal names as adoption, land rights and kinship are sensitive topics. Since most Wogeos see my work as 'writing Wogeo history', descriptions with pseudonyms are not an option.
5 Cf. Howell (1995) about the silent existence of matrilineages among the Lio.

References

Anderson, Astrid, 1996 Men Play Flutes, Women Bear Children. Sharing Places and Sharing Blood: Concepts of Belonging, Growth and Fertility in Wogeo, Papua New Guinea. Unpublished Cand. Polit. thesis, University of Oslo.

——— 2001 Adopsjon og tilhørighet på Wogeo, Papua Ny-Guinea. *Norsk Antropologisk Tidsskrift* 12(3): 175–188.

——— 2003a Landscapes of Sociality: Paths, Places and Belonging in Wogeo Island, Papua New Guinea. In: Ingjerd Hoëm and Sidsel Roalkvam (eds) *Oceanic Socialities and Cultural Forms*, Oxford: Berghahn.

——— 2003b Wogeo Landscapes: Place, Movement and the Politics of Belonging. Unpublished Dr. Polit. dissertation, University of Oslo.

Brady, Ivan, 1976 *Transactions in Kinship*, Honolulu: University of Hawaii Press.

Carroll, Vern (ed.) 1970 *Adoption in Eastern Oceania*, Honolulu: University of Hawaii Press.

Carsten, Janet and Stephen Hugh-Jones (eds) 1995 *About the House*, Cambridge: Cambridge University Press.

Harrison, Simon, 1990 *Stealing People's Names*, Cambridge: Cambridge University Press.

Hoëm, Ingjerd and Sidsel Roalkvam (eds) 2003 *Oceanic Socialities and Cultural Forms*, Oxford: Berghahn.

Hogbin, H. Ian, 1935 Native Culture of Wogeo. *Oceania* 5: 308–337.

—— 1935/36 Adoption in Wogeo, New Guinea. *Journal of the Polynesian Society* 44,45(4,1): 208–215, 17–38.

—— 1939 Native Land Tenure in New Guinea. *Oceania* 10(2): 113–165.

—— 1970 *The Island of Menstruating Men: Religion in Wogeo, New Guinea*, Scranton: Chandler.

—— 1978 *The Leaders and the Led*, Melbourne: Melbourne University Press.

Howell, Signe, 1995 Rethinking the Mother's Brother: Gendered Aspects of Kinship and Marriage among the Northern Lio, Indonesia. *Indonesia Circle* 67: 293–317.

—— 2001 'En Vanlig Familie': Utenlandsadopsjon I Norge, Et Stadig Voksende Fenomen. In: Howell, Signe and Marit Melhuus (eds) *Blod – Tykkere Enn Vann?* pp. 73–98. Bergen: Fagbokforlaget.

Hviding, Edvard, 1996 *Guardians of Marovo Lagoon*, Honolulu: University of Hawaii Press.

Keesing, Roger M., 1993 'Earth' and 'Path' as Complex Categories: Semantics and Symbolism in Kwaio Culture. In: Boyer, Pascal (ed.) *Cognitive Aspects of Religious Symbolism*, pp. 93–110. Cambridge: Cambridge University Press.

Lévi-Strauss, Claude, 1983 The Social Organization of the Kwakiutl, *The Way of the Masks*, pp. 163–187. Seattle: University of Washington Press.

Lindstrom, Lamont, 1984 Doctor, Lawyer, Wise Man, Priest: Big-Men and Knowledge in Melanesia. *Man* 19: 291–309.

Parmentier, Richard J., 1987 *The Sacred Remains*, Chicago: University of Chicago Press.

Roalkvam, Sidsel, 1997 Pathways to Hardness: Values of Body, Gender and Place in Onotoan Social Life. Unpublished Dr. Polit. dissertation, University of Oslo.

Strathern, Marilyn, 1988 *Gender of the Gift*, Berkeley: University of California Press.

Tilley, Christopher, 1994 *A Phenomenology of Landscape*, Oxford: Berg.

Wagner, Roy, 1974 Are There Social Groups in the New Guinea Highlands? In: Leaf, Murray J. (ed.) *Frontiers of Anthropology*, pp. 95–122. New York: D. van Nostrand.

Chapter 9

Adoptions in Micronesia
Past and present

Dietrich Treide

Introduction

In 1980, Philip Kraeger presented his study entitled *Traditional Adoption Practices in Africa, Asia, Europe and Latin America* for the International Planned Parenthood Federation. He compared a Western stereotype – adoption and fosterage as a secondary and peripheral phenomenon – with non-Western cultures. In these cultures, adoptions do not only have the purpose of solving a crisis (such as childlessness) but are embedded in the general principles of joint use of essential resources (such as food), with groups rather than individuals performing the adoption. Kraeger confirmed the difficulty of differentiating in some cultures between adoptions and fosterage or other forms of family support. He also quoted examples from Oceania, based on the anthologies published by Vern Carroll (1970) and Ivan Brady (1976), which give a picture of the main features of adoption in the pre-colonial and early colonial era in Micronesia. These include:

- the relatively frequent occurrence of adoptions
- the function of adoption as part of more comprehensive systems of exchange and the joint use of cultivated land, mobile goods, information and people
- the reversibility of adoption if the obligations assumed with adoption are not met
- the traditionally often high regard for adopted children.

In contrast with this, the following major characteristics of Euro-American adoption were noted:

- its relatively rare occurrence
- a low estimation of adoption (a child was likely to be adopted from a life on the 'edge' of society)

- asymmetric relations between the adopting and the adopted
- the separation of adopted children from their birth family, disrupting the biography of adopted children.

To discuss some of these statements I shall reflect on the social life of the people of Yap State in western Micronesia. It is possible to gain a relatively reliable historical picture of the content and forms of adoption on Yap from historical and ethnographic records, dating back to the work of Pater Salesius (Johann Gustav Haas, 1907) and ethnologist Wilhelm Müller (1917), who stayed on Yap for nine months in the course of the 1909–1910 South Sea Expedition. The picture that emerges is of fairly frequent adoption as a form of exchange, and of the importance of name-giving, with adopted children receiving their names from a pool of names belonging to a place, estate and the ancestors of the place (who could pass as 'ghosts' into women during pregnancy).[1] During the Japanese colonial era (1914–1944), adoption appears to have remained a frequent occurence on Yap, and to have retained many of its features in subsequent decades. A pioneering work by Joseph Weckler (1953), using genealogies and life histories from Mokil, an atoll to the east of Pohnpei, revealed the importance of adoption in establishing relations between neighbouring islands, the adoption of sailers and whalers in the nineteeth century and the association of special forms of adoption with production for the colonial market.

Adoption and fosterage in Oceania

In the 1960s and 1970s, studies of adoption and fosterage became a major subject of anthropological research in Oceania. Cross-regional comparisons within Oceania and, above all, comparison with adoption in the USA constituted an important aspect of these studies. In her introductory statements to the anthology *Adoption in Eastern Oceania* (1970), Vern Carroll pointed out that it was very difficult to provide a cross-cultural definition of the phenomenon of adoption. She referred to major differences between Oceanian examples and adoptions in the USA and suggested that vernacular terms be used in local studies. Terms like adoption, fosterage or care of a child can often only be differentiated with reservation. She emphasised that adoptions or cases of fosterage are elements in more comprehensive systems of mutual obligation, and that the phenomenon of parenthood is also a cultural construction. Finally, Vern Carroll pointed out that – with the exception of cases in which land law issues were involved – adoptions in Oceania were not usually officially registered (Carroll 1970: 3–15).

The second anthology on adoption and fosterage in Oceania (edited by Ivan Brady 1976) also includes two articles on Micronesia. Mac Marshall undertook his studies on the Namoluk atoll (Chuuk/Truk) between 1969 and 1971. He confirmed the high adoption rate and the adopting of the children of relatively close kin with the aim of strengthening social relations already in existence, probably not least in the face of increasing fragmentation of land ownership with a then growing population. In his opinion, infertility is not an adequate explanation of the relatively large number of adoptions, and he saw adoption as part of a more comprehensive system of joint use of resources, such as land, food, possessions and, increasingly, money and people's skills and knowledge (Marshall 1976: 31–47). According to Marshall (1976: 34):

> Namoluk adoption is always customary. There has never been a legally registered adoption on the atoll, in spite of the provision for this in Trust Territory jurisprudence. This is not surprising since Namoluk people have no need for legal adoption. Adoption is an act of generosity – a form of sharing among relatives – and, as such, legal trappings are superfluous. Indeed, such trappings would imply a lack of trust and solidarity, and run counter to the very essence of adoption transactions.

In the late 1960s and early 1970s, ethnographic monographs were written on Yap which, together with data collection, produced new interpretative approaches (Labby 1976) and attempted an analysis of social change (Lingenfelter 1993). When discussing the extensive exchange of women, children, labour and land use, Labby wrote (1976: 20):

> The exchange of children for land took place as a woman became pregnant on the man's estate and bore children. If the woman produced no children, or bore fewer children than were desired, then the exchange could be accomplished through adoption (*pof*). The preferred method of adoption was for a woman to receive a child from her own clan sisters so that exchange relations between clan groups would be maintained and the proceeds of the woman's labors could still go to her own clan group. It was considered least desirable to take a child from the man's clan relatives.

While Labby gave adoptions a place in his model of the structure and relations of exchange, Lingenfelter presented a differentiated picture of the phenomenon of adoption which also considered individual cases. He referred to two forms of adoption, *cowiy* and *pof*, characterising the former as a barely formalised taking-in of children of relatively close kin. In his view, *pof* adoptions were primarily made with the aim of ensuring that land rights and titles or functions were passed on and that elderly people were looked after. The adopted children left the estate of their biological parents and thereafter held only very limited rights to this estate. But, as adults, they maintained relations with both their adopted parents and their birth parents (and their relatives).They liaised between the two sets of relatives, but when conflicts arose, they sided with their adoptive parents. Giving children away for adoption to distant relatives or non-relatives could be seen as 'throwing them away' according to Lingenfelter (1975: 36–40). Sometimes *pof* adoptions were supported by exchange of stone money, which 'anchored' them, so to speak.

The children of *pof* adoptions did not learn who their birth parents were until they were in the process of becoming adults. In general, they were seen as being special, since they were wanted and had been chosen – they had been thought about and arrangements had been made for them. Apart from the fact that they might be faced with conflicts of loyalty, their position was by no means worse than that of birth children.

The practice of giving away children for adoption because there are too many children in the family is expressly described by Lingenfelter as a contemporary phenomenon (1975: 37). This is undoubtedly connected with the growth in the population registered since the end of the Second World War and especially since the 1960s,[2] and possibly also with the increasing formation of nuclear families which are becoming more and more self-contained.

Adoption and fosterage on Yap

Kirkpatrick and Broder (1976) based their special study of adoption and fosterage on Yap on field studies which they had conducted in two settlements on the relatively isolated island of Rumung in 1972. They appear to have primarily covered traditional forms of adoption, fosterage and 'help' which were still little affected by the new era. The authors also mentioned the terms *pof* and *cowiy* but showed – using individual cases – that forms and content of adoption were dependent to a not inconsiderable extent on specific situations and constellations.

Kirkpatrick and Broder (1976) were able to show that the relations between an adopted child, its biological and adopted parents were constantly renewed and strengthened on Yap. This was done by them working for each other, giving each other things, and in other ways. Like

Labby, they saw adoptions as part of a chain of transactions. In the data collected by Kirkpatrick and Broder and in their analysis, adoptions to compensate for childlessness played a relatively minor role. Numerous adoptions were, however, performed to ensure that elderly people were looked after. Whether such cases represented a reaction to the beginnings of dissolution of traditional solidarity is difficult to say. If the obligations undertaken with an adoption were not met, such as care of elderly people, the adoption could be reversed.

It is quite clear that children were not only adopted to solve special problems (to integrate illegitimate children, for example, or children of marriages which had dissolved) but also to secure land utilisation rights, and – last but not least – to provide a brother for a sister and vice versa. It is the Yap belief that there should be children of both sexes in a nuclear family. In this way, one's own household was maintained and normal relations established or strengthened with other households and descent groups.

Kirkpatrick and Broder also mentioned that the Yapese regarded adopted children as wanted in many cases. They were able to liaise between groups of relatives but they also became involved in conflicts of interest as 'in-betweens' – which the authors illustrated with specific examples. Although some biological parents would try to 'forget', their adopted children, as far as they could, adoption was not necessarily permanent. Names could be taken away again if obligations associated with name-giving were not met. Kirkpatrick and Broder also discussed fosterage, in which care of a child was limited to a certain period from the onset, and and involved an obligation to care for children under certain conditions, in order to 'help', the children and their relatives.

The analyses made by Kirkpatrick and Broder enabled them to confirm and explain that, together with the consideration and, in some cases, manipulation of names, land histories or descent relationships, there were on Yap numerous ways of establishing and strengthening relationships between individuals and groups and of dissolving them again. It is hardly an exaggeration to say that there were, in this respect, a substantial number of relationships established predominantly through ties to land.

When I was recording life histories on Yap with my wife in 1996 and 2000, we frequently met with the phenomenon of adoption. Francis Defngin, the author of a study on name-giving on Yap (1958), confirmed a number of points also set out in the ethnographic literature, namely the adopting of relatively close kin, often for reasons of succession, the giving of a new name on adoption, the possible return of adopted children to their biological parents and, the adoption of children who were already quite old, as well as the relatively more frequent occurence of adoption on the neighbouring islands to the east of Yap.

When we talked to Defngin's former teacher, Louis Pitmag, we learned that Pitmag had been adopted by a high-ranking family in the neighbouring settlement of Gachpar. When he was about ten years old, he moved to the school in the town of Colonia, where two adults looked after him, but Pitmag did not know at the time that they were his birth parents. One day, he heard a conversation between one of his brothers and a Japanese resident, who openly talked in his presence about him being an adopted child, not realising that he already understood Japanese well. This was a terrible time, Louis Pitmag told us. Later he talked to his biological parents about the matter and they assured him that, according to tradition, it would have been impossible for them to have told him the truth.

Whereas the feelings of adopted children were not usually discussed in ethnographic studies, they can certainly play a role in a person's own life narrative. However, even Louis Pitmag found it difficult to talk about his childhood. As a result of adoption, Pitmag found himself, both consciously and unconsciously, in a special position as a person between two families, several descent groups and two influential villages.

In 2000, we also tried to record life histories of people no longer alive, such as Joachim Falmog, who died on 20 July 1985. He was President of Yap Islands Congress (established 1959), President of the Yapese District Legislature (first session in June 1969), Delegate to the Yap State Constitutional Convention (1981). Falmog too was born in the Japanese era, in the years after 1920. Tharngan adopted him as a brother to his son Faimau. Falmog was the son of Faimau's wife's brother. In this way, he was adopted into the genealogical generation of his father. After the deaths of Tharngan and Faimau, Falmog became the representative of his kin group but Pitmag, Faimau's son, did not. Thus no gap in a descent sequence was closed by this adoption. There were very probably particular reasons for Falmog gaining an influential position. Through the adoption, he moved from the settlement of Merur to the settlement of Taeb. Merur was and still is a very respected settlement and connected with Taeb, one of Yap's three traditional social centres. Louis Pitmag was adopted in the same way, moving from Wanyan to the settlement of Gachpar, another centre of social and political life on Yap. It is perhaps possible to see both cases as strategic adoptions.

The first governor of the State of Yap, as part of the Federated States of Micronesia, was John Mangefel. At the age of about ten years, he was adopted from the settlement of Gal (in the region of Kanifay) to the settlement of Ateliu (in the region of Fanif), from which his mother came. This was undoubtedly a special case, since Mangefel himself said that it was not common for men to bring the children of their sisters back to their own settlement, to their own estate, by adoption. The reason may have been that Gal was near the Japanese airfield, which was repeatedly bombed during the Second World War. The relatively late adoption points in this direction. As Mangefel said, he can still obtain the very much coveted – and not always available – breadfruit from his biological family in Gal, since relations have always been maintained.

On Yap today 'traditional' and 'modern' ways of life coexist. Both forms have a certain interactive effect on each other, as illustrated by the phenomenon of adoption. In a not insignificant number of cases, adults are adopted to support older people, not least widowed men, until their death. First, it can be assumed that some families have few people available today – many younger Yapese leave the island because they cannot find any paid work there or because they are no longer satisfied with living conditions, above all when they have graduated from high school. Second, only the people on Yap who were in paid employment have any benefits in old age. In return for caring for an elderly person or an elderly couple, adopted adults can inherit land shares. But if they fail to meet their care obligations, they can lose the land claims which they have acquired through adoption. They can be deprived of the name inseparably linked to the land, as can birth children in comparable cases. So the status acquired with adoption is certainly not necessarily permanent and its duration depends on the fulfilment of the obligations associated with adoption.

Alongside adoption, children have always been brought up by others on Yap, without any change of name or relationship status – a form of mutual assistance or help. Currently, there seems to be a possibility for non-Yapese to improve their status. Under the Yap constitution, foreigners are not allowed to acquire land. As a result, joint ventures have been formed, in which the land comes from a Yap owner and the money and know-how from a foreigner. A foreigner may now bring up the child or children of a Yap couple in order to be able to use the land.

When the Yapese leave their island, and this also applies to the inhabitants of the outer or neighbouring islands, they are usually no longer able to meet their traditional obligations, above all their obligation to show deceased relatives the necessary respect. A woman from Guam married into a high-ranking family on the island Mogmog (Ulithi atoll to the east of Yap). When she moved to Yap with her husband some years later she would no longer have been able to meet her obligations to her relatives by marriage on Mogmog. So she was adopted into a Mogmog family which subsequently performed all the duties on behalf of this woman and her family on Guam, to her relatives by marriage on Mogmog. It should be noted that this is a special form of adoption and that the woman was neither given a new name nor lost contact with her birth parents.

The 'view from the outside', as Yap informants say, has not thrown a very favourable light on traditional adoption practices. Today, parasitic forms of misuse of traditional relationships contribute to this view. Economic reciprocity is neglected in such cases, the social network injured (Hezel 1999). This frequently happens when people, including adopted people and their families, benefit from the individual income of relatives, without rendering any services in return as prescribed by traditional norms. It is certainly possible that increasing isolation in nuclear families will bring about new forms of adoption. As an example of poor treatment of adopted children, Marcus (1991) quoted a case on Yap in which a boy was adopted by his paternal grandfather after the death of his father and his mother's remarriage. Both his grandfather and, subsequently, his stepfather, failed to take care of him, so the boy ran away.

Representatives of Christian churches have repeatedly complained, and still complain, that children are separated from their birth parents, that they are not informed of this until very late, if at all, and that they frequently learn about their adoption from others before the appointed time, which can come as a shock to them. While this is true, we should also have in mind that following a comprehensive analysis of adoptions on Fais, one of Yap's, neighbouring islands, Rubinstein (1991) comes to the conclusion that adopted children are introduced to a larger circle of people who can look after them and educate them. On Fais, relations with birth parents are not broken off after adoption.

Less is known about the emotional effects of adoption on mothers giving up their children. In the opinion of the Yap people, these mothers act 'generously', and they are respected. However, detailed studies on Palau, the neighbouring group of islands to the south, have also indicated that women were, and are, not always in agreement with adoption decisions, a fact that might not be recognised by anthropological studies in which no women are involved (Smith 1977, 1983). It is certainly possible that the gradual emancipation of women (Lingenfelter 1993) will influence adoption on Yap too in the long term.

Yap was a part, but the dominant part, of a larger unit, the so-called Yap Imperium. Besides Yap, numerous atolls and some high islands, the outer or neighbouring islands, belonged to this Imperium. These outer islands were bound to a few villages on Yap through an elaborate system of tributes, patronage and the exchange of goods. As part of this system, groups and individuals from the outer islands had an obligation to bring certain products to their patrons in Gachpar or Wanyan, for which they were given other items in return. For their part, the patrons had an obligation to support their people, notably following devastation on the outer islands caused by typhoons and in other emergencies (Alkire 1965; Lessa 1966; Hunter-Anderson and Yigal Zan 1996). This reciprocal *sawei* relationship continues right up to the present day, though subject to constant modification. According to Al Fanechigiy, director of the Historic Preservation Office of Yap, there are adoptions between the outer islands and Yap, but only between the two villages in Gagil, Gachpar and Wanyan, which have the *sawei* relationship with the outer islands. Families in the surrounding villages might also adopt, but this would only be in the situation where the adopting families have connections with families in Gachpar or Wanyan. The adopted child would be given a new name.[3]

It is also important to note that Yap has about fifteen villages in which the residents do not own any land. They live on the land of their lords or patrons in other villages (de Beauclair 1968; Kirkpatrick and Broder 1976). The Yapese without land (*milingai* or *pimilngay*), practise adoption among themselves. It is rare for *milingai* to be adopted into a Yap family that owns land. One of the Yapese informants confirmed this and reported the following story which he witnessed when he was young:

> The *malob*, or 'sea-hawk', whose name was Anafel, for Gachlaw village in Gilman municipality, was said to have adopted a *milingai* girl from Gachlaw. My father asked Anafel why he adopted the girl, and Anafel said so that she could look after him in his old age. The girl was given a name, Laamang, from Anafel's platform when she was adopted, and accepted into the family as the adopted daughter of Anafel. She subsequently married someone from the *daworchig*, one of the 'middle' ranks on Yap.
>
> (B. N. Weber, personal information, 18 February 2002)

According to this informant, adoption of a *milingai* by a non-*milingai* involves the ceremony of cleansing. The chief of the village, or any person from the family who is adopting but with the chief's knowledge, would put red clay, or *eryaa'*, on the forehead of the adopted person. There is also 'enchantment' purifying the adopted person. A name from the new family would also be given as part of this ceremony. The Yapese phrase *ngin arow nag e milngay*, 'move inland a *milingai*', is the phrase that the informant used to describe the symbolic moving of the low caste person from the forbidden area, or *ta'ay*, which an upper caste person could never enter, to the *arow*, or area occupied by the non-*milingai* (B. N. Weber, personal information, 18 February 2002).

In 2000, we had the opportunity of talking to a *milingai* about his adoption and about adoption on Yap in general. T. was adopted by an elderly childless couple in 1936 during his mother's pregnancy. They were closely related to the biological parents and lived in the same settlement. T. became suspicious when he was about ten years old and asked both his adopted mother and his birth mother. His birth mother assured him that she loved him but that tradition did not permit her to reveal anything. His adopted mother explained the situation to him. When T. was twenty-one, he spoke to a sister about his position but not to his biological mother again and he never spoke to his adopted father about his adoption. The two families were close. In T.'s opinion, the relevant patron could be told about the adoption but there was no obligation to do so.

T. confirmed that adopted children were frequently appreciated and treated well on Yap and that they could be a 'bridge' between two families. He said that adoption elevates a child to a higher social ranking, and confers belonging to a respected place. He explained that there had been fewer adoptions on Yap during the past thirty years and attributed this fact to increasing individualisation of life. In his opinion, more attention is paid to the competence of adoptive parents and he said that nobody liked to give children to families in which alcohol was important. T. confirmed that adults were also adopted to care for the elderly.

The new political order introduced on Yap since the end of the Second World War and the legal system based on the US model have barely influenced adoption practices. Only in exceptional cases do the Yapese approach the Yap State Court to have adoptions confirmed. This happens, for example, if young people leave Yap to be educated (on Guam, Hawaii or elsewhere); then an official record of the names of their guardians is required. Confirmation of adoptions may also be necessary if Yapese living abroad have insurance with a private employer and there needs to be clarification of who is entitled to insurance benefits. Also, adoptions of Yapese by Americans or Japanese are documented in the State Court (B. N. Weber, personal information, Yap, 10–11 May 2000). American, Filipino or Japanese citizens have not been adopted on Yap, although there was an Israeli (Egal), who was on Yap for two years and who was given a Yapese name, 'Go'psan', by a Yapese family in Toruw village, in the municipality of Maap (B. N. Weber, personal information, 18 February 2002).

Yap adoptions in historical context

Depopulation during the colonial eras, resulting from various causes, including temporary or permanent departure from the island to perform contract work, created a need to fill gaps in the generational sequence. The restriction of ceremonial exchange actions (*mit-mit*) by the German colonial authorities made the adoption of a sister for a boy appear less essential. Following termination of the relatively frequent violent conflicts between settlements or settlement alliances during the German colonial period, it probably became possible not only to marry but also to adopt children across greater distances, but mostly within the framework of the alliances. No answer can be supplied to the question as to whether the number of *pof* adoptions increased in consequence. Perhaps there were greater opportunities of using adoptions for a specific purpose, to create or strengthen social ties.

As a result of missionary work and actions against native belief in ancestors as 'ghosts', it possibly became simpler to give children or adults a new name through adoption. On the other hand, the connection of names to certain rights, primarily land inheritance rights, and duties seems to have determined name-giving and name-changing for a long time, and in some ways it still does today.

With the current rise in the loss of any ties extending beyond the nuclear family, the interest in adoptions to solve 'family-specific' problems has probably not fallen – despite a general rise in the population and birth rate. Mention has already been made of the typical phenomenon of adoption of adults for care of the elderly. As already pointed out above too, people in Micronesia apparently pay more attention today to whether adopting parents can give the child or children 'proper' care from a contemporary viewpoint. No assessment can yet be made of the effects which more liberal opinions towards and attitudes of women will have on future adoptions, although it is precisely women on their often laborious path to emancipation who are dependent on external help in caring for their children on a more or less long-term basis.

The Yapese appear to still be resisting any sustained and comprehensive formalisation of new aspects of social life, as shown by avoidance of official registration of adoptions. This may really be an expression of insistence on a traditional behavioural code of mutual trust. Relatively frequent adoption still maintains a fixed place in public culture, despite the often negative attitude of Christian churches, and it remains part of the island's cultural identity. On the other hand, there seem to be an increasing number of opportunities and incentives to abuse adoption. Adoption is becoming a one-sided matter, losing its character as part of a system of interaction and transfer, of sharing of resources, information or goods.

Lessons from Micronesia?

We are currently seeing changes in Western understandings of adoption. Adoption as a way of removing children from the more marginal areas of society has declined in importance or has been replaced or supplemented to a certain degree by transnational adoption. In view of the increasing adoption of children from Third World countries since the end of the Second World War, especially in Europe and the USA, and simultaneous development of a 'trade in children', there was a need for rulings going beyond national law. These agreements are predominantly 'soft law' which is not mandatory for the countries concerned. But now a process is under way to convert soft law into binding legal practice, even if it is applied differently in different regions (Marx 1993).

Since the United Nations Convention on the Rights of the Child (1989), the UN Declaration relating to the Protection of Children with Special Reference to Foster Placement and Adoption (1986) and the Hague Treaty on the Protection of Children and Co-operation in Respect of Intercountry Adoptions (1993), the increased consideration of children's well-being has also had an effect on adoption. This includes better understanding the emotions, problems of cultural orientation, and identity formation of adopted children. In this context, such children are increasingly being granted the right to learn about their origins and history (Scharp 2000).

Where international adoptions are concerned, a tolerated or assisted search by adopted children or young people for their identity and their roots also takes them to different cultures. Currently, there is more forceful expression of the opinion that adopted children also have a 'right' to comprehensive knowledge of their origins and this raises the question as to whether so-called 'weak' adoption should not be recognised in Western countries too, and need not be converted into full, legal adoption. Such 'weak' adoption has remained common practice in many non-Western countries. It restricts but does not sever the ties of adopted children with their birth parents. It is a matter for discussion whether this status of being an adopted child linking two families, as in Oceania, can provide a model for the West. Of course, in such cases, the families concerned are still frequently intact and adoption often involves 'extended families' and related groups rather than individuals or nuclear families.

To conclude, in Oceania, the economic content of adoption appears to be gaining more and more significance and the boundaries between adoption, fosterage and temporary care of children are becoming increasingly blurred. The suitability of the adopting parents also seems to be subject to an assessment which was not previously customary. Finally, there is no mistaking the fact that adoption increasingly relates to children in certain critical situations, whereas this aspect was previously of less significance. On the other hand, there seems to be a trend in Western societies towards informing adopted children about their origins, recognising that children's rights can also include an entitlement to learn about their history and, if applicable, about their origins in a different culture. The associated opportunity of making and maintaining contacts with their birth parents or with their birth mother matches traditional behaviour in a substantial number of non-Western societies, in which adopted children formed, and frequently still form today, a link between two families or, even more, between two groups of kin.

Notes

1   Cf. Defngin 1958; Kirkpatrick and Broder 1976.
2   See also Gorenflo and Levin 1991.
3   B. N. Weber, FSM High Court, Yap, personal information, 16 July 2002.

Bibliography

Alkire, W. H. (1965) *Lamotrek Atoll and Inter-island Socioeconomic Ties*, Illinois Studies in Anthropology, 5, Urbana: University of Illinois Press.

de Beauclair, I. (1968) 'Social Stratification in Micronesia: The Low-caste People of Yap' (reprinted from *The Bulletin of the Institute of Ethnology*), *Academia Sinica*, 25: 45–52.

Brady, Ivan (ed.) (1976) *Transactions in Kinship, Adoption and Fosterage in Oceania*, Honolulu: University of Hawaii Press.

Carroll, V. (1970) 'Introduction: What does "Adoption" mean?', in V. Carroll (ed.) *Adoption in Eastern Oceania*, Honolulu: University of Hawaii Press, pp. 3–17.

Christmann, H., Hempenstall, P. and Ballendorf, D. A. (1991) *Die Karolinen-Inseln in Deutscher Zeit, Bremen Asia-Pacific Studies* (Wagner, W. ed.), Universität Bremen, 1, Münster, Hamburg: Lit Verlag.

Defngin, F. (1958) 'Yapese Names', in *The Use of Names in Micronesia, Anthropological Working Papers*, 3, Guam: The Office of the Staff Anthropologist, Trust Territory of the Pacific Islands.

Fischer, J. L. (1970) 'Adoption on Ponape', in V. Carroll (ed.) *Adoption in Eastern Oceania*, Honolulu: University of Hawaii Press, pp. 292–313.

Gorenflo, L. J. and Levin, M. J. (1991) 'Regional Demographic Change in Yap State, Federated States of Micronesia', *Pacific Studies*, 14: 97–145.

Hezel, F. X. (1999) 'American Anthropology's Contribution to Social Problems Research in Micronesia', in R. C. Kiste and M. Marshall (eds) *American Anthropology in Micronesia*, Honolulu: University of Hawaii Press, pp. 301–325.

Hunter-Anderson, R. L. and Yigal Zan (1996) 'Demystifying the Sawei, A Traditional Interisland Exchange System', ISLA: *A Journal of Micronesian Studies*, 4: 1–45, University of Guam.

Kirkpatrick, J. T. and Broder, Ch. R. (1976) 'Adoption and Parenthood on Yap', in I. Brady (ed.) *Transactions in Kinship, Adoption and Fosterage in Oceania*, Honolulu: University of Hawaii Press, pp. 200–227.

Kraeger, P. (1980) *Traditional Adoption Practices in Africa, Asia, Europe and Latin America*, International Planned Parenthood Federation, London: International Office.

Labby, D. (1976) *The Demystification of Yap*, Chicago: University of Chicago Press.

Lessa, W. A. (1966) *Ulithi: A Micronesian Design for Living*, New York: Holt, Rinehart & Winston.

Lingenfelter, S. G. (1975) *Yap: Political Leadership and Cultural Change in an Island Society*, Honolulu: University of Hawaii Press.

Lingenfelter, S. G. (1993) 'Courtship and Marriage on Yap: Budweiser, U-Drives, and Rock Guitars', in R. A. Marksbury (ed.) *The Business of Marriage, Transformations in Oceania Matrimony*, Pittsburgh and London: University of Pittsburgh Press, pp. 149–174.

Marcus, M. N. (1991) 'Child Abuse and Neglect in Micronesia', *Micronesian Counselor* 2, Micronesian Seminar Publications, Kolonia, Pohnpei, FSM.

Marshall, M. (1976) 'Solidarity or Sterility? Adoption and Fosterage on Namoluk Atoll', in I. Brady (ed.) *Transactions in Kinship, Adoption and Fosterage in Oceania*, Honolulu: University of Hawaii Press, pp. 28–50.

Marx, A. (1993) *Perspektiven der internationalen Adoption*, M.B.H., Neue Folge, 38, Frankfurt am Main: Verlag für Standesamtswesen.

Müller, W. (1917) *Yap*. Vol. II, B, 2, *Ergebnisse der Südsee-Expedition, 1908–1910*, (ed.) Georg Thilenius, Hamburg: Friederichsen, de Gruyter.

Rubinstein, D. H. (1991) 'Adoption in Micronesia: A Lesson in Cultural Psychology', University of Guam, CAS Research Conference Presentation, copy on file in the Micronesian Area Research Center, University of Guam, Mangilao, Guam.

Salesius (Haas, J. G.) (1907) 'Die Karolinen-Insel Yap', *Zeitschrift für Kolonialpolitik, Kolonialrecht und Kolonialwirtschaft*, 8: 196–203, 375–422, Berlin.

Scharp, D. (2000) *Die Auswirkungen internationaler Regelungen auf das deutsche Adoptionsrecht*, Diss. Universität Münster (Westfalen), Aachen: Shaker Verlag.

Smith, De V. R. (1977) *The Ties that Bind. Exchange and Transactions in Kinsmen in Palau*, Ph.D. dissertation, Bryn Mawr College.

Smith, De V. R. (1983) *Palauan Social Structure*, New Brunswick, NY: Rutgers University Press.

Weckler, J. E. (1953) 'Adoption on Mokil', *American Anthropologist*, 55: 555–568, Menasha, Wisconsin.

Part III

Central and South America

Chapter 10

"The one who feeds has the rights"

Adoption and fostering of kin, affines and enemies among the Yukpa and other Carib-speaking Indians of Lowland South America

Ernst Halbmayer

A common modern understanding of adoption is based on the idea of a person or a couple looking after someone else's child on a long-term basis (fostering), and the acquisition of fictive but juridically binding "kin" relationship between such "parents" and the adopted child. This chapter deals with strategies and cultural notions of adoption, fostering and cosmo-sociological integration that go beyond such an understanding. Through an examination of empirical cases of adoption among the Yukpa and comparative evidence from other Carib-speaking Amerindians I identify some restrictions and weaknesses in current theoretical concepts. I argue that adoption does not necessarily imply a process of consanguinization of the adoptee, and consequently inclusion as a child is not the only possible outcome of adoption and fostering.

Local notions of adoption and fostering are embedded and shaped by broader concepts concerning constituting principles of sociality and the person. At least two different and opposed notions of Amazonian sociality may be identified: one focusing on morality and affective notions of conviviality and the other on symbolic notions of alterity. The first tends to associate relations beyond the local everyday creation of sociality with the unsocial realm (Overing and Passes 2000) whereas the latter argues for a cosmo-social medium that expands beyond humanity, and nature becomes part of an encompassing sociality (Descola 1996; Viveiros de Castro 1998).[1] This medium is based on specific cross-cutting relations, forms of exchange and according to Viveiros de Castro, on a "symbolic economy of predation" (1993: 184–192).

Predation and taming are understood as two complementary forms of animal assimilation by humans.[2] Amazonian peoples contrast game animals to tamed family animals[3] of the same species. Tamed family animals are generally the young of killed animals, cared for by the hunter's spouse (Erikson 1987). Descola (1994: 339) argues that three types of relations are structurally homologous: that between game and family animals; a second one between affines and consanguines; and a third one between enemies and captive children. Fausto expands his formula and advocates the idea, indicated already by Erikson, that the shamanic appropriation of helper spirits follows the same logic of transformation of enmity into familiarity and that the "adoption of captive children and animal young are only particular cases of a wider relational structure that involves the familiarization of human spirits in warfare and of animal spirits in shamanism" (Fausto 1999: 949).

Adoption and cosmo-sociological reproduction

Processes of inclusion and exclusion are central for the reproduction of such cosmo-sociological systems. Adoption and fostering are obviously processes of inclusion and internal reproduction, which I see as a selective socio-cultural inclusion of persons[4] into existing households or familial relationships, which go hand in hand with the establishment of close kinship ties.

In contrast to merely temporal or functional inclusion based on specific roles, jobs or tasks in modern organizations, such incorporation into households, familial relationships or indigenous groups includes persons in all their aspects. In indigenous South America this may include the incorporation of a *dead* enemy's multiple aspects, such as body-parts (head, teeth,[5] meat), his spiritual dimensions (souls, energy, life force) or his onomastic identities (names) for the (re-)production of persons.

Contemporary Carib-speaking Indians

Ethnographically, my focus will be on the Carib-speaking peoples of South America, one of the main indigenous language families in the Lowland. Of these groups I will especially refer to the Yukpa, among whom I did a total of two years of field research between 1988 and 2001. I will interpret the Yukpa data in the light of comparative evidence from other Carib-speaking groups.

There are few studies focusing on adoption among Carib-speaking

Indians despite its prevalence in the region.[6] The discrepancy between the lack of anthropological attention and the empirical frequency of the phenomenon may arise for several reasons: (1) the fostering and raising children does not imply the substitution of a "biological" with a "fictive" kin relationship; (2) adoption does not lead to the erosion of the former kin relationship; (3) adoption among related, co-resident persons and families is very common and obviously unproblematic; (4) the question of the social integration of war captives was for a long time hardly understood as a specific form of adoption.

The regional unimportance of descent and genealogical reckoning is reflected in the fact that adoption lacks the notion of "substitution of kinship". The absence of corporate groups, such as lineages, among the Carib-speakers (Rivière 1984) makes a replacement of one filial relationship by a "fictional" one irrelevant for social progeny and inheritance.[7] Therefore some authors – using a definition based on the substitution of filiative relations – argue that adoption is absent among Carib-speakers: "Children living in households other than the one of their parents, are not adopted; adoption is not known in Carib-society," writes Peter Kloos of the Maroni River Caribs (Kloos 1971: 119). Ellen Basso argues along comparable lines: "For the Kalapalo, filiation is a permanent relationship which cannot be changed. Adoption is entirely absent; although fosterage is common on the death of parents, the foster parent and child do not, in fact by definition cannot, participate in a filiative relationship" (Basso 1970: 406).

However, most other authors apply the notion of adoption. Menget (1988: 64f.) makes use of the term in a sense that is worth following. He acknowledges that the child may acquire a new father but states that it never looses its original filiation. Accordingly, adoption does not imply a break with the original family: it is not a substitutive kinship or a mimetic relation of natural filiation. Adoption is the complementation and addition of social relationships, but not their substitution and displacement.

My data for the Yukpa confirm the lack of substitutive kinship. Children raised by others than their physical parents know – like everyone else – who their parents are. The filiative link is stressed among Yukpa by the fact that their own children are designated by specific kinship terms terminologically distinguished from other relatives of the first ascending generation, such as brothers' and sisters' children. Children remain children of their parents, even if adopted by others.

If parents no longer raise and feed a child they renounce their rights over that child, and are unable to interfere in decisions concerning their offspring. This renunciation is not a formal act but a subsequent and continuously ongoing transfer of rights to the foster-parents based on the care, food and material items provided for the child. In recompense, social parents may enjoy the help and labour of elder children and have the possibility of expanding their social influence through the uxorilocal residence of a future son-in-law, or the possibility to give an adopted girl to their own son and thereby enable his consequent virilocal residence. This "political economy of persons" (Rivière 1984) may also explain why girls seem to have fewer problems being adopted or fostered than boys.

Even "natural filiation" is a gradual concept and implies multiple parenthood. This multiplicity is based on the idea that each sexual act during pregnancy contributes to the formation of the foetus, and a child therefore may have several, more or less intensive, filiative links with men, who all contributed to its formation.[8] While among some groups, multiple parenthood is explicitly valued, in others it has to be avoided as it causes illness (Kalapalo) or leads to the birth of undesired twins (Yukpa, Akawaio). In any case, multiple filiation implies the need for a social definition of the child's social father, and normally this is the role of the mother's husband.[9]

Adoption among the Yukpa: the case of Yurmutu

Yurmutu is a small Irapa-Yukpa village at the headwaters of the Tukuku River in the mountains of the Sierra de Perijá near the Colombian–Venezuelan border. The inhabitants have a permanent intermediary contact with the mission station, which is about an eight hours walk down the non-navigable river. The only "modern" institution within the village is a small school, irregularly visited by a teacher from the Lowland, in which till 2001 no one had learned to read or write.

At the beginning of 2001 seventeen households belonged to the community, ten formed the village, whereas seven were located outside but within the community's territory. Movements between the village and secondary houses near the fields are common and people often reside some weeks near their fields and the village may appear to be abandoned. Community boundaries are in reality fuzzy.

Houses among the Yukpa are generally small and inhabited by a single hearth-group,[10] or household. Such a household normally consists of a couple or a polygamous family, its unmarried children, step-children and adoptees. Marriage goes hand in hand with the establishment of a new, preferentially uxorilocal household. Nevertheless, uxorilocality and

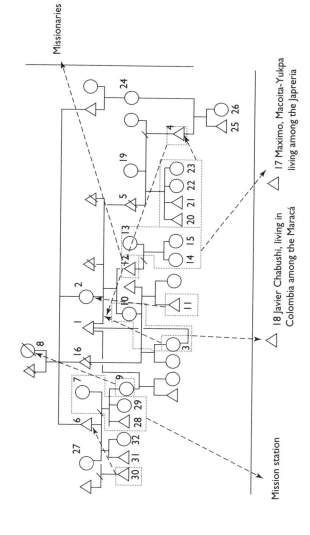

Figure 10.1 Cases of adoption in Yurmutu, Irapa-Yukpa.

virilocality may become the same within the village and access to better land may change the uxorilocal ideal to an ambilocal residence practice.

Eighty-four people live in these seventeen households and forty-eight of them are unmarried children. Nine of these forty-eight children (almost a fifth), are not raised by their biological parents. Additionally one is living with his mother and step-father, and four of the community's adults were themselves raised by others than their biological parents. I will present the cases of adoption involving residents of Yurmutu in some detail, as they are representative of the situation encountered among contemporary Irapa-Yukpa (see Figure 10.1).

Case 1

In 1988 Nupe (1), who was at that time between forty-five and fifty years old, lived with his wife, Nippe (2), some years older than himself, his second young wife Christina (3), and a still unmarried adolescent, called Alejandro (4). Alejandro is Nippe's son's son, and Nippe his paternal grandmother. Alejandro's father, Noupaka (5), gave the boy to his mother after his wife had left him, and Nippe and Nupe raised him.

Case 2

In 1990 Akio (6) and his wife at that time, Esperanza (7), decided to settle in the Lowland near the mission station. Akio's aged mother Matshukapshi (8) had become a widow only about one year earlier. She complained that her son was going to leave her alone – although several of her other children lived in the village. She asked that Akio's oldest daughter, the already eleven or twelve-year-old Oroshi (9) should stay and live with her "to help her, so that she will not be alone". So Oroshi stayed in the village with her father's mother while her parents and siblings left. In 1991/92 the marital situation of Nupe (1) had changed, Nupe and his elder wife Nippe (2; see Case 1) had separated and Nippe was now living on her own. Nupe had married another second wife: the very young Oroshi (9), after she had reached puberty. So Matshukapashi (8), who was also Nippe's mother (2), had again become his "mother-in-law", as she – as Nupe said – "gave" Oroshi to him.

Case 3

The change mentioned in Case 2 had the consequence that Nippe (2) was now living alone, and therefore asked her daughter Parenete (10) that her young son (11) be given into her care to be raised by her. From that time on the boy was sleeping in the hut of his maternal grandmother, but during the day he was regularly switching between the hut of his grandmother and his parents.

Case 4

Nippe (2), today between seventy and seventy-five-years-old, had had three children from two previous marriages before she had married Nupe: Noupaka (5), Parenete (10) and Ignacio (12). Parenete once told me that when she was a very small child the Capuchin missionaries came to the village. She was told to hide together with some other children, so that the missionaries would not see her. The Yukpa already knew that the Capuchins wanted to carry away their children to raise them in the mission boarding school. This appeared the easiest and most effective way of spreading the Catholic faith among the Yukpa. Despite the protests of Tema, Nippe's father, they took Ignacio with them and he was raised in the missionary school. Later he returned to live alternatively in Kanowapa, a neighboring village, and in Yurmutu. While he is the only one who knows to read and write in Yurmutu he lacks the common agricultural and cosmological knowledge and remains an intermediary person between the mission station and the villages at the headwater. While valued for his knowledge of the *watia* (non-indigenous people) he has lived a sort of outlaw's life without a wife for an extremely long time in these traditional villages. He is still unsuccessful as a hunter or cultivator and hardly capable of producing what is necessary to sustain a family.

Case 5

Nevertheless Ignacio (12) was married for rather short periods. He was married to Adelina (13), who came originally from the Macoita-Yukpa but was raised in the missionary school. After she left school she lived with him in Yurmutu and had two girls (14,15). They separated after some time and Adelina married Maximo (17), also a Macoita-Yukpa, who is today the teacher among the Japrera, the most northern Carib-speaking group in the region. Adelina and Maximo raised Ignacio's daughters and they live today among the Japreria and are already married.

Case 6

Christina (3) the wife of Nupe, was a daughter of Parenete (10). Her father, Pashruma (16), had died and was Nippe's (2) brother. So Pashruma had married his sister's daughter, a legitimate marriage among the Yukpa. It turned out that Nupe had been married to two wives (2, 3) who were, depending on the calculation, grandmother and grandchild, or brother's daughter and father's sister to one another. How did this happen? Parenete had left her husband Pashruma with whom she had had two daughters and went with young Christina to live with Javier Chabushi (18) at the Colombian side of the Sierra among another Yukpa subgroup, the Maracá. There they had an additional child. But this marriage ended in a quarrel, Parenete was beaten with a machete and flew back to Yurmutu without managing to take the children with her. In Yurmutu the three women, Matshukapshi, Nippe, and Parenete repeatedly complained and cried for the small Christina, who had been left in Colombia without close relatives. Finally they convinced Nupe, at that time influential Cazique of Yurmutu and son-in-law of the famous healer and Matshukapashi's husband, Tema, to go to Colombia and bring Christina back. He went and managed due to his enormous oratory skills to bring the child back. The second small child remained with the father in Colombia. Back in Yurmutu, Christina was adopted by Nippe and Nupe, as her mother was still without a husband. When Christina became a marriageable woman Nupe took her as a second wife.

Case 7

The already mentioned Noupaka (5), son of Nippe (2), married a second wife (19) and they had four children (20–23). Noupaka died suddenly in 1998 and left his wife and four children. These children are now fostered by Alejandro (4), Noupaka's son from his preceding marriage, and his wife Juanita (24) together with their own two small children (25, 26).

Case 8

Chokwe was living in the neighboring village of Pishikakaw. His oldest daughter married a man called Sapo, who is originally from Yurmutu, where his mother and brother live. After his marriage he went to live near his father-in-law in Pishikakaw. In 1997 however he had returned to Yurmutu and was living there with his wife and a son. In 2001, after

Chokwe had died, Chokwe's daughter and her husband Sapo were raising Chokwe's four orphaned children in addition to their two sons.

Case 9

A man called Jototshi, who was already married to a daughter of Chijishi – one of the senior men of the community – asked for another of the latter's daughters. This girl was still young and probably about seven years old. Chijishi gave him the daughter with the words "raise her yourself" (*ajapsa tojeka*). He raised her, but she did not like him and she left Jototshi when she was grown.

Forms of adoption

Several forms of adoption may be distinguished in these nine cases:

Adoption by classificatory parents

Same-sex siblings of parents are generally classificatory (or diminutive) parents among Carib-speaking groups. Due to the principle of bifurcate merging, classificatory parents are terminologically distinguished from the parents' cross-sex siblings. Classificatory parents are logically the first and closest relatives to adopt their same-sex siblings' children. So it seems rather surprising that among the cases outlined there is not a single case of adoption by classificatory parents, although this form of adoption would be entirely consistent with the Yukpa's principles of kinship classification.

Adoption by real or classificatory mother's sisters or father brother's wives is the most common way to raise orphaned children among the Txicão (Menget 1988: 64), and among the Yekuana adoption by classificatory parents is documented of the mother's sister, the father's brother and for the mother's co-wives in a polygynous household (Arvelo-Jiménez 1971).

Adoption by (elder) siblings

Cases 7 and 8, outlined above, demonstrate adoption by elder siblings. In Case 7 Alejandro raises his deceased father's children and half-siblings, whereas in Case 8 Sapo's wife raises her siblings together with her husband. Arvelo-Jiménez mentions two cases: a Yekuana son who cares for his father's wife and daughter (his half-sister) and a daughter who adopts

her sibling. It is obvious from the general ethnography that the relationship between terminologically distinguished elder and younger siblings
may take the form of care and protection and especially elder sisters may
assume a mother-like role toward their younger siblings.

Among the Yukpa adoption by elder siblings becomes terminologically
equivalent to adoption by close grandparents, due to a system of alternate
generations inscribed in their kinship system. The term for elder brother
may also be used by male speakers to refer to close grandfathers of the
second ascending level (eB = FF, FFB) and the term for younger brother
is also used for close grandchildren of the second descending genealogical
level (yB = BSS, FBSSS, . . .).

Intergenerational adoption by "grandparents"

Adoption by grandparents is a common phenomenon among the Yukpa,
especially by the father's mother (Cases 1 and 2) and the mother's mother
(Cases 3 and 6). The prominence of such intergenerational adoption
is also recorded for other Carib-speaking groups, such as the Yekuana,
where a preference for adoption by the father's mother seems to exist
(Arvelo-Jiménez 1971: 77f.). Among the Yekuana the principle of
adoption by grandparents also expands to classificatory grandparents,
generally same-sex siblings of the grandparents. Also, among the Bakairi,
the Txicão and the Barama River Caribs adoption by grandparents is
reported as common.

Adoption by grandparents is not only to care for (orphaned) children.
It is also a form of assistance for old women and couples and it is quite
common for daughters to give a child to their mother or parents, to avoid
having them live "alone", without children. To live alone is not only
undesired, but considered to be an unsocial state of existence. Adoption
is an option for changing such a situation. Another option – hardly used
among the Yukpa – would be the integration or adoption of the elderly
persons into their children's households by the extension of the hearth-
group. The Yukpa prefer to give a child to their parents for adoption than
to adopt the parents into their household. As adoption also includes
an aspect of power, dependency of the adoptee, and loss of autonomy,
Yukpa avoid transferring their parents into such a position. Through the
adoption of children, senior households have the possibility of continued
autonomy through access to an additional work force, help and support
by a young boy or girl and consequently even the support of a son-in-
law in the case of an adopted girl's marriage.

Among the Waiwai this sort of "domestic assistance" for elderly childless couples is described by (Fock 1963) as "curious custom" and a specific institution called *anton*. Fock interprets it as "an effective means of counteracting the haphazard division of large and small families and of equalizing the consequent differences in economic obligations and practical services", and argues that "by bringing into the family an unrelated person it (the *anton* custom) can also become a short-cut to marriage" (1963: 154). Although the Yukpa do not recognize a specifically named institution, the practice of providing old or childless couples with children is basically the same, although the adopted children seem always closely related to the grandparents.

The most general cause for such adoption is the lack of children in the household, either due to advanced age or infertility. So, it has to be emphasized that Cases 1 and 6 may not – in contrast to Cases 2 and 3 – be interpreted in terms of help for an elderly couple. At the time of Alejandro's and Christina's adoption, Nupe and Nippe were an active, highly productive and respected couple, and Nupe was even the settlement's headman. Nevertheless, Nippe and Nupe remained childless, as their only child died shortly after birth. Adoption of two of Nippe's grandchildren, offspring of children from previous marriages, was a way to compensate for this lack.

While adoption does not regulate inheritance and social progeny among Carib-speaking Indians it regulates access to work force, children, sons-in-law and even to spouses. Intergenerational grandparental adoption sets up a whole range of social phenomena through its relationship to marriage.

Adoption as a shortcut to marriage: adoption of potential in-laws

Future children-in-law may be adopted and integrated into a household prior to marriage. This holds true for both potential daughters-in-law and sons-in-law. Fock (1963: 154) mentions a Waiwai mother, presenting to her adopted son a just-adopted girl, saying: "Here is your wife, train her yourself." Among the Apalai, girls are occasionally "given to her future mother-in-law to rear and train for her son". Koehn (1975: 103) and Arvelo-Jiménez (1971: 79) mention two orphaned Yekuana girls who were brought up by their future husband's mothers. Such adoptions – as Arvelo-Jiménez outlines – may lead to "the advantages of virilocal residence for their sons" (1971: 122).

The other form of adoption is that of potential sons-in-law. Such incorporation is also known under the label of "children marriage", in fact a "marriage" which often excludes[11] a sexual relationship between the child-couple until the girl reaches puberty (Halbmayer 1998; Rivière 1969). Among the Yukpa, Wavrin (1953: 269) described an eighteen-year-old man who was married to a five or six-year-old girl: "he had asked for her, while she was still very young. Marte (the father-in-law . . .) gave his daughter to him. Since then [they] play household together, sleep abreast in her parents' hut and under their surveillance.She has a little sister (. . .) who sleeps with the engaged ones" and observes all their activities. According to Wavrin they have to abstain from sexual intercourse till the girl is pubescent. The son-in-law has to obey and work for his future parents-in-law, receives food from them and is their "domestique" (Wavrin 1953: 269f.). Such cases of pre-marital adoption by parents-in-law have been reported among the Yukpa (Halbmayer 1998), the Panare (Henley 1982: 108) and the Txicão (Menget 1977: 131).

These examples make it obvious that marriage, as long as it involves residence with the parents-in-law and bride-service, is a – stronger or weaker – form of adoption, including the well-known aspects of dependency and inferiority of the son-in-law.

This relationship is also expressed in the kinship term for son-in-law. Among the Yukpa this term – used equally for reference and address – is equivalent to the term of a sister's son for male speakers, namely, depending on the subgroup, a form of *patu/pa'te/pachi*. This is the equivalent of the term *pito*, discussed for the Guianese Carib-speakers.[12] This term for son-in-law has a wide semantic range, from war captive (Kloos 1971: 51; Gillin 1948: 849) to equal and a "universal affinal connotation" (Rivière 1977). Besides the adoption of in-laws, two other forms of "adoption-marriage" have to be mentioned and both may also be child marriages.

Adoption of a spouse

Among the Yukpa adopted children may also become the (future) spouses of the adopters, as the Cases 6 and 10 demonstrate. The Yukpa generally note that raising a wife-child has an important advantage: the wife will become accustomed to the future husband and therefore no marital problems will arise.

The meaning of the notion *yenétojeka* (to raise) is close to yento (to approximate). The verb consists of *yené* (to make) and *tojen* (to eat). The basic meaning of the term is "to make someone eating". *Tojeka*, including the suffix *–ka* expressing intensity and emphasis, is translated into Spanish as "*arrancar*". "*Arrancar*" has a double meaning: to obtain by coercion, or to dig up, and to start up or to begin with. Both, the idea of coercion of the adoptee and the beginning of a formation, a training and taming, are thereby expressed. It indicates that fostering and raising a child depends not only on providing food and care, but also on coercing someone to accept the offered food and to be formed.

It is important to note that these girls are fostered as affines. Despite the fact that Christina was raised by Nupe, she never became a daughter or any other sort of consanguinial relative to him. She remained a perfectly marriageable *pahte* (the category of marriageable women, including the classificatory cross-cousins and the sister's daughters), whereas Nippe, Nupe's wife, had adopted her as a *piki* (a broad term, used among others for sister, and daughter's daughter). Jototshi (Case 9) also raised his young second wife – although unsuccessfully – as an affinal woman and as he was already married to her sister, he established thereby a sororal polygynous household.

So in such cases the difference between adoption and marriage is a temporal one.[13] Rivière discussed child marriages among the Trio and refers to them as "avuncular adoption" preceding a sister's daughter's marriage.[14] "The man is said to be the girl's *arimikane*, her nurturer, and this term must be distinguished from husband (*inyo*), which implies a sexual relationship" (Rivière 1969: 161). In most cases this form of nurturing adoption seems to be associated with secondary unions and the establishment of polygamous families.

Mother–daughter polygamy

The adoption of a future spouse may not only lead to a sororal polygamous household as in the case of Jototshi, but also to mother–daughter polygamy. These polygamous unions are repeatedly reported among Carib-speakers and they indicate once more the smooth transformation from adoption to marriage. Mother–daughter polygamy has its foundation in a man marrying a mother and nourishing/marrying her daughter from a preceding union. Gillin (1948): 850) noted in the *Handbook of South American Indians* "the marriage with the step-daughter" as a feature of the indigenous groups of Guiana. Polygamous unions with a mother and her daughter are variously reported for the Waiwai, the Kapon (Patamona; Akawaio: Butt 1954: 26), the Trio (Rivière 1969: 161), the Apalai (Koehn 1975: 99), the Wayana (Lapointe 1970: 105) and for several of the Yukpa subgroups (Irapa, Macoita, Iroka, see Halbmayer 1998: 205f.).

Among the Yukpa the condition for such a marriage with mother and daughter is that the marriage with the mother is not a leviratic one. It is important that the girl's father and wife's former husband is no classificatory brother of the new husband. In such a case the wives' daughter would be unmarriageable, as she would be a brother's daughter and the new husband at the same time the girl's classificatory father (FB). In this case we would not be dealing with a mother–daughter marriage-adoption but with adoption by a classificatory parent. What is striking in these cases of spouse adoption and its polygamous version of motherdaughter adoption is that the "step-daughter" stands in a completely different and affinal relationship to the adopter. From a male point of view she is an affine, marriageable "step-wife", rather than a consanguine step-"daughter".

Adoption and the simultaneous reproduction of consanguinial and affinal relationships

These cases demonstrate that a single case of adoption among the Yukpa may have two strikingly different meanings in terms of relationship. These forms of adoption may be divided into two classes: a consanguinial, filliative form of adoption by classificatory parents, elder siblings and grandparents, and an affinal form of adoption of/by future in-laws and spouses. Whereas primary marriages are generally a form of adoption by future in-laws, secondary marriages may achieve the adoption of a second wife without being adopted by in-laws. In the first case marriage depends on being included into the family of in-laws, whereas secondary marriages achieve marriage and avoid (further) inclusion by in-laws.

A single adoptive operation may at the same time reproduce two of the mentioned forms of adoptions. This may be demonstrated by several examples: in the case of adoption by classificatory parents, such as the mother's sister, the relationship between the children and the mother's sister is clearly a consanguinial one. But this is not necessarily the case for the mother's sister's husband. If he is not a consanguine, for example a classificatory brother of the children's father, the girls are his marriageable wife's sisters' daughters (WZD). The same logic operates in case of polygamous mother–daughter marriages. If the deceased wife's husband was a classificatory brother of Ego his wife's daughter is an unmarriageable classificatory daughter and not a marriageable affine. In case of adoption by elder siblings this is even more obvious as Ego's siblings are Ego's spouse's affines: a case as we have seen that may lead to sororal polygamy.

Such a system allows very close marriages, without altering the distinction between the affines and consanguines, and the reproduction of both consanguinial and affinal relationships in a single act of adoption. In contrast to the common wisdom presented in the literature, where adoption or familiarization goes hand in hand with consanguinization (Descola 1994; Fausto 1999), the Yukpa state that the children of others are raised as *akono* (classificatory male cross-cousin) or as *pahte* (classificatory female cross-cousin and sister's daughter). Adoptees are therefore, except in cases of a pre-existing relationship of "classificatory parenthood" or "siblingship", raised as affines.

The Yukpa put no stress on the consanguinization of affines but rather expand and maintain affinal relationships. This goes hand in hand with a highly dispersed settlement structure, the lack of concentrated and integrated villages and high endemic internal violence (Halbmayer 2001). Even more important, consanguinization would reduce options for close marriages by reducing the number of potential marriage partners (Menget 1988: 65). The Yukpa solve this problem – in contrast to other Carib-speakers – by adopting others as affines, and by reproducing the distinction between affines and consanguines. The production of nearness among the Yukpa does not rely on consanguinization but on co-substantiation, based on sharing and the incorporation of the same food. Three such levels of co-substantiation may be distinguished: (1) the level of the hearth-group, whose members incorporate food cooked at one fire and "dug out" from the household's fields; (2) the obligatory sharing of meat and freshly harvested maize co-substantiate the local residential units consisting of a number of households; (3) feasts co-substantiate temporary regional groupings through the shared consumption of maize beer. This is today the highest level of such integration. Were there traditionally any other forms of integration?

The adoption of enemies

To draw a clear distinction between social units and insiders/outsiders is often problematic in indigenous Lowland South America. Menget (1988) introduced a distinction between internal and external adoption in his analysis and located it at the edge of the Txicão as a socio-cultural group. Among the Yukpa it is more difficult to establish such a distinction, as they are internally differentiated into different subgroups living in different river valleys on the eastern and western slopes of the Sierra de Perijá. These subgroups traditionally conceived of each other as enemies and war-raids and the theft of women among these groups was common.

In contrast, contact with the neighbouring Chibcha-speaking Barí in the south was completely avoided, as for a long time were marriage relations with the Barí, Guajiros and *watia* (non-indigenous people). Adoption in relation to warfare and the incorporation of killed enemies' children and women took place among the Yukpa between different subgroups.

Among the Yukpa movements across the subgroups' borders have greatly increased due to missionary activity and so-called pacification. As we have seen today even the movement of children to other subgroups (e.g. Cases 5 and 6) is tolerated at least as long as a close relative or parent moves with them. This situation changes however as soon as a child moves to or remains within another subgroup without such relatives, as Cases 6 and 4 indicate in different ways.

Ignacio was as a small boy carried away by the Capuchin missionaries and raised by them – as the people state today – against the will of his close family. Such a forced external adoption was conceived as a form of robbery and loss. Yet times have changed, systematic forced adoptions by missionaries no longer occur and many Yukpa have tried to establish bonds with the missionaries so as to have better access to Western goods. Those raised in the mission boarding school tend to stress the support they received rather than their forced appropriation – itself an indication of their successful adoption. With raising consciousness of indigenous rights and political self-determination this interpretation seems to be slowly changing. In the remote villages the connotation of loss is still strongly alive when a child moves out of the community, for instance to the boarding school in the Lowland. In fact, hardly any children of these villages are raised there. The feeling of loss is also exemplified in the example of Christina, who was left in Colombia among a different subgroup without close relatives as her mother fled back to Yurmutu.

There is a significant difference between an adoption by and of outsiders. Adoption by outsiders has to be avoided and is conceived as loss, robbery or predatory intervention while the adoption of specific outsiders is generally welcome and in some cases, such as among the Txicão, even a highly valued resource for increasing the group's available names and identities. So whereas adoption of those who are not too different is valued, an inclusion by external others has to be avoided. The general principle of such symbolic predatory relationships is a negative reciprocal one, based on the hope of keeping away and shunning a reciprocal counter-predation. Such logic relies on the idea of incorporation without being incorporated. Although the threat of counter-predation is present, inclusion at this outer level should ideally be a one-way inclusion.

Enemies were generally killed outside the village and remained at the place they were killed. Children and wives of the enemies would be taken to the village and adopted and taken as spouses but not killed. Among the Yukpa this practice has disappeared. The only eyewitness account of a war captive I am aware of is provided by Bolinder (1958: 146f.). He saw a Socomba-Yukpa Indian living among the Maracá-Yukpa "as an indentured servant of his . . . master. He was required to work for him but, as slavery is unknown to Indian cultures, he was allowed to keep everything he made as well as the harvest from the patch of cornfield which had been allotted to him. His captors also selected a wife for him". Reichel-Dolmatoff refers to a murderer and his victim's son. During a feast, a drunken Cazique killed three men, among them the father of a young boy. The boy and his mother left the settlement to live in a faraway village. When the boy was grown he returned to the settlement and killed his father's murderer and stayed in the village. A relationship of "mutual dependence" developed between the avenger and the six-year-old boy of the killed murderer. The avenger became the protector of the child, they stayed together all the time and he taught him a lot. "The child seemed to consider him as substitute of his father" (1945: 66). This supports Erikson's idea that familiarization is a strategy to minimize the antagonism between the killer's and victim's group, between prey and predator, and to avoid the inversion of this relationship.

Conclusion: the logic of adoption and cosmo-social reproduction

Adoption among the Yukpa contradicts the common wisdom that adoption and familiarization are processes leading to consanguinization, as adopted and familiarized persons generally remain or become – if no prior relationship existed – affines. Only if a prior consanguinial relationship existed it is maintained. Adoption is understood as a complementation of relationships based on co-substantiation through the exchange of food and co-residence. It produces increasing sameness and goes hand in hand with the transfer of rights and obligations over adopted children but not with terminological consanguinity. As in a single act of adoption consanguinial and affinal relationships may be reproduced, adoption may under such conditions easily culminate in marriage and be a short cut for the establishment of a marital relationship.

Notes

1 For a discussion of this assumption see Halbmayer (1998, 2004).
2 This may be contrasted with the exchange of children versus domestic animals among the Maasai (see Aud Talle, Chapter 5 in this volume).
3 Called *yeki* among the Yukpa and with more or less related terms among other Carib-speaking groups: *yeken* (Pemon), *yiki* (Panare), *(y)ekë*, *ayekï* (Kariña), *jekï* (Wayana), *egu* (Txicão), *itolugu* (Kalapalo).
4 The notion of persons is not restricted to the notion of humans, as the attribution of personhood cross-cuts the distinction of human/non-human in Amazonia.
5 Called for example *egu* among the Txicao, the same term is used for family animals, captives and the bamboo flutes used during initiation which are the *egu* of the flute players (Menget 1977: 156).
6 (Menget 1988) on the Txicão is one of the few studies in this area.
7 As the deceased's personal goods are burned or otherwise disposed of and land is generally not an inheritable item, inheritance is hardly an issue.
8 As among the Txicão, Arara, Yekuana, Wayana, Akawaio, Waimiri-Atroari and Kuikuro, for example.
9 A number of these features are also shared by the contemporary urban working-class population as Claudia Fonseca (Chapter 11 in this volume) writes: a "mother is who brings you up" and fosterage creates "a bond which may rival but is never confused with blood ties" and "mothers were multiplied rather than substituted".
10 A term used by Henley (1982).
11 Not so in the Xingu where "'arranged' marriage(s) between a girl engaged before puberty and an older man" are common and related to the giving of a bride-price. This is called *mázope itsomitá*, "he marries a girl in puberty seclusion" (Basso 1970: 413).
12 See Kirchhoff (1931 126f.), Rivière (1977 641f.), Whitehead (1988: 188f.).
13 The groups of the Upper Xingu are an exception as girls frequently have sexual relations during the long seclusion period but without being adopted during that time into a future husband's household.
14 For the high frequency of ZD marriages among Carib-speaking Indians see Henley (1983/84).

References

Arvelo-Jiménez, N. (1971) 'Political relations in a tribal society. A study of Ye'cuana Indians', unpublished Ph.D. dissertation, Ithaca.
Basso, E. (1970) 'Xingu Carib kinship terminology and marriage: another view.' *Southwestern Journal of Anthropology* 26: 402–416.
Bolinder, G. (1958) *We Dared the Andes*. London and New York: Abelard-Schuman.
Butt, A. (1954) 'Systems of belief in relation to social structure and organisation', unpublished Oxford: Ph.D. dissertation, University of Oxford.
Descola, P. (1994) 'Pourquoi les Indiens d'Amazonie n'ont-ils pas domestiqué

le pécari? Généalogie des objets et anthropologie de l'objectivation', in Latour, B. (ed.), *De la préhistoire aux missiles balistiques*. Paris: Ed. La Découverte.

Descola, P. (1996) 'Constructing natures. Symbolic ecology and social practice', in Descola, P. and Pálsson, G. (eds), *Nature and Society*. London and New York: Routledge.

Erikson, P. (1987) 'De l'apprivoisement a l'approvisionnement: chasse, alliance et familiarisation en Amazonie Amérindienne.' *Techniques and Culture* 9: 105–140.

Fausto, C. (1999) 'Of enemies and pets: warfare and shamanism in Amazonia.' *American Ethnologist* 26: 933–956.

Fock, N. (1963) *Waiwai*. Copenhagen: The National Museum.

Gillin, J. (1948) 'Tribes of the Guianas and the left Amazon tributaries', in Steward, J. (ed.), *Handbook of South American Indians*, Vol 3: 799–860. Washington: Smithsonian Institution.

Halbmayer, E. (1998) *Kannibalistische Sonne, Schwiegervater Mond und die Yukpa*. Frankfurt am Main: Brandes & Apsel.

Halbmayer, E. (2001) 'Socio-cosmological contexts and forms of violence. War, vendetta, duels and suicide among the Yukpa of North-Western Venezuela', in Schmidt, B. and Schröder, I. (eds), *The Anthropology of Violence and Conflict*. London: Routledge, pp. 49–75.

Halbmayer, E. (2004) 'Elementary distinctions in world-making among the Yukpa.' *Anthropos* 99: 1–17.

Henley, P. (1982) *The Panare*. New Haven and London: Yale University Press.

Henley, P. (1983/84) 'Intergenerational marriage amongst the Carib-speaking peoples of the Guianas: a preliminary survey.' *Antropológica* 59–62: 155–182.

Kirchhoff, P. (1931) 'Die Verwandtschaftsorganistion der Urwaldstämme Südamerikas.' *Zeitschrift für Ethnologie* 63: 85–193.

Kloos, P. (1971) *The Maroni River Caribs of Surinam*. Assen: Van Gorcum.

Koehn, S. S. (1975) 'Apalaí kinship and social behavior.' *Arquivos de Anatomia e Antropologia* 1: 79–108.

Lapointe, J. (1970) 'Residence patterns and Wayana social organization', unpublished Ph.D. dissertation, Colombia University.

Menget, P. (1977) 'Au nom des autres. Classification des relations sociales chez les Txicao du Haut Xingu', unpublished Ph.D. dissertation, Université de Paris X.

Menget, P. (1988) 'Note sur l'adoption chez les Txicao du Brésil Central.' *Anthropologie et Sociétés* 12: 63–72.

Overing, Joanna and Passes, Alan (eds) (2000) *The Anthropology of Love and Anger*. London and New York: Routledge.

Reichel-Dolmatoff, G. (1945) 'Los Indios Motilones.' *Revista del Instituto Etnológico Nacionale* 2: 15–115.

Rivière, P. (1969) *Marriage among the Trio*. Oxford: Clarendon Press.

Rivière, P. (1977) 'Some problems in the comparative study of Carib societies.' *Anthropological Papers of the University of Arizona Press* 28: 39–43.

Rivière, P. (1984) *Individual and Society in Guiana*. Cambridge: Cambridge University Press.

Viveiros de Castro, E. B. (1993) 'Alguns aspectos da afinidade no dravidianato Amazônico', in Viveiros de Castro, E. B. and Carneiro da Cunha, M. (eds), *Amazônia: Etnologia e História Indígena*. São Paulo: Universidade de São Paulo, Núcleo de História indígena, pp. 149–210.

Viveiros de Castro, E. B. (1998) 'Cosmological deixis and Amerindian perspectivism.' *Journal of the Royal Anthropological Institute* (N.S.) 4: 469–488.

Wavrin, M. D. (1953) *Chez les indiens de Colombie*. Paris: Plon.

Whitehead, N. L. (1988) *Lords of the Tiger-Spirit*. Dordrecht, Holland: Foris Publications.

Chapter 11

The circulation of children in a Brazilian working-class neighborhood

A local practice in a globalized world[1]

Claudia Fonseca

Anthropologists doing research on traditional societies have pondered over practices related to the circulation of children since the early days of the discipline. The quandary of children living with parents unrelated by blood has been a key element in rethinking the naturalized conjugal family and formulating alternative models for the study of kinship organization. Many of these studies, however, might well be classified under what Ginsburg and Rapp have called the 'natural history' approach to reproduction: the 'fine-grained, local-level, holistic analysis [whose] strength – its focus on cultural specificity – was sometimes also its limitation' (1995: 1). Few researchers have studied informal circuits of child circulation within complex societies where the state and global processes have a clear impact.

In recent years, there have been several anthropological studies on adoption from the point of view of adoptive families in Europe and North America. Researchers have systematically criticized the value-laden ideologies that influence adoptive parents' attitudes, denouncing, for example, the 'myth of abandonment' and, for intercountry and transracial processes, the reification of a child's 'cultural origins'. They have likewise relativized the identity problems of adopted children, raising innovative theoretical perspectives on 'enchained identities', 'multiple authorship', 'heterotopic families' (Yngvesson 2000), pluripaternity (Ouellette 1995), and 'self-conscious kinship' (Howell 1998). My work is designed to contribute to this line of investigation, deconstructing the naturalized categories linked to family and, in particular, the adoption process. However, my point of departure – poverty-stricken Brazilian women who have given a child to be raised by others – necessarily leads me to develop a slightly different perspective on the question. I seek to understand the

place adoption holds in the life experience of these women and, by extension, the way the laws which govern legal adoption (authored by people
generally of a different class, if not of a different country) relate to their
way of seeing the process.

Following this line of investigation I examine a local practice – the
circulation of children in working-class neighborhoods of a large Brazilian
city – by situating it within the wider context which includes national and
international adoption. Such an approach does not preclude ethnographic
description, and so the first part of this chapter will involve narratives
based on the accounts of concrete flesh-and-blood people. But it does
oblige us to ponder the 'cultural' specificity of these people in relation
to the representations of other groups, such as Brazilian legislators or
European adoptive parents – that is, in relation to the representations of
those who have the power to influence, directly or indirectly, the destiny
of children in poor families throughout the globe. The Brazilian case is
particularly suitable for this sort of investigation. During the 1980s, Brazil
was in fourth place among the world's main providers of internationally
adopted children (behind Korea, India, and Colombia). During that
decade, more than 7,500 Brazilian children, many of whom came from
families like the ones we describe in this chapter, were sent to France,
Italy, and – to a lesser extent – the United States (Kane 1993). This rate
doubled during the 1990s when, in the first five years of the decade, over
8,500 were adopted internationally.[2] The subject has received a great deal
of publicity in various Brazilian newspapers – both salvationist *pros* and
xenophobic *contras*. Little if any interest has been shown, however, in
the lives of birth parents, much less in the way their experiences relate
to national policies and international laws. This chapter is designed help
fill in this gap, depicting poverty-stricken women in a Brazilian slum as
relevant actors in contemporary world processes.

Child circulation in a Brazilian *favela*

It was during my field research in a neighborhood of poverty-stricken
squatters (rag pickers, beggars, and an occasional construction worker)
in Porto Alegre,[3] that I first became aware of the circulation of children.
There, approximately half the women had placed at least one child
with a substitute family or at the state orphanage. Five years later, I began
a second phase of research in a less miserable working-class district, composed of artisans, janitors, maids, bus drivers and other lower-income
employees, where better-off families had an average income of around
$200 a month. Here, I encountered a surprising number of women who

had at some time taken in a child to raise. But a fine line divided 'fosterage' from 'adoption' as many children who had embarked on a short sojourn in the foster household just 'stayed on'. All in all, in more than 120 households canvassed during my field research, I took note of nearly 100 people who had, during their childhood, alternated residence in the households of godmothers, grandmothers, and other sorts of mothers de *criação*.[4] Of these, not one had been legally adopted.

Whereas during the first phase of research my analyses had been centered on the immediate circumstances surrounding child circulation – the need to place children as a survival strategy and the frequent disputes which arose between a child's different mothers, ten years later (in the mid-1990s), I returned to the field, rekindling old as well as making new contacts, in order to better understand the long-term repercussions of this practice. The following story, a sort of exemplary case, is drawn from this second round of field experience.

Networks and survival

Inez was 38 years old when I met her. At the time her husband was distributing newspapers while she worked as an attendant at the neighborhood day-care center. As a preamble to her life story, she mentioned the odds she had been up against during her early childhood: nine of her sixteen brothers and sisters had died in infancy. 'My mother was very poor', explained Inez. 'She didn't get enough to eat so the babies would be born undernourished.' Inez was lucky enough to have been placed with her godmother, Dona Joana, early on. As she tells it: 'They took me to visit my godmother and when it was time to go home, I grabbed on to a table leg, and nobody could pry me loose, so they just let me stay on.'

Dona Joana, despite being infertile, had always been surrounded by children, brought in by her activities as a midwife and foster mother. Twenty years before Inez entered her life, Dona Joana had acquired a son, an 'abandoned' child whom she'd registered as though he were own flesh and blood. This son became, for a short period, Inez's stepfather, making her a sort of granddaughter in the three-generation household. However, for a good part of her childhood, Inez had called the elderly woman who cared for her neither 'godmother' nor 'grandmother', but rather 'mother'. When eventually Inez's birth mother demanded her daughter's return, the conflict had to be settled in court.

The coexistence of different sets of parents is hardly easy, especially when a child is placed during 'crisis' circumstances. Conflicting interpretations of events may well arise between biological and foster mother as to the terms of the placement. Rather than 'abandon' her child, most women will try to place it with one of the many neighbors who earns a living by boarding the children of working mothers. However, the question then arises: if a woman cannot afford to support her child in her own home, how is she to pay for its upkeep in someone else's house? We may reasonably assume that Dona Joana, who earned her living as a foster mother paid either by the state or directly by her wards' mothers, was supposed to be compensated for taking in Inez, and that it was precisely the non-payment of this debt which led Joana to claim maternal rights. It is no coincidence that Dona Maria (Inez's birth mother), when recounting her version of the story, underlined the fact that Dona Joana was an elderly widow. In an evident attempt to reverse the flow of obligations she presented the transaction as a sort of gift she was making this solitary old woman, providing her with the gracious company of a little girl. Evidently, the ambiguous terms of the contract implicitly written into the circulation of children leaves the transaction open to contradictory interpretations.

Notwithstanding the various disputes which result from this 'invented kinship', the bonds it forms appear to be more long lasting than the grudges. Well into old age, Dona Joana, finding herself with no retirement benefits, no property, and incapable of making a living, was taken in by her former rival, Inez's mother, Maria. At the time of our interview, she was reigning as proud grandmother over an extended household which included at least four nuclear families (those of Maria and three of Maria's married children). The fact that she possessed no biological tie to the other members of the family appeared to trouble no one, exactly because the tie binding her to this family was so evident. '*Mãe é quem criou*' ('mother is whoever brings you up'), her family members explained, using an adage known to all. The implication is that to give food and lodging to another person carries with it all sorts of affective and symbolic consequences, creating a bond that may rival, but is never confused with, blood ties.

Child circulation is undeniably linked to the question of mutual-help networks. Networks are mobilized to ensure the child's survival, but the contrary also holds true. Children, as objects of exchange which themselves carry memories, have been fundamental in counteracting the centripetal forces that tend to splinter family members off. A woman, for example, may receive periodic aid from her divorced brother in exchange for raising his children. A grandmother will see her own married children far more often if she is raising one of their offspring. By taking in a poor cousin or an orphaned nephew, an upwardly mobile relative will demonstrate to his kin group that he is not getting 'uppity', nor does he intend to sever ties. Finally, the circulation of children also serves to expand the kin group to neighbors and unrelated friends, such as Dona Joana, as momentary affinities are transformed into lifelong relationships through the sharing of parental responsibilities.

Blood and other family ties

The story of this family underlines the socially forged nature of kinship; it also serves to illustrate the enormous weight attributed to blood ties. Of Inez and her six siblings, only the last two were raised by their biological parents. How then was I to explain the fact that the Sunday I arrived unexpectedly to interview Maria, the mother of this family, I found her at a backyard barbecue, surrounded by six of her seven offspring? (The seventh, who had spent the night at Maria's, was having lunch with his parents-in-law). With no hesitation, they all chimed in to piece together their family saga. Two of them had been raised by Dona Joana. A third, carried off by his paternal grandparents, was chased down twenty years later by his brothers and sisters who simply followed a tip on where the (now) young man's father worked. Still another recounts how, as a baby, he endured the mistreatment of a negligent wet nurse, before being brought back to live with his mother and step-father. The oldest brother had simply run away from home at age eight, 'never to be seen again'. In fact, despite this gloomy forecast, Maria's children eventually all found their way back, but the oldest's arrival, after a ten-year silence, had become a sort of family legend. His sister recounts in vivid detail the day she ran into this 18-year-old youth, pushing his bike up the hill:

> He waved me over and asked, 'Listen, you don't happen to know a Dona Maria who lives around here? A woman with a whole lot of kids?' I said, 'I guess you're talking about my mother. She's the only Dona Maria around here and she has a pile of children. I don't know if it's her, but I'll take you to see.' I didn't pay much attention; I just left him with Mom saying, 'This boy says he wants to talk to you.' When I came back a couple of minutes later, my mother introduced us: 'This is your brother.'

Six years later, working as a night watchman, the boy was still living (with his wife and two children) in a house he had built in his mother's backyard.

This story is far from exceptional. Innumerable times I ran into a family ostensibly united – where the mother lived side by side with several of her married offspring with whom she interacted daily and celebrated the usual family rites – despite the fact that the children, spread out among different 'mothers', had not grown up together. *Mãe é uma só* ('mother, there's but one'), they will tell me in order to explain this situation, thus reaffirming what, for this group, seems to be fundamental belief in the biological connection.

It is as though the tie between a person and his blood relatives, going beyond individual acts of volition, cannot be broken. Birth mothers and adoptive mothers alike espouse the view to which one birth mother gives voice: 'Even though my son doesn't know I'm his mother, every time he sees me, I know I attract his attention, I feel it (. . .). Because it's like my mom says, it's the blood – the drawing power of blood (*o sangue puxa*).' The symbolic nature of this bond dispenses with the necessity of a person's physical presence. Small children will be taught, through photos on the wall or birthdays recalled, to remember their siblings who are living elsewhere. The bond thus entitles apparent strangers to become sudden intimates. As Inez said, describing her re-encounter with one of her long-lost brothers: 'When we met, I knew right away he was my brother. We hugged with all the emotion of brother and sister, even though we'd spent all those years apart.'

For the outside observer, the banality with which people treat child circulation is striking. A good number of children claim to have decided themselves just where they wanted to live. It is not unusual to hear an 8-year-old explaining: 'Auntie asked me to visit, I liked it, so I told my mom I was just going to stay on.' People will include in their own life histories a list of various households in which they lived as a child – with a predictable variety of commentaries. Some foster parents are remembered as wicked slave drivers, some as fairy godmothers, but most are described in quite matter-of-fact terms. Many, many people will speak of two, three, and four 'mothers' with no embarrassment or particular confusion. In one particular example, a woman wanting to spend the weekend at the beach left her two-week-old daughter in the care of a neighbor. The unpaid babysitter, whose two adolescent children were just becoming independent, called in her sister to wet-nurse the child. A triangular sort of arrangement ensued which had lasted, when I met them in 1994, for at least eight years. As the foster mother said, 'She sleeps and eats in my house, and I'm the one she calls mother.' The child herself, called momentarily away from her playmates to speak to me, appeared delighted with the great number of mothers she had. 'Three,' she gleamed: 'The mother who nursed me, the mother who raised me and the mother who gave birth to me.'

As children scatter among different foster families, they acquire new parents and siblings. Such additions do not necessarily imply a rupture or replacement of previous relationships. Rather, just as with ritual kin (which adds godparents to a child's list of relatives) so foster arrangements serve to enlarge the pool of significant others in a person's social universe. New mothers do not cancel out the old ones. However, 'the mother who raised me' is never mixed up with 'the mother who bore me'.

To sum up we can say that, for the members of the working-class population we studied, the circulation of children is embedded within a particular set of family values. This practice, well documented in the literature on Brazilian history from colonial times up through the nineteenth century (Fonseca 2002a), has evolved through time. Like any other cultural practice, it is dynamic, contains internal contradictions, and adjusts to the changing historical context, undergoing constant re-elaborations. However, it does seem to be a fairly constant part of the group's experience, and therefore demands to be considered when members of the working class are subjected, through different forms of legislation and social work, to national and international forms of intervention.

State intervention in the field of child circulation

The cases of child circulation I have cited up to now involve adults of more or less equal status. In the working-class districts of Porto Alegre, it would be difficult to distinguish a class of child donors, separate from a class of child recipients. Many women who, as young mothers, placed their children in a substitute family, end up taking in somebody else's child to raise. The slight financial advantage enjoyed by foster mothers is often due to factors linked to the life cycle rather than to social stratification. The events – accords and disputes – take place in a cultural idiom comprehensible to all concerned. As we move away from the in-group networks, however, and closer to national legislation and cosmopolitan sensitivities, we come into contact with other perceptions which link considerations of survival, mother rights, and relationships in an entirely different way. The conflicts I witnessed during the 1980s, between *favela* mothers and the administrators at the state orphanage furnish an apt illustration of this difference.

Ever since the 1964 *coup d'état*, the military regime had manifested its concern for children and youth through a state-run service, the *Fundação Estadual de Bem-Estar do Menor* (FEBEM) which, aside from sponsoring a series of private and philanthropic institutions, basically limited its action to the institutionalization of poor, orphaned, and refractory children. Much to my surprise, the slum dwellers I was studying neither feared nor resented this agency. Rather, they used it to their own purposes. There were an infinite number of reasons a woman might want to institutionalize a child: if she was going through a particularly bad financial period (which was often), if she was without a place to live, or if she remarried and her new companion rejected or threatened her children with violent behavior. Parents might also use the threat of internment to keep their disobedient children in line. If institutional authorities attempted to impose obstacles, alleging that the establishment was not meant to be a simple 'boarding school', a woman could deploy new strategies, claiming her child was in danger of rape by a new stepfather or simply a menacing neighbor (Fonseca 1986). At any rate, the mothers I knew who had institutionalized a child generally considered the arrangement temporary, and expected to bring the child home 'as soon as things got better'. Women who showed up at the orphanage, ready to resume their motherhood after (sometimes) years of absence, would be stupefied when told that their child had been declared abandoned and given away for adoption. Even those who had signed a paper 'consenting' to their child's adoption, did not seem to grasp the idea that they had been stripped of their motherhood and that the child had disappeared forever. From their point of view, they had left their children in the care of the institution in the same way they would have resorted to a grandmother or neighbor. These substitute mothers, at times, also insisted that the transfer of parental responsibilities should be permanent, but experience proved them wrong. In the great majority of cases, the birth mother and child would eventually end up in contact; the child would not be 'lost' to its kin group. Sooner or later, he or she would be back, looking up old contacts.

One might ask, however, if, in their informal patterns of behavior, women always saw child placement as a temporary measure? Did they never have the intention of giving up their children in the terms imagined by orphanage administrators? Consideration of another lengthy example will help to answer this question. Whereas the case of Inez and her family illustrates the comings and goings of children within the deep-rooted fosterage culture prevalent in Brazilian working-class neighborhoods, with Eliane we see a woman who, faced with intolerable conditions, 'voluntarily' gave up her third-born child on a permanent and irrevocable basis. By examining her gesture, which bears close resemblance to legal adoption as it is known to most people in the First World, we come one step closer to thinking about the different perceptions of birth parents and of adoptive parents, which may possibly be involved in the process of intercountry adoption.

Clandestine adoption: shaping the law to localized perceptions

Eliane, a tall, thin black woman, received us in the front room of her little wooden house where she lives with her husband, a junkman, and her four children. Between chuckles and sighs of exasperation, she had chatted with us for well over an hour about the exploits of her various offspring when suddenly she fell silent. Taking a long puff on her cigarette, tears welling in her steady gaze, she let out an almost inaudible whisper, 'I forgot to tell you. Now that you mentioned adopted kids . . . I gave one away . . . [pause] . . . I gave one away.'

Eliane tells a story not much different from that of many other mothers from the outskirts of the city. Her extended kin group had been able to absorb her first two unprogrammed children, but still unmarried and living with her mother when she got pregnant a third time, Eliane had reached the limits of her family's endurance. Furthermore, she had no way of paying a non-relative to keep her child. Even were she to work, for example, as a maid, she could not expect to receive more than one or two minimum salaries ($60–$120 a month), hardly enough to feed and pay for the daycare of three children. Thus, Eliane had no choice but to give her newborn child away.

The young woman went searching among relatives and acquaintances for her future child's adoptive parents and, shortly before giving birth, found what she was looking for. Her choice fell upon the baby's paternal aunt, a woman who, after years of trying to get pregnant, had recently lost a stillborn child. Eliane recalls the circumstances of this encounter with amazing detail: the hesitation, the tears and the respect with which the potential mother treated her: 'She said, "Look Eliane, we don't want to force you." She gave me liberty to do what I wanted.' But, after a week's soul-searching and mutual support, the decision was made. As Eliane tells it, she went to the would-be mother's house, and the two women sat there crying – the baby between them, in his crib – until Eliane drew herself to say, 'No, you keep him.'

The drama of this moment runs high exactly because, contrary to most of the cases we mentioned before, it is understood that Eliane's child will not return to his birth family. Unbeknownst to the state authorities, the child's adoptive parents will take out his birth certificate as though they were the birth parents, and he will learn only the details of his biography that they are willing to furnish him. Eliane, too, will be bound to secrecy. The proof? Six years later, although she has found a stable companion and clearly improved living conditions, her son treats her as a 'stranger': 'As far as he's concerned, I'm no one. At least not his mother. When I go by to visit, he calls me "Auntie".'

By participating in this clandestine form of adoption, Eliane and the adoptive parents of her child have technically committed the crime of 'ideological falsity', punishable by up to six years in jail. However, the illegality of this act does not seem to intimidate most potential parents. According to some estimates, this *adocão à brasileira*, until very recently, was much more common than legal adoption, a fact easily understood by those who recognize that the Brazilian working-class population has traditionally lived on the margin of state bureaucracy. Even today, at the turn of the century, nearly one-third of births are not declared within the legal deadline, and many children acquire a birth certificate only when they enter first grade or do their military service. In these circumstances, it is not difficult for adoptive parents to pose as birth parents.

The fact that birth mothers prefer Eliane's method of placing children is understandable. Closer to cosmopolitan sensitivities than to local cultural dynamics, the Brazilian adoption laws, more and more centered on a narrow definition of the conjugal family, have more or less shunted birth parents aside. Until 1965, an adopted child simply added on the adoptive filiation to the biological filiation, maintaining the two sets of parents. During the past thirty years, plenary adoption, based on the idea of the adoptive parents' exclusive parental rights, gradually took root, being declared, with the 1990 Children's Code, the country's sole legal form of adoption. All trace of a child's original identity is now to be struck off an adopted child's birth certificate, and the secret of the biological parents' identity divulged only when the Court deems fit.

Thus if Eliane, for example, appeared at the state's official adoption services, she would no doubt be advised to think twice before 'abandoning' her child. However, once she took the decision, she would have absolutely no say in the decisions concerning its future. After a court decision stripping Eliane of her parental authority, an efficient service of psychologists and social workers would take her child in tow, and she would have no further contact with or information about her child. Although the informal practice of *adoção à brasileira* likewise erases a child's biological parents from the birth certificate, it gives them much greater leeway in their actions: not only will they be able to play an active role in the choice of their child's birth parents but, in all probability, they will be able to watch, from a respectful distance, as he grows up.

Why adoptive parents might prefer this modality is not much harder to understand. For many years, performing this legal sleight of hand was the only way people with other (biological) children could guarantee full inheritance rights to their adoptive offspring. Furthermore, legal adoption was long hemmed in by a series of restrictions which, in many cases, simply did not fit their circumstances. In 1988 the new constitution facilitated adoption and prohibited any discrimination between biological and adoptive children. However, at least in Rio Grande do Sul, the number of national legal adopters has yet to increase. It is possible that many potential adopters still do not feel at ease with the interviews and bureaucracy involved in the state adoption process. They may imagine, perhaps with reason, that they are too poor, too old, single or otherwise unacceptable by the adoption service's usual criteria for good parents. It is no coincidence that a recent study showed that whereas upper-middle class parents go through official procedures at juvenile court, lower-income couples tend to adopt in the traditional (and illegal) *adoção à brasileira* (Weber 1998). If the state authorities enjoyed an aura of superior authority or greater legitimacy in their 'gate-keeping' role, poorer people might make greater use of their services. But this does not appear to be the case and *adoção à brasileira* continues to be an extremely popular way of acquiring a son or daughter.

In the past decade, with the increasing attention drawn to international and, by extension, national adoption, successive members of the judiciary and social services have waged an ever-growing campaign against *adoção à brasileira*. The imposition of a state-run monopoly is seen as prerequisite to the professional regulation of adoptions and, among other things, the protection of poor women against pressures from 'baby traffickers'. It is nonetheless interesting to observe that the cases of abuse (in which children are removed from their homes too quickly and with insufficient justification) which appear in the national press seem to involve overzealous judges and state social workers just as much as venal intermediaries (Fonseca 2002b).

One might wonder if, with the 1990 Children's Code, the nation's lawmakers have been more successful in blending child welfare and local family dynamics. In fact, the Code foresaw radical changes in policy concerning the institutionalization of children. The big orphanages were to be dismantled and replaced by little units; in no case was a child to be placed (with or without its parents' consent) simply for reasons of poverty. Poverty would likewise not be a sufficient motive for stripping a mother or father of parental authority, and adoptable children would be destined first and foremost for Brazilian families.

Despite the humanitarian intentions of these reforms their result has been ambiguous. A study of children's dossiers at the state orphanage shows that the sort of mother who, during the 1980s, would be classified as merely 'poor' began, after the 1990 Children's Code, to be labeled 'negligent' and 'abusive', thus maintaining the legal fragility of her maternal status (Cardarello 2000). We also see that the 'small, family-like units' in which children are presently placed have become so costly that the state is highly motivated to keep the number of institutionalized children to a minimum. Ironically, the program of state-sponsored foster mothers (who, like Dona Joana, would receive a modest sum of around $30 a month per child) has been all but phased out. For children from poverty-stricken families the present, progressive solution appears to be adoption.

One of the indirect implications of this new mood is that poverty-stricken mothers who in the past sought some sort of mutual understanding with local state authorities, foster and/or adoptive parents, are now up against a decision-making force which extends to the other side of the world. It is this stretch which justifies our chapter's final considerations on the cosmopolitan sensitivities which guide the policies of most gate-keepers in the contemporary field of adoption.

Cosmopolitan sensitivities

It is not possible to do justice to the complexity of laws and attitudes concerning international adoption in receiving countries, located mainly in Western Europe and North America. However, to complete our argument, and perhaps indicate a few possibilities for future research, we wish to evoke three lines of discourse presently being developed in these countries.

The first discourse presents international adoption as a way of saving children from Third World misery and violence, and is particularly common in popular news media. Critics hold that it is an example of how those who possess the upper hand, rather than recognize inequality as a fundamental element of the adoption process, activate mechanisms which translate the process into moral terms. The rhetoric on intercountry adoption which revolves consistently around 'huge numbers' of 'homeless' or 'abandoned' children, indirectly asserts the birth parents' irresponsibility, absence of moral fiber (inability to 'plan' their family), or lack of sexual constraint.[5] Not only does this sort of argument generally ignore the existence of the many frustrated people in sending countries who have been turned away by local adoption agencies, it summarily dismisses the alternative of placing children in local foster families.

In a similar vein, the idea that because of their financial security affluent couples make better parents (having 'so much to offer a child') is implicit in countless European and North American texts. Although no adoption agency, public or private, would explicitly give voice to such consumer logic, the qualities they require of a worthy adoptive parent usually include superior financial solvency. Gailey (1999), in her study of North American adoptive parents (responsible for well over half the world's international adoptions), gives us a concrete example of such attitudes. With an average annual income of $110,000, her interviewees were distinctly more affluent than those who adopted locally-born children and, with rare exceptions, had little compunction in linking their affluence to their right to adoptive parenthood. Not only did they tend to present this right as obvious, in function of the wealth and social status they could provide a child, these adoptive parents also implied that, considering the high price they were willing to pay ($10,000 at least), they expected to get high quality goods: light-skinned babies in good mental and physical health. Gailey's account demonstrates how 'salvationist' attitudes coexist in dangerous proximity with the commodity logic historically abhorred by the field of adoption workers (Zelizer 1985).

Signe Howell (1998), in her study of Norwegian parents who adopted a child from overseas, describes a discourse quite different from the first – one that is based on the idea of a gift relationship. Whereas the 'salvationists' consider birth parents and sending countries to be of secondary interest, those who engage in this second discourse see themselves as actively involved in a reciprocal exchange with 'child donors'. Acutely aware of the financial disparities which provoke the North–South flow of children, these Norwegian parents band together to send money to orphanages in the country from which they received their adopted offspring, thus establishing what they consider to be a 'long-distance fostering relationship'. The fosterage arrangement is seen as opening the circle of protagonists, providing for an indirect return, delayed in time, to those institutions perceived as the donor agents.

While there are evident merits to this approach, one cannot but wonder at the ease with which birth parents, flesh-and-blood people, are substituted in the adoptive families' imagination by the mediating agents or agencies, or even by a folkloric image of the child's birth country – 'abstract entities and not a partner with whom the gift has created a bond' (Ouellette 1995: 162). Of course, in certain cases it would be impossible to proceed otherwise since, because of particular historical circumstances, the child has no traceable relatives. But people are often overly hasty in seeing this sort of circumstance as typical of all adoptions, ignoring cases such as most of those in Latin America where 'orphans' became available for adoption for no other reason than the sheer and utter misery of their parents. In Brazil, at least, evidence leads us to believe that a good number of the children given in adoption have living and identifiable parents (or other relatives) who, given the opportunity, would relish contact with or knowledge about their offspring.

A third discourse on adoption is centered precisely on the spiny question of the coexistence of two different sets of relatives. Researchers in this line remind us that, at least in North America, the notion of a restricted conjugal household is so entrenched in the people's minds, that the very idea of sharing represents a fundamental violation of parenthood.[6] They also contend that it is exactly the average American's belief in the overriding appeal of blood relationships that leads people to fear the continued presence of birth parents in their child's existence. (One does not take the trouble to banish what one does not fear.) This fear was largely responsible for the consolidation, during the 1960s, of certain legal institutions: the child's pre-adoption biography was hidden, the court and adoption workers were guardians of this 'secret', and a radical distinction arose between adoptive and foster families (Carp 1998; Modell 1994).

The North American panorama, however, has changed vastly in the past thirty years. In the more progressive adoption services, adoptive parents are no longer selected according to rigid criteria, but rather they are 'prepared' for the task. 'Fostadopt' programs have sprung up permitting foster families to adopt their ward and, in like fashion, permitting potential adoptive parents to foster a child while awaiting the legal pronouncement making him or her 'adoptable'. Adoptees, for their part, joined hands with birth mothers' associations to challenge what they considered the state's authoritarian monopoly on information surrounding the adoption process. Although it was generally agreed that judicial files should be confidential – available only to the concerned parties – court-controlled *secrecy* was seen as an abusive use of power. Furthermore, although controversies still rage over the issue, 'open adoption', associated by certain researchers with the empowerment and self-affirmation of birth mothers, seems to have come to stay. Today there are literally hundreds of agencies adhering to the policy that not only should a birth mother be able to meet her child's adoptive parents, she should also participate in choosing them. The more enthusiastic advocates suggest that relations should not stop with one or two meetings, but rather that open adoption should entail full disclosure of identifying information and a commitment to lifelong relatedness.[7]

It is ironic that exactly this third discourse which directly addresses the problem of comparative parental worth does not seem to have spread to issues concerning international adoption where, according to at least one specialist, the 'clean break' principle (positing a complete rupture in the adopted child's identity) is 'increasingly dominating adoption as a global practice' (Yngvesson 2000). Brazil serves as a case in point. The secret of a child's origins has been part and parcel of the legal process ever since the first embryonic version of plenary adoption (1965). Up until recently, only an occasional birth mother who showed up at the adoption board having 'changed her mind' might complain about the secrecy involved in the adoption process. Such incidents appeared to have little influence on policy makers. However, as more and more children adopted by foreign families come of age and seek to discover their origins, the panorama may be changing. At the end of 1999, Brazilian national TV carried frequent programs on the re-encounter of some adoptee, raised abroad, with his or her Brazilian birth family, and state adoption agencies report they are being regularly approached by individuals from overseas looking for their blood relatives. Not surprisingly, the controversy over sealed birth records is emerging for the first time in Brazilian history – as a response, one might say, to consumer demand. Yet, the revelation of information follows a one-way track. It only occurs when the adoptive family (never the birth family) takes the initiative, in the desire to furnish necessary 'background' elements for a child's development. Significantly, open adoption, which would involve the active participation of birth parents (much as in traditional practices of child circulation) remains an untouched issue.

Conclusion

The comparative perspective afforded by anthropological research proves particularly useful to our analysis of child circulation among Brazilian slum dwellers, not only to bring out particular dynamics in family organization, but also in understanding how these 'local' dynamics fit into hegemonic currents of thinking. It is no longer possible to limit ethnographic descriptions to a natural history approach, focused on the quaint customs of a supposedly isolated or archaic group. In today's world system, localized practices are recognizably embedded in asymmetrical power relations which have a bearing on both local and global realities. We have tried to show that the people we interviewed possess notions of family and individual identity in keeping with their particular historical context, and that these notions do not always coincide with those of conventional contractual law. In the normal procedures which make children available for adoption (the sentence of abandonment or the term of release signed by birth parents), we may be overly hasty in presuming a certain understanding between the different parties concerned.

On the basis of these remarks, we may outline a program of research which covers three major questions. First, we might ask what ideological mechanisms – what scientific and professional biases – have silenced local dynamics which diverge from the hegemonic norm? A second question concerns the difference in national policies on adoption: to what extent are these differences due to specific local realities, and to what extent do they depend on the particular position each country occupies in the world system of production and distribution of children? A third question addresses the enormous concentration of research focusing on adoption to the detriment of other forms of placement such as fosterage or 'traditional' practices of child circulation. Considering the increasing popularity of international adoption, and in the interest of forging just procedures, it is of urgent importance to map out the different forms of placement, not only so that they will be respected in faraway exotic places, but also so that they may be recognized as viable alternatives within today's world, thus permitting a rewriting of modernity's hegemonic script.

Notes

1   A modified version of this chapter was published in French in *Anthropologie et Sociétés* 24(3): 24–43 (2001). I would like to thank Chantal Collard and Françoise-Romaine Ouellette for their throughtful reading of this material.

2   From 1994, the number of children adopted by foreigners went into decline, sinking by the year 2000 to one-fifth the peak rate of the late 1980s. For an analysis of this about-face, see Fonseca 2002c.

3   Porto Alegre is the capital city (with one and a half million inhabitants) of the Brazil's southernmost state, Rio Grande do Sul.

4   The verb *criar* in Portuguese means both 'to raise' and 'to create'. Kin ties formed by caring for one another are labeled '*de criação*'. I have loosely translated the term here as 'foster relatives'.

5   The Brazilian case undermines the simplistic reasoning that links adoptable children to lack of birth control. In the last twenty-five years, the birth rate has been cut in half. In 1996, Brazilian women could expect to bear an average of 2.7 offspring (bringing the country's birth rate close to that of Sweden). And yet, for most of this period, international adoption increased steadily. On this subject, see also Selman 2000.

6   Modell 1994: 47; see also Wegar 1997.

7   See also Avery (1998) for an overview of open adoption.

References

Avery, R. J. (1998) 'Information disclosure and openness in adoption: state policy and empirical evidence', *Children and Youth Services Review* 20(1–2): 57–85.

Cardarello, A. D. L. (2000) 'Du "Mineur" a "l'enfant–citoyen"': Droits des enfants et droits des familles au Brésil', *Lien Social et Politique* 44: 155–66.

Carp, E. W. (1998) *Family Matters*, Cambridge, Mass.: Harvard University Press.

Fonseca, C. (1986) 'Orphanages, foundlings and foster mothers: the system of child circulation in a Brazilian squatter settlement', *Anthropological Quarterly* 59(1): 15–27.

—— (2002a) 'Inequality near and far: adoption as seen from the Brazilian favelas', *Law and Society Review* 36(2): 101–134.

—— (2002b) 'The politics of adoption: child rights in the Brazilian setting', *Law and Policy* 24(3): 199–227.

—— (2002c) 'An unexpected reversal: charting the course of international adoption in Brazil', *Adoption and Fostering Journal* 26(3): 28–39.

Gailey, C. (1999) 'Seeking "Baby Right": race, class, and gender in US international adoption', in A. Rygvold, M. Dalen and B Sætersdal (eds) *Mine, Yours, Ours and Theirs*, Oslo: University of Oslo Press.

Ginsburg, Faye D. and Rayna Rapp (eds) (1995) *Conceiving the New World Order*, Berkeley: University of California Press.

Howell, S. (1998) 'Is blood thicker than water? Some issues derived from transnational adoption in Norway', paper presented during the Wenner–Gren symposium 'New Directions in Kinship Studies: A core concept revisited', Mallorca, 27 March–3 April.

Kane, S. (1993) 'The movement of children for international adoption: an epidemiologic perspective', *The Social Science Journal* 30(4): 323–339.

Modell, J. S. (1994) *Kinship with Strangers*, Berkeley: University of California Press.

Ouellette, F.-R. (1995) 'La part du don dans l'adoption', *Anthropologie et sociétés* 19(1–2): 157–174.

Selman, P. (2000) *Intercountry Adoption*, London: British Agencies for Adoption and Fostering (BAAF).

Weber, L. N. D. (1998) 'Famílias adotivas e mitos sobre laços de sangue', in L. N. D. Weber, (ed.) *Laços de Ternura*, Curitiba: Santa Mônica.

Wegar, K. (1997) *Adoption, Identity, and Kinship*, New Haven: Yale University Press.

Yngvesson, B. (2000) '"Un niño de cualquier color": race and nation in intercountry adoption', in J. Jensen and B. de Sousa Santos (eds) *Globalizing Institutions*, Aldershot: Ashgate, pp. 247–305.

Zelizer, V. (1985) *Pricing the Priceless Child*, Princeton: Princeton University Press.

Chapter 12

Person, relation and value

The economy of circulating Ecuadorian children in international adoption[1]

Esben Leifsen

Introduction

Drawing on ethnographic material from Ecuador this chapter discusses the process by which abandoned, orphaned or handed-over children are readied for international adoption. I will be concerned with the adoption process in the children's country of origin,[2] in which children come into circulation and a new social relation is constituted between adoptee and adoptive parent or parents. A crucial concern for prospective adoptive parents is to build a strong emotional tie with the adopted child, and to incorporate this newcomer into their kinship circle (Modell 1994; Schneider 1984). Hence the adoptive parents tend to conceive of the child's value as one of sentiment, of personal and inherent qualities and of moral character, incomparable with any monetarized value or market price. The adopted child is, as Zelizer (1985) puts it, priceless in the eyes of the adoptive parents. A closer look at the way the adoption process is carried out in the Ecuadorian context, however, makes the issue of value less unambiguous. During its circulation from birth or original parents to future adoptive parents, the adopted child, or rather its case, passes through a series of legal procedures within the Ecuadorian state bureaucracy. The child is stored and cared for by orphanages or substitute families, and it is exchanged and connected to a price in the market. The adoptee is at different stages in its circulation valued differently, and as a result brought closer to and farther from its objectified form.

This chapter analyses the process by which the adoptive relation is constituted as one where the person (adoptee) is circulated in a shifting and differentiated moral economy (cf. Kopytoff 1986). In other words I am interested in how the person is circulated in social contexts where the cultural conception of the value of the adoptee changes. These social contexts consist of central actors in the adoption process: birthparents and their relatives, functionaries in the state bureaucracy, representatives from private adoption agencies, people involved in work at orphanages, temporary substitute caretakers and the prospective adoptive parents themselves. Here I will concentrate on state functionaries, representatives from agencies and adoptive parents. My point of departure is that the objectification of the adoptee is an important mechanism, although not the only one, occurring at different stages in the adoption process. I will look more closely at two distinct but interlinked forms of objectification: (1) the commodification of the child as it is transferred from birthparents to adoptive parents, and (2) the de-socialization of the child within the Ecuadorian legal system as a necessary step in constituting the new adoptive relationship.

The economy of circulating Ecuadorian children is related to the expansion of commodity markets and the influence of money into spheres considered beyond the market: the family and the legal system. Such an expansion implies that economic interests and concerns have a bearing on the way people take decisions, act and respond within the family and the state bureaucracy. There are limits to the ways children are objectified and commodified; as Zelizer (1985) remarks, the market does not exclusively contribute to the shaping of ideas concerning the value of an adopted child. Conceptions concerning the child's lack of a price, its potential and human qualities as a builder of emotional ties and as a moral being, also influence and restrict the way children are connected to exchange value in the market.

However, the valuations and valuators that modify market influence seem to be less influential than the ones enhancing economic interest when a child is adopted. The adoptive parents, for example, can stress the emotional dimensions concerning the adoption, but they cannot significantly annul the money transaction involved or influence the size of the adoption fee. Similarly the birthparents cannot control the ways their child is connected to formal and informal payments from the moment they give up the baby. Neither can the adoption agencies eliminate irregular economic activity in relation to the adoption process. Indeed, in adoption persons and not objects travel, but in order to do so they have to be turned temporally into objects, and they have to undergo commodification.

Ecuadorian adoptions and the market

It may be controversial to state that children are exchanged in the market during the legal adoption process. A common view is to think that this is what happens in illegal practices, and a distinction is often made between baby-trafficking and the legal transfer of children. "The differentiation of an adoption fee and a purchase price", of a non-profit and a profit-making arrangement hinges, as Zelizer points out, "on defining the payment as compensation for professional services" (Zelizer 1985: 205).[3] The role of the adoption fee is thus crucial in defining the value created in relation to the transfer of an adopted child, that is in determining if the payment involved enhances personal value or transforms it into a standardized economic value. The adoption fee is ambiguous in this respect precisely because it intertwines a market transaction with deeply emotional and personal motivations related to the transfer of a human being. In more general terms Simmel (1978) discusses this ambiguity between a person's whole value as a human being ("value") and obtained price in a market ("purchase") in situations where exchange of money is related to the transfer of persons.[4] In order to distinguish between value and purchase, he argues, we have to look at the definite social character the payment has in the way it is transacted. If the actors involved in the transfer of the person modify the influence of the market by protecting the value of the person against the standardizing effects of putting a price on them,[5] value would be rescued. If the actors put a price on the transfer in order to follow economic interests and obtain a gain, the transfer would be made into a purchase. Concerning the transfer of the adoptee the meanings and effects of the fee paid does not solely depend on the amount of money involved but also on the potential this amount offers to create different kinds of value. In relation to this, the interests and motivations of the crucial actors in the transfer of the adoptee, namely representatives from adoption agencies as well as the adoptive parents, have to be investigated.

Among the legally approved agencies in Ecuador there are both those who, according to Simmel's logic, rescue the person's value and those who purchase babies, as well as those who do a bit of both. Almost all the international adoption agencies operating in Ecuador have only one representative in the country.[6] They are Ecuadorian citizens, largely from the upper middle class with advantageous positions and networks within the justice system and political milieu. A majority of them are women. Just one of the agencies employs a bigger staff, and also implements, maintains and evaluates its own social programs for abandoned children.[7] This agency is the only one with the characteristics of an international non-governmental organization (NGO). On a scale based on the value–purchase distinction it comes close to the value side because it converts money and resources into social benefits for children at risk. Through its social programs it supports families, reunifies abandoned children with their birth parents or other relatives, places children in foster families, and carries out national adoptions.[8]

At the other extreme, at least one agency is suspected among other things of forcing or actively encouraging birthmothers to give up their babies in exchange for some kind of compensation. It also manipulates the legal system in order to get children quickly and efficiently through the adoption process, securing a high delivery rate. In order to demonstrate ethnographically the market exchange of children in adoptions, I will choose an agency in-between these two opposed poles as an example, a European agency operating in Ecuador.

The agency, let us call it MAM, charges a relatively moderate standardized fee for an adoption.[9] According to MAM some countries are more expensive than others when it comes to adoption, and its official discourse, the one the applicants are presented with in the agency's preparative courses, is that the sum of money paid reflects the level of expenses existing in the respective countries of origin. Latin American bureaucracies are presented as inefficient and slow which, according to MAM, means that it has to invest resources in building up and maintaining an infrastructure and a contact network of persons who can assure that the adoptions are completed in an efficient and professional manner. MAM presents itself as a non-profit organization, and the Ecuadorian representative confirms that she works for the agency not because of the money but because it gives her an opportunity to give some of the most needy children in her home country a better life. The representative is a lawyer with her own practice, who also runs a real estate agency for clients in the upper economic strata in the capital Quito.

The adoption fee MAM takes is substantially less than the total sum of money the adoptive parents have to pay: it does not include the investigation and elaboration of the social report on the parents, which is made by a private company in the agency's home country, nor does it cover travel, housing and living expenses in Ecuador. The parents also pay a daily amount of money for the child's maintenance to the orphanage from the day they are granted custody. The adoption fee only covers expenses related directly to the adoption in Ecuador, including judicial and technical assistance, paperwork and, although not stated publicly, bribes to functionaries within the system. These costs do not amount to more than 6 or 7 per cent of the total of the fee. The rest goes presumably to MAM's representative in Ecuador, to the four persons working at the agency's main office, to those who are contracted to organize the preparative courses, and on additional administrative expenses, office rental and equipment.[10]

Although difficult to evaluate, it seems clear that MAM's adoption fee produces a modest profit. Fransisco, who had the adoption of his daughter from Ecuador arranged by MAM during a longer stay in the country, reflects on the topic in the following way:

> The theory I have is that [the way adoptions are carried out] serves to consolidate these kinds of service companies with a facade of non-profit non-governmental organizations, with few people employed who earn a middle range income . . . it is not that they are accumulating a lot of capital in this way, they are not really enriching themselves, but multiply the cases from Ecuador in which we know the real expenses for an adoption . . . multiply it with the 23 couples who are coming after us on the list, and with the parents who have already got their children, multiply all these with \$5–6,000, take away the real expenses involved and what the representative in Ecuador receives [approximately \$1,700], and it becomes clear that this is a business, its evident.
>
> (Personal communication)

What is clear is that contrary to what MAM says, it is the agency and people running it, and not the adoption process in Ecuador, which consumes the lion's share of the adoption fee. Taking into account that the only work the agency does is to arrange the preparative courses and carry out the adoption, and knowing that as much as 93 per cent of the total sum could go to the agency, it is fair to say that MAM generates an economic surplus out of the money it receives directly for the transfer of the adoptee. Although this is a moderate amount of money compared to what some of the US adoption agencies make,[11] it would still be correct to talk of a market exchange and hence commodification of the adoptee in relation to the fee MAM charges for an adoption.

Economic interest becomes an even clearer motivation if we look at the agency's Ecuadorian representative and how she operates. The representative receives a fixed sum for each adoption she finalizes, which means that her income is directly related to the number of children she manages to process.[12] This is distinct from practices in other agencies that pay the representative an honorarium independent of the number of adoptions completed. The difference between these two forms of payment is that the former connects a sum of money to the exchange of a child; the honorarium contributes directly to putting an individual price on the child. This arrangement could easily stimulate the representative to find ways to increase the number of adoptions for economic gain.

The honorarium, however, is not the only income the representative can expect from the adoption. As the owner of a real estate agency, she arranges lodging for the adoptive parents in Ecuador. She also invites the prospective parents to take advantage of their stay in the country and offers them a cruise to the Galapagos Islands on the family company yacht. Income from adoptions is neither unimportant nor crucial to this person and her family's economy. It is a supplement to other economic activities and as such integrated into a family enterprise characterized by several sources of income. Furthermore it would be incorrect to portray her as purely profit-minded, since she identifies strongly with a charitable attitude to children and poverty, in which adoption is looked upon as one solution to a grave social problem. Her central position as a supplier of babies and door-opener to childless prospective parents also allows her to exercise a kind of (non-economic) power. Among these multivalent personal motivations, however, the economic plays an important part.

Fransisco experienced a series of surprises in his contact with MAM's representative during the period his adoptive daughter's case was processed. One of the most shocking was that the Ecuadorian representative suggested helping him formalize an illegal adoption. In order to save time, she offered to give him the names of a couple who specialize in handing over children from marginal parts of the city for national adoption. Fransisco's job would be to find an Ecuadorian couple who would accept to formally take care of the child, and then hand it over to an indicated orphanage in the historical centre. She would have the nuns at the orphanage "reserve" the child for her, to guarantee that the child was connected to Fransisco and his wife, and take the necessary formal steps to legalize the adoption. She let Fransisco understand that he would have to spend some money on such an "operation", and admitted, "although this is not immoral it is illegal, and so we have to act with caution".

The problem with such an irregular practice could not be reduced to a problem with the Ecuadorian representative's moral standards and proclivity to get things arranged outside the law. MAM's staff are aware of this practice and have not taken steps to change it. Furthermore, initiating the adoption process irregularly is not a problem unique to MAM. A small number of agencies are probably involved in such a practice because it increases the total number of children available for international adoption.[13]

In this case the possibility for the adoptee to be exchanged and valuated in the market is enhanced. The child welfare authorities in the agency's home country could be said to increase this possibility by giving MAM the exclusive right to carry out international adoptions without exercising control over their activities.[14] On the other hand MAM has to weigh its practices against Spanish adoptive parents' expectations and demands. It carefully maintains an image of being a non-profit professional service institution, providing couples with what is of crucial importance to them, namely the legally, socially and economically sound transfer of a child. This image implies that MAM's staff have to be cautious about what they tell and show adoptive parents during the process, which in its turn modifies their actions and the amount of money they can charge as an adoption fee.

International adoption to this European country does not leave the applicants with a choice of agency because of MAM's exclusive right. The situation is totally different in the USA where numerous private adoption agencies and adoption lawyers offer their services, which in principle are open to any applicant regardless of place of origin. Hence the variation in types of adoption agencies is considerable and applicants have an opportunity to make a choice that matches their values and expectations. How this choice is made, however, is restricted by the knowledge the adoptive parents have of the agency and baby's country of origin, as well as by the image and information the agency presents. Apart from a few especially well informed applicants, most people would not conceive of their choice as one between a corrupt, a profit-oriented, and a law-abiding agency but, for instance, between an agency that offers adoptions of young babies with special characteristics, one presenting a discourse on adoptions as a way of bridging the gap between cultures or as a solution to Third World poverty, and one with a social program in the country of origin.

It is impossible to generalize concerning parents' motivations for adopting children, but it seems reasonable to argue that very few would see their child as having a market value, or would legitimize payments for adoptions with "symbolic expressions of sentimental concern" (Zelizer 1985: 207). A higher payment would not be envisaged as an increase in the symbolic expression of love (see also MacTaggart 1980). Few would agree with the argument that a free market in babies would be the best way to solve the problems related to illegal adoption practices, although such an argument has been put forward by economists at the Chicago School of Economics (Landes and Posner 1978 in Wolfe 1989). Furthermore, few prospective adoptive parents would pay the fee required by a US agency operating in Ecuador, if they knew about the contracts they are suspected of making with pregnant women for delivery of newborn babies, and about the ways they speed up the adoption process by manipulating the system in order to supply high price young, healthy babies. Adoptive parents' motivations and choices are conditioned by the limited access they have to information about agencies and their practices. On the other hand, as Fransisco comments in my interview with him, there are also limits to what the adoptive parents want to know:

> The adoptive parents don't want to know too much. Basically they want a child, they want a boy or a girl, and that is it. They are convinced that although they are doing themselves a favour, they are also helping an abandoned, ill-treated child, and that is all they want to know.

Adoptions and the Ecuadorian legal system

Let me now turn to the Ecuadorian adoption bureaucrats as another set of actors who connect children to a different context of valuation. The aim of the formal adoption process is to make the child available for adoption, and this availability is assured by following a judicial procedure that connects a series of documents to the adopted person. Hence the adoption process makes apparent one of various ways the state, through its legal system, contributes to the constitution of the person. Without certain documents linking the child to a set of legal categories, bureaucratic registers and institutions, the child is formally invisible.

The lack of documents is a serious obstacle for a child's possibilities for action in a legal world, and it conditions its circulation. Custody of a child cannot be transferred from birth to adoptive parents without adequate documentation and investigation. The investigative work is meant to make clear the social situation of the child, which implies identifying the child's family and kinship relations. In present practice orphanages, adoption agencies, the social service of the *Tribunal de Menores*, and the special department of the police dealing with child affairs, *DINAPEN*, carry out investigations. The birth certificate, an indispensable document in this part of the adoption process, is the formal statement of the child's biological origins. The various reports on the child would often indicate why the persons who are biologically related to the child could not offer the child the care needed for its survival and well-being.

Interestingly, however, many of the children cleared for adoption do not live with their original parents but in institutions where the possibility of being enclosed in a legally unclear state is relatively high. If the investigation is carried out in a formally correct way any doubt about the child's biological and social connections would be reduced or totally eliminated.[15] This clarification of the child's situation, what is termed the clearing of the child's state of abandonment and adoptability, could lead to the reunification of the child with its original family, or result in adoption. If the formal procedures are not followed properly the legally diffuse situation of the child can be used to fabricate fictive biological relations. In some of the detected cases of illegal child-trafficking fictive birth certificates have been created for children who for different reasons are not cleared for adoption. Non-related persons, sometimes contracted by interested parts, appear as birthparents to the child in official registers, and the birth certificate, with or without the conscious acceptance of the public official, is produced as if it were authentic. Why this is necessary becomes clear if we take into consideration Ecuadorian adoption law.

According to the law children can only be adopted if they are abandoned, if birthparents have consented to give up parental responsibilities, and other near relatives their care-giving role. In situations where a child is abandoned or relinquished by birthparents, the justice system has formally to dismantle the child's original kinship relations. This de-socialization follows a legal procedure that culminates with a declaration from the *Tribunal de Menores* stating that the child is suitable for adoption. If this declaration is not made the process cannot proceed. In the irregular cases, then, the production of the birth certificate and hence the fabricated kinship relationship serve as the imitation of the child's original social situation which has to be dismantled in order to construct a legally recognized and 'real' adoptive relationship.

Let me now introduce another economic aspect of the legal adoption procedure into the discussion. This procedure should be free of charge, however the state's creation of an adoptable child tends to have a price. Various well established but informal payment arrangements within the bureaucratic system are in common use. As mentioned above, different types of reports have to be officially processed in relation to the de-socialization of the child, including a police report based on an investigation, social and health reports, all of which have to be submitted together with the child's birth certificate. It is on the basis of this documentation that the Tribunal makes its decision. Different persons, who are involved in the elaboration of reports and in the work with the declaration of the child's aptness for adoption, regularly receive money informally. The ones receiving money are primarily functionaries and lawyers at the Tribunal. Those paying bribes are basically the adoption agencies, lawyers working for these agencies and certain orphanages.

In most cases the aim of the bribes is to shorten the time it takes to carry out an adoption, and avoid cases being delayed or put aside on a semi-permanent basis. The child temporally "stored" in an orphanage or substitute family grows older while waiting for its case to be finalized. Motivated by their concerns for the child's psychological and emotional well-being, prospective parents put pressure on the adoption agencies to get the formalities over quickly and effectively, which can serve to "nourish" an informal payment system. Functionaries at the Social Welfare Ministry, at the Tribunal and in the police, often regulate the time used in carrying out the adoptions by slowing down or speeding up the process. By accepting payments they convert the scarcity of time into a surplus generating object of exchange.

Irregular practices apply to the whole adoption process, including the legal formation of the adoptive relationship. Ideally this part of the process should proceed in the following way: the adoption unit at the Social Welfare Ministry appoints an "assignment" committee responsible for connecting a child with applicants. The committee consists of representatives from the Social Welfare Ministry and the Tribunal, the leaders of the orphanages where the adoptable children have stayed, and a representative from one of the adoption agencies. Before putting together the committee the adoption unit at the Ministry decides which agencies will be asked to carry out adoptions of children declared adoptable at that moment. An important principle in the Law of Adoption is that the child should not be connected in any way to its prospective social parents before the assignment committee has made its decision. Ideally the state reserves for itself the right to complete the first socially constitutive work with the adoptive relation and to secure a principle of arbitrariness in the selection. According to the law the adoption unit at the Ministry should maintain two lists, one with the names of the children declared suitable for adoption by the Tribunal handed over by the orphanages, the other with the names of applicants handed over by the agencies. On the basis of these two lists the assignment committee is supposed to link the child to the most appropriate among the applicants.

In practice this principle has proved difficult to implement, and two of the most influential adoption orphanages have obtained a special authorization from the state to carry out the matching before and even without the help of an assignment committee. One reason why it is tempting for these orphanages to acquire control over the flow of children to adoptive parents is that they can ensure that the children they clear for adoption go to agencies they represent. To invest time and money in bureaucratic work without the security of disposing of "their" own children would be to follow an altruistic principle that would be beyond the economist logic of these representatives.

After the child is connected to new social parents they are called to an audience at the Tribunal. On the basis of the observations and conversations at this meeting, and a re-evaluation of all documentation in the case, the Tribunal issues an act for full adoption. Having issued the act, the case passes to the national register where the child's original birth certificate is annulled and a new so-called actualized one created. In this way the birthparent's names are erased and replaced by the names of the new adoptive parents (cf. Corporación de Estudios y Publicaciones 1999).

The legal procedures described here are essential for the circulation of the adopted child, and they could be characterized as the specific mechanisms that make the child move from abandoned, orphaned or handed-over infant, to objectified adoptable person, and finally to reconstituted adoptee. In this process time becomes crucial; it becomes important to delimit and economize it. This use (and misuse) of time links to the system of bribe payments based on a certain economic logic within the bureaucracy, and is interlinked with other payments based on the economic logic of the market.

The constitution of relation and the objectification of person in the adoption process

In a polemical article Triseliotis (1999) asks what kind of exchange is or should be involved in intercountry adoption: is the adoptee a commodified and globally traded object or an altruistically given and received gift? An answer to such a question could be that the value connected to the child as it circulates changes. The shifting and differentiated moral economy in which the child is adopted is shaped by various social actors or valuators with different interests, concerns and personal projects. Hence, the child could be given up by its birthparents or relatives involuntarily and in despair, or be given away voluntarily motivated by hopes for a better future for the child, or simply out of indifference. It could be handed over by temporal caregivers in an act of altruism, objectified and even commodified in the process by bureaucrats and agencies' representatives, and received by the adoptive parents as a desired gift.

If a defining distinction between commodity and gift exchange is the absence or presence of a social production of relations (cf. Gregory 1982), then the adoptee as a circulating person/object is linked to both types of exchange. In the first part of the international adoption process the values and resources related to the market and the state bureaucracy are used by some actors more efficiently in objectifying the child, than others manage to humanize, socialize and personify her or him.[16] When persons are connected directly to a market price through a general means of exchange, they are also compared to a standardizing measure of value, money. Hence the unique value of the person, which makes her or him incomparable and not exchangeable, is temporally suspended.

Furthermore, the way the adoptee is objectified through the legal system's adoption procedures dismisses the relations that make the person into a specific social being. Formally the state does not recognize birthparents and their kinsfolk as persons socially significant to the adoptee. Several stages in the process contribute to the separation of original kin from adoptive parents, finalized by the cancellation of the original birth certificate and its replacement by a new actualized one. The child's birthparents are by this last operation made non-existent; biological facts are overwritten by social facts. In this sense the adoptee is not *filled* with relations as it circulates (cf. Strathern 1988; Gell 1999). Adoption in the formalized intercountry form does not produce a person constituted of a multitude of relations. It is a much more controlled process of separation, objectification and re-constitution, one where relations are replaced and social discontinuity created. Thus the socially constitutive work going on in the adoption process is characterized *by the making of one relation*.

Apart from the child's relation to its birthparents there are several other potentially significant others who are set-aside in the adoption process, children interned and adults working in orphanages and caretaking persons partaking in kinds of fosterage arrangements are some of them (cf. Cardoso 1984; Fonseca 2002). Only the adoptive relation, which is the outcome of the process, is reckoned as decisive for the child's sociality. The other social connections are seen to be a means to create this one relation, and hence they are successively dismantled as the adoptee circulates.

Objectifying the person through de-socialization always takes into consideration a social relation, either the relation to the birthparents that is dismantled, or the relation to the adoptive parents that is constituted. A combination of being the product of relations and becoming separated from them seems therefore to be essential in the making of the adopted person. These observations could challenge generalizations made about specific Western notions of the person. Strathern (1988) argues that such notions are based on ideas about the person as a unity, a microcosm with attributes "intrinsic to his or her identity" (Strathern 1988: 135). Social relations are external to this unity, they connect the person to a social world, but they do not fundamentally create or produce the person. The argument in this chapter, however, is that the adopted person seems to be fundamentally produced by one social relation which changes during the process. This suggests that relations are both inherently constitutive to as well as separable from the person. Furthermore one could observe that the uniqueness of the person is temporally modified by the other form of objectification taking place in the adoption process, namely the commodification of the adoptee.

Notes

1 I would like to thank participants in the workshop on gifts and commodities at the conference held by the Norwegian Association for Anthropologists at Lillehammer in May 2000, and the participants in the workshop on cross-cultural approaches to adoption at the EASA conference in Krakow in July 2000 for helping me to develop the analyses in this chapter. I would also like to thank Torhild M. Andersen, María A. Guzmán, Sarah Lund, John McNeish, Aud Talle and Kari-Anne Ulfsnes for constructive comments to earlier drafts of this chapter.

2 The chapter is based on data produced during four months of fieldwork in the Andean capital of Quito, Ecuador, in 1999, with child labour migration and international adoption as main themes of investigation.

3 Although Zelizer has worked with historical material on national adoption in the USA, parts of her analysis are relevant to issues concerning international adoptions.

4 Simmel discusses such payments especially in relation to the transfer of women in marriage arrangements.

5 Standardizing here refers to the way a person's (unique) value is reduced to a standard money value.

6 In 1999, 25 legally approved adoption agencies operated in Ecuador.

7 Holt International Children's Services Ecuador.

8 The income Holt Ecuador has on its international adoptions by no means covers the costs of running its programmes. The organization does not charge any fee for national adoptions.

9 Around $6,000 for an adoption from Ecuador carried out in 1999.

10 Adoptions from Ecuador are not the only source of income for MAM since it carries out its services in a series of countries in Asia, Africa and Latin America.

11 According to Gailey (1998) international adoptions to the USA are solely carried out by private agencies and adoption lawyers, and according to information gathered by the National Adoption Information Clearinghouse, a public service agency within the Children's Bureau of the US Department of Health and Human Services, the costs of an international adoption range from $25,000 to $63,000, with $42,000 as an average.

12 Only 20–25 per cent of the honorarium the representative gets goes to cover expenses related to the adoption. Since MAM's representative in Ecuador is a lawyer she has no extra expenses related to judicial assistance.

13 The formal justice system in Ecuador restricts the number of adoptions each agency is allowed to carry out through a system of repartition. The informal

practices within that same justice system make it possible to manipulate the order established by this repartition.

14 These authorities never seriously investigated accusations made by adoptive parents concerning irregularities in MAM's practices.

15 Contrary to the image of the abandoned child as "the child of nobody", the investigation in most cases reveals some or even extensive information about the child's family situation.

16 An acknowledgment of this situation in the 1980s and 1990s resulted in international efforts to introduce mechanisms of control of the market in adopted children through the implementation of the UN conventions for children's rights into national laws of countries involved in international adoption (cf. Triseliotis 1999).

References

Adopsjonsforum (2000) *Råd og veiledning i adopsjonsprosessen*, Oslo: AF.

Cardoso, Ruth C. L. (1984) 'Creating kinship: the fostering of children in *favela* families in Brazil', in Smith, Raymond T. (ed.) *Kinship ideology and practice in Latin America*, Chapel Hill: University of North Carolina Press, pp. 196–203.

Corporación de Estudios y Publicaciones (1999) *Codigo de menores*, Quito: Corporación de Estudios y Publicaciones.

Fonseca, Claudia (2002) 'Inequality near and far: adoption as seen from the Brazilian *favelas*', *Law and Society Review* 2 (36): 397–431.

Gailey, C. W. (1998) 'The search for baby right: race, class, and gender in US international adoptive kinship', paper presented at the Wenner Gren symposium no. 123 'New directions in kinship study: A core concept revisited', 27 March–4 April.

Gell, A. (1999) 'Strathernograms, or the semiotics of mixed metaphor', in *The Art of Anthropology*, London: The Athlone Press.

Gregory, C. A. (1982) *Gifts and commodities*, London: Academic Press.

Kopytoff, I. (1986) 'The cultural biography of things: commoditization as process', in Appadurai, A. (ed.) *The social life of things*, Cambridge: Cambridge University Press, pp. 64–91.

Landes, E. M. and Posner, R. A. (1978) 'The economics of the baby shortage', *Journal of Legal Studies* 7: 323–348.

MacTaggart, L. (1980) *The baby brokers*, New York: Dial Press.

Modell, J. S. (1994) *Kinship with strangers*, Berkeley: University of California Press.

Schneider, D. M. (1984) *A critique of the study of kinship*, Ann Arbor: University of Michigan Press.

Simmel, G. (1978) *The philosophy of money*, London: Routledge & Kegan Paul.

Strathern, M. (1988) *The gender of the gift*, Berkeley: University of California Press.

Triseliotis, J. (1999) 'Inter-country adoption: global trade or global gift?', in Rygvold, A. L., Dalen, M. and Sætersdal, B. (eds) *Mine – yours – ours and theirs*, Oslo: University of Oslo Press, pp. 14–31.

Wolfe, A. (1989) *Whose keeper?* Berkeley: University of California Press.

Zelizer, Viviana A. (1985) *Pricing the priceless child*, Princeton: Princeton University Press.

Chapter 13

Choosing parents
Adoption into a global network

Huon Wardle

A mother is a dear loving person to their children: a child who don't have a mother they lost everything. But this mother I have got from God is a real good mother. She is better than the mother that birth me. Make I tell you this: your mother don't must be your mother. The one that feel the pain sometime is not your real mother but the one that don't feel the pain is the real good mother. Because she does not feel the pain to carry me here, but she treat me as if is she carry me into this world.

In 1991, in response to my suggestion that she tell me her life history, Jeanette, a Jamaican in her thirties, taped for me the recollections of childhood relocation and adoption reproduced in this chapter. The central theme of Jeanette's narrative is her loss, search for and providential discovery of a mother and a family. Around this is woven a moral story of cruelty and kindness, ill fortune, good luck and personal strategy.

As a mechanism, adoption tells us a great deal about the ways social life is organised and reproduced in the Caribbean, but the West Indian experience is also of some significance when compared to adoption practices in richer nation states with more extensive programmes of social welfare. Jeanette's story emphasises cruelty and neglect but it also shows up the pragmatism and moral incorporativeness of Jamaican family life. Adoption in the West Indies has classically been understood as a reaction to familial 'crisis' (Goody 1978). However, at the end of this chapter I draw out some of the positive features of child shifting in Jamaica by comparison to Britain where ideas about and practices of adoption are institutionalised by the state to a far higher degree. However, before presenting Jeanette's account for comment, I want to establish a certain amount of contextual detail concerning child shifting and family organisation in Jamaica and the West Indies more generally.

Adoption in the West Indian context

Fostering and adoption are extremely common in the Caribbean. In some case studies up to a third of children in Creole working-class families have been relocated from the birth parent elsewhere (Roberts and Sinclair 1978; Gordon 1987; Barrow 1996; Sargent 1998). Children are typically transferred from resource poor, averagely younger family groups, to older wealthier/more economically diverse groupings. There is usually a cognatic kinship connection involved but relocation to the households of unrelated friends and others is also frequent. Most shifting is informally arranged but some takes place via state institutions (as in Jeanette's case). Child relocation is an open-ended and fluid process describing a wide variety of experiences. These range from brief fostering-then-return-to-birth-parent to permanent relocation. What is striking is the relative prominence of child shifting as a social strategy and the freedom parents feel to relocate children as they feel necessary and appropriate. However, the forms of displacement involved in child shifting are integrated within much wider patterns of West Indian social life and culture.

Since slave emancipation in the 1830s, Creole social life has been structured around the continuum of rural–urban–cosmopolitan relations created by transmigration. Jamaican family life is patterned on networks of ties between members linking (for instance) Kingston with a rural migrant base as well as with metropolitan centres such as London, New York and Toronto. Historically, the migration of (predominantly male) family members has led to a range of strategies of child care. Women have been integral in shifting children to the locations where they can be supported. In Kingston this kind of child movement is in no sense considered aberrant. It simply complements the continual flow of household life in which bilateral family members arrive from the country or abroad, give and receive assistance, then stay or move on again. Organised around a relatively stable core of personnel, 'family' in Kingston is a dynamic equilibrium where the emphasis is on dynamism. The accumulation and dispersal of new family members through fostering/adoption is one factor in the typical family flux.

Caribbean sociality is individuated to an exceptionally high degree (Wardle 2000). Gonzalez (1984) has pointed out that while Macfarlane's (1980) model of English individualism depends on the triadic nuclear family, in Creole kinship individuals are linked together in overlapping networks of dyads – child–mother, child–auntie, child–father, child–grandmother, for instance. This again reflects the dyadic linkages of social life more generally (Mintz 1973, 1996). In this context terminology is flexible – an elder brother in an authority role may be referred to as 'papa', for instance (Gonzalez 1969: 60). Much emphasis is placed on the child's (and adult's) capacity to link into extended social networks rapidly and successfully. Kinship from a subjective point of view is highly voluntaristic. In terms of fostering, first parents, adopters and children all underline their influence and choice. Children often voice their preference for staying with one or another parent. And these personalised affective linkages between child and potential parent very often determine the outcome. The biographical individuality of, and the assertion of personality by, children is thus assumed and encouraged. This is of particular interest when compared to the 'closed adoption' practised historically in Britain where the child was understood ideally to be a *tabula rasa* for socialisation or behavioural moulding by adoptive parents.

The idiom of kinship in working-class Kingston is again exceptionally broad-minded – with ultimate appeal to the ideal of other Jamaicans as 'brethren and sistren'. Hence, there is plenty of room for strategic refiguring of given people as parents or relatives. And a central persona in this organisation of family networks is the charismatic woman. In Jeanette's story, Miss Mills, is one such organiser. Since the 1960s Miss Mills, a working-class Kingstonian, had built up a large family of adopted children between the United States (where she worked half the year) and Jamaica. Because child shifting is ubiquitous, informal, and seeks to avoid the intervention of state agencies, the charismatic organiser is an absolutely integral figure in restoring and establishing family networks. And the collapse of the Jamaican economy since the late 1970s has meant that charisma has maintained its dominant position vis-à-vis bureaucracy in the allocation of care.

Ideologically in this cultural milieu, individualism and the displacements built into social networks are reflected in a strong belief in providence and an, often apocalyptically phrased, focus on the present (Wardle 2000, 2004). Since the events leading to a person's co-option into a kinship network may often be highly contingent, providence is frequently called upon as an ultimate rationale for how events turn out. At the same time individuals know that they will have to use skill and strategy to find their way into relationships of friendship or family that will satisfy them.

Adoption is understood as a form of reciprocity between known individuals and family groupings but, within the framework of Kingstonian social life, it is an open-ended one. In day-to-day life, tension often builds up around the sense of lack of reciprocity between individuals linked through networks of family or friendship. The extensiveness of adoption shows the degree of openness to social exchange, but child shifting can also lead to accusations that others have failed to reciprocate or more broadly 'cooperate'. When, for instance, the partner of my friend Lee died, Lee moved one of his children into the care of a local cousin. Lee told me that his cousin was now complaining about the lack of cash support Lee was giving, but Lee, in turn, emphasised the number of exchanges-in-kind that he had given to his cousin. Sadly, Lee himself died recently and while his daughter is now staying at her mother's natal home in Trelawny, his son lives with one of Lee's brothers.

The tensions involved in social displacement are countermanded by ideologies which stress human generosity and which tie individuals into networks through the workings of providence. Sindy was a niece of Miss Mills, my landlady. Sindy's father had been shot and killed by the police and her mother was finding it impossible to look after her. In 1991 Miss Mills took over care of Sindy and when Miss Mills died Sindy moved in with Jeanette, Miss Mills's adopted daughter. In her new home, Sindy responded to previous maltreatment by mischief and deceit on a massive scale. It seems likely that in Britain Sindy would have entered long-term care at an early stage and have been very lucky to find her way out again. It is a credit to Miss Mills, Jeanette and the general pragmatism surrounding fostering in Jamaica that she still has a home and a reasonably happy family life a decade later.

Though it is not meant to represent the norm (whatever that might be), Jeanette's story shows up persuasively both positive and negative features of child shifting in Kingston (according to local and exoteric standards). Jeanette describes how her mother gives her away with deliberate cruelty to a woman in the countryside. A doctor eventually has Jeanette removed from this woman and Jeanette is then placed in the limited care of a state orphanage. Finally, at Jeanette's own suggestion, Miss Mills, a woman with whom Jeanette had had some early contact, agrees to take her in. The narrative demonstrates both the open-ended and contingent character of kinship and the need to assert personality in relation to it. It also recognises the value of certain close relationships in the face of this contingency and open-endedness. As Jeanette says 'the child that don't know parents – you have to stick where you get to stick'.

Jeanette's story

This is a story about a little girl named Jeanette. My name is Jeanette, my mother's name is Ariadne Clarke and my father's name was Samuel Taylor. Now as I was told about my mother, this I don't know of but I

hear about it as I grow older, my mother worked at a hospital. I understand that she meet my father whose name is Sam. Sam came to Kingston
as a tourist guide. My mother and him become friend. After becoming
friend for a while, them go on dating each other for a while 'til my mother
became pregnant and have a baby. That baby is me – Jeanette.

Now I understood that after my mother got pregnant and have
me, my father treated her so badly that they have to part. My mother did
not care about me because of my father. She say, as she look at me she
remember Sam. She say I look so much of him and she hates me for that.
My mother did not care at all about me. Now there was this lady named
Miss Mills who my mother rent a room from. Now this lady used to take
good care of me. So when my mother beat me she would beg for me and
say 'don't beat her'. But my mother still beat me. Sometimes I would
have to sleep over at the lady's house as a little child. Now as I grow older
I understand for myself. My mother used to tell me bad words and tell
me 'now get away from me you ugly this, you ugly that; I hate you so
much'. But as a child I did not understand: I try to make her love me but
there was no love in her heart for Jeanette.

But this lady Miss Mills would look after me – cook, give me dinner,
give me a bath and send me to school – she would do everything for me
as a mother. Now my mother keep on beating me: sometimes she come
and she find me eating something she would put it and throw it away.
Now Miss Mills say to her 'Nicey [her nickname] if you don't want this
child why don't you give her to me?' She said, 'no, I will not give her
to you because you will treat her too good and that's what I don't want:
I want to find someone who have hog and goat. I want her to go and
look after hog and goat because that is what she is about [what she is
good for] – just to feed hog and goat.'

One day, my mother call me and say 'go to the bathroom'. After
finishing in the bathroom I come back. And she and this little man named
Bishop take me to the bus stop and we take the bus to Gordontown.
When we reach Gordontown, my mother took me and gave me to this
old lady Miss Mailer. Miss Mailer live on a very high hill and a long walk.
This lady does not treat children good either. Someone told my mother
about her and my mother give me to her. While I was there I was so
unhappy: all my thoughts was on how to get back to Miss Mills. Anyway
my mother leave me there.

I have to wake every morning at five o'clock . When Miss Mailer wake
me I have to wash out pig pen, feed the pig, tie out the goat. After tie
out the goat I have to carry water about half a mile. After carrying the
water I have to go with her and plant gungu [a pulse], weed grass. When

I am not weeding grass I am picking pine [pineapple]. When I am not picking pine I am always on the move. So sometimes after finish carrying water I feel so tired, but I cannot say that I am tired. She sent me now down to the river to carry sand. She is not building a house, she don't want the sand for anything, but you still have to carry the sand. Sometimes I so tired that I would lie down by the river and drop asleep and if I stay too long she would beat me with electric wire.

One time I run away from her to Kingston to find my mother. But my mother was not there. But I find Miss Mills's sister. She did not know anything about me so she has to take me back to Miss Mailer. After taking me back, Miss Mailer gave me a proper beating with electric wire. The electric wire burst my lip and I have to go to the clinic at Gordontown for an injection. After getting that injection, with the lip burst and everything, I have to go to the market and call out 'scallion and thyme': I have to sell scallion and thyme for her. After selling, I have to pack up and go home. She don't give me shoes. I have two dress: I have to wash one, dry one. She hardly give me food to eat: sometimes when I am hungry she give me a bottle of drinks and a bun and that have to serve me the whole day. She don't let me sleep on her bed. She spread two old sheet on the floor. She have two double bed: she sleep on one and nobody sleep on the other one. Sometime the floor so hard I consider what to do. Sometime I run away from her and sleep under the house bottom. Sometimes I sleep on the bushes just to hide from her.

She treat me so cruel: she used to beat me with coconut and beat me onto my head. Sometimes I feel like dying, but I have to carry on because the child that don't know parents – you have to stick where you get to stick. Now I remember once she beat me to climb a mango tree. After climbing the mango tree, and pick the mangoes, and give to her, I could not come down, and she leave me and go to the market. After she gone this man that live next door named Uncle hear me crying and come to see what was wrong. And when he saw what had happened he go into the bushes and cut two piece of wood and make a ladder and climb up the tree and carry me down on his shoulders. When she come back Uncle ask her why she did that and she says 'none of your business'. People stick up for me sometimes when she do wrong things to me. Sometimes I am so glad when someone talk up for me.

She have this shop where she sell coal, coconut, and all sorts of things. Sometimes when I am so hungry, while I am round the back cleaning out the shop, I would steal her biscuits and eat them and stuff them into a corner. One time when she was cleaning out the shop she find a whole heap of biscuit paper and she call me and ask me about them, and I say

I eat them because I was hungry. And she beat me so terrible that I step back on a sardine tin and cut my heel back. And I have to go to the clinic again for an injection, and for a whole month I could not walk. And I have that mark on my heel back 'til death do.

She didn't have a bathroom on the shop: she had to go next door to use the bathroom. But she and the people didn't agree because they have a fight. Now she have a pint glass, first time [original style] pint glass. She pass her urine in it behind the counter of the shop and hide it in a cupboard. I clean out the shop but I did not see it. It was there for days and she come back and buck it up [found it] and ask me 'Jeanette, you couldn't throw away the urine from the pint glass?' I said I did not remember it was there. She beat me with a piece of wire and say, 'you must be saving it up to drink – so drink it'. And she keep beating me and all I could do was drink the urine from the pint glass. And for the whole day I have a stomach ache. And all that went on.

It so happened that one day I was so hungry I was dying for hunger. They take me to the hospital and the doctor say 'this child is so hungry and underfed'. As soon as the doctor treated me he take me to the police station because there was nowhere to keep me. So I have to sleep at the station for a month and the policemen there find something for me to eat. Now when they do get space I went to the children' home and I was there about three months. And it was like I hold in a prison: you couldn't go out to play, they lock the door and all you could do is peep out through the window. They give you food, OK, yes, but the place was like a prison – you couldn't have no fun, no nothing. Now after all that, one day I hear someone call out my name and they open the door and let me out. There was a lady looking for a child to adopt. But when I went and they ask me if I would like the lady to be my mother, I say 'no, I do not want to be with her, I will not go'. They say yes I have to go because the place is full up. I say if I have to go I will run away. They say they see so many children run away from foster parents that they will not send this one because 'she let you know she will run away'.

Another time I hear my name call out and I went out. They ask me, 'do you know anyone who would take care of you – do you have a family?' I say, 'I don't have a family, only a mother and she does not like me, but there was this lady Miss Mills who used to treat me so good: she bring clothes for me when she come from foreign and thing'. They say, 'where is this lady now?' I was so small I did not know. If I see a number at this time I didn't know a number. So I did not know the number of the gate where she was living. Anyway, I describe the place to them and they go to find out.

The same day the police came and asking for Miss Mills, the same day she coming out of a taxi coming from foreign. Now, they told her that they have this little girl and I say that she would look after me, and would she take me? She say yes. The Wednesday was the court, and when I come to court the Wednesday I see her sitting on the bench. But I did not know her that day: I did not remember her. So there was this police lady have us in a line to go inside the court room. I hear someone say 'Jeanette' and I turn round and say 'fine thank you ma'am'. And by the time I reach a couple of chains I realise it was Miss Mills and I run back and hug her up and I start to cry. Then the police lady grab me by my neck-back and drag me away and say 'you have to wait until you get time to speak to her: you are going into court now and afterwards you can speak to her'.

And when her time came, and they call Miss Mills, the Judge say, 'Miss Mills, you seem like a nice lady, you take care of Jeanette, and Jeanette, you take care of Miss Mills', and the judge send us out. When we was leaving the court, they say the dress I wear to court they need it for another child. And Miss Mills say, 'when I come I don't carry no dress for this little girl: I did not know nothing about her 'til yesterday, I cannot take her on the street naked'. So they say, 'OK Miss Mills, you can keep the dress, but we must have the shoes for another unwanted child'. But Miss Mills say, 'I cannot take her on the bus with no shoes on: it would look so bad'. Anyway the judge let me keep the shoes. But the frock was so big, that Miss Mills was so ashamed to walk with me with that big dress, she send me ahead and she walk behind.

So when I reach home that day she take me in the bathroom, she gave me a bath. And she have a sewing machine and she sew me a fine loving dress to put on that day. And the next day she take me down to town: she buy me some brand-new dresses, shoes, and ribbon, and bubbles to put in my hair. And she get round that sewing machine and she sew me some fine clothes to wear.

After being there for a time, one day she say to me 'Jeanette go and wash up all the dishes'. That night I did not feel like washing up the dishes. So I went inside and start crying. And she ask me say, 'why are you crying?', and I did not answer. And I went into my room and I took the scissors and I cut off all my hair: I cut it right down to the skull. When she saw me she say, 'why did you cut off your hair?' I said because I did not want to wash the dishes. She say, 'you cut off your hair, you don't want to wash the dishes: tomorrow I am taking you back where I take you from'. She take me back the next morning. And when she take me back I was crying when I see her leaving. They say, 'Miss Mills can't you give her another chance?' She say, 'no, I leaving her here because she seems to be rude'. The officer ask me 'do you want to stay here?' I say 'no!, no!, no!' He say 'do you want to go with that man over there?' I say 'no, no, no, I want to go with Miss Mills'. And after that they call Miss Mills and beg her and plead with her and in the end she agree to taking me back home.

After taking me back home she carry me to the barber to shape up my hair. She get me to a school. When I go to school the children did mock me about my hair. I would cry and come back and say 'Aunt Erica, you know what, they are teasing me about my hair'. And she say 'good for you: we treat you so good, who tell you to use the scissors in your hair?' After that, every night she comb the hair, tying it back: and my hair catch up so good. And that lady – from that day until today I am thirty years old – she love me so much and take good care of me and she treat me like I am a baby until today.

A mother is a dear loving person to their children: a child who don't have a mother they lost everything. But this mother I have got from God is a real good mother. She is better than the mother that birth me. Make I tell you this: your mother don't must be your mother. The one that feel the pain sometime is not your real mother but the one that don't feel the pain is the real good mother. Because she does not feel the pain to carry me here, but she treat me as if is she carry me into this world.

Commentary: disjuncture, ambiguation, commitment

As Jeanette tells it, her early life was characterised by a series of dyadic relationships; with a cruelly indifferent mother, with the abusive Miss Mailer, and with the loving and nurturing – though sometimes punitive – Miss Mills. Jeanette makes only passing reference to other kin. She pictures herself as significantly alone in her struggle with chance and fate. Even after arrival at Miss Mills's house, the narrative does not mention her foster siblings. However this sense of individuation adds to and confirms the picture of her success as a strategist: as a small girl, on her own, Jeanette manages finally to get what could have been so easily achieved to begin with – to live with Miss Mills. And she emphasises in the story that it was she who chose Miss Mills, first in opposition to other foster parents, then in the face of Miss Mills's own disenchantment.

These emphases – on people's subjectedness to arbitrariness and fate, their aloneness in the world, but also their capacity to find and choose happiness through a struggle – contrast with, but do not contradict, the image of people linked into networks of kinship presented earlier. Had I, instead of suggesting that Jeanette recount her life story, asked her to 'please give me a list of your relatives' (Smith 1988: 31) the resulting narrative would have been very different. In that case Jeanette would have told me about a wide range of people. She would have noted her 'blood' relations via her birth mother's other *babyfather* (one of the fathers of her mother's children), her 'in-laws' via her own babyfathers, and her relatives in Miss Mills's family. In fact during the period that Jeanette made this tape she was also re-establishing her relationship with her mother and her brother (half brother in Anglo-American terms). Kinship is a powerful, open-ended, and inclusive idiom in Kingstonian life, but it does not contradict the sense that many like Jeanette have of being fundamentally alone with God and against fate. In the frame of reference provided by her story, Jeanette expresses herself as, and clearly is, individuated. Within another referential scheme, the inclusive language of kinship, she finds herself within a network.

The family that Jeanette is co-opted into has important features. It is extended spatially across the boundaries of the Jamaican nation state: the children and grandchildren of Miss Mills's sisters have created second and third generation linkages between Jamaica and the USA and UK. Similarly, Miss Mills has built up property and resources between New York and Kingston. Jeanette has had to position herself within this framework of nurturance and economic support – and to negotiate the reciprocities demanded. Her local strategies give onto these wider processes.

I have suggested that adoption practices can be considered a microcosm of Creole culture and social life more broadly. In Jamaica, and in many other Caribbean states, there is a poor integration between state and civil society. Especially under recent conditions of structural adjustment, lower class Jamaicans look to transmigrant social networks for support rather than towards amelioration by state institutions. The Creole culture characteristic of this context tends to be expressed triadically (Wardle 2002) – either as commitment (to valued relationships), as ambiguation (the negotiation of values through fantasy humour or symbolic displacement, Wardle 2002, 2004) or as disjuncture (expressing the insuperability of conflicting claims). Jeanette's narrative calls on all these modes as she attempts to synthesise a definition of Aunt Erica as her mother – not as the one that 'feel the pain' but as instead the one who 'treat me as if she carry me into this world'. While Jeanette's narrative is characterised by a sense of disjuncture and ambivalence the end is marked by this striking expression of synthesis and commitment.

Conclusion

Economic and political conditions in Kingston are excessively harsh both on individuals and family groups, but there are nonetheless instructive conclusions to be drawn from the response to these conditions. Comparisons here with the situation in Britain are suggestive only (since I am not strictly comparing like with like), but if I were to extract a number of positive features from the picture of child shifting in Kingston these would include:

1   The lack of stigma attached to adoption in working-class Jamaica. In Britain adoption continues to be viewed as a practice of last resort reflecting an entrenched idealisation of the nuclear family and the consanguinity of parent and child: the priority is for children to stay with birth parents at all costs while adoption for reasons other than the infertility of adopters is rare. By contrast, in Kingston, child movement is not aberrant and the emphasis is on leaving the networks of family life as open as possible.

2   The identification of adoptees as individuals with biographical histories. In Britain this appears to be increasingly important – adopted children are encouraged to recognise their pre-adoption histories; though the exercise is subject to careful social control.

3   The visibility of the moral/social relations involved. The classic system of 'closed adoption' in Britain and the USA emphasised the absolute barrier between the stigmatised birth parent and the new adoptive parental environment: even now the system of social/moral reciprocities involved is far from transparent. Jamaican child shifting is noticeable for the visibility of the exchanges involved, the relative egalitarianism and voluntariness governing these and, once again, the lack of stigma implied.

4   The flexibility and pragmatism of child shifting arrangements. Child relocation has a strategic role in the organisation of dispersed family relationships in Jamaica. It is not assumed that shifting a child between family environments is in itself damaging to the child, and indeed there is no evidence that this is so. In the absence of state institutions to inform them otherwise, Jamaicans consider themselves competent to organise these movements. Sometimes, as in the case of Jeanette's birth mother, child shifting turns into deliberate child abandonment (Brodber 1974). In the great majority of cases children are relocated into family networks where they will receive support.

208   Huon Wardle

References

Barrow, C. 1996. *Family in the Caribbean*. Oxford: James Currey.

Brodber, E. 1974. *Abandonment of Children in Jamaica*. Mona: Institute of Social and Economic Research, University of the West Indies.

Gonzalez, N. 1969. *Black Carib Household Structure*. Seattle: University of Washington Press.

—— 1984. 'Rethinking the Consanguinial Household and Matrifocality'. *Ethnology*, 23: 1–13.

Goody, E. 1978. 'Delegation of Parental Roles in West Africa and the West Indies'. In Shimkin, D., E. Shimkin and D. Frate (eds) *The Extended Family in Black Societies*. The Hague: Mouton.

Gordon, S. 1987. '"I Go to Tanties": The Economic Significance of Child-shifting in Antigua, West Indies'. *Journal of Comparative Family Studies*, 18: 427–443.

Macfarlane, A. 1980. *The Origins of English Individualism*. Oxford: Blackwell.

Mintz, S. 1973. 'The Caribbean as a Socio-cultural Area'. In Horowitz, M. (ed.) *Peoples and Cultures of the Caribbean*. New York: The Natural History Press, pp. 19–46.

—— 1996. 'Enduring Substances, Trying Theories: The Caribbean Region as Oikumene'. *Journal of the Royal Anthropological Institute*, 2: 289–313.

Roberts, G. and S. Sinclair. 1978. *Women in Jamaica*. New York: KTO Press.

Sargent, C. 1998. 'Bad Boys and Good Girls: Gender and Child Health in Jamaica'. In Scheper-Hughes, Nancy and Carolyn Sargent (eds) *Small Wars: The Cultural Politics of Childhood*. Berkeley: University of California Press, pp. 202–228.

Smith, R. T. 1988. *Kinship and Class in the West Indies: A Genealogical Study of Jamaica and Guyana*. Cambridge: Cambridge University Press.

Wardle, H. 2000. *An Ethnography of Cosmopolitanism in Kingston, Jamaica*. New York: Edwin Mellen.

—— 2002. 'Ambiguation, Commitment, Disjuncture: A Social Analysis of Caribbean Cultural Creativity'. *Journal of the Royal Anthropological Institute*, 8(3): 493–508.

—— 2004. 'A City of Meanings: Place and Displacement in Urban Jamaican Self-framings'. In Fog Olwig, K. and J. Besson (eds) *Caribbean Narratives of Belonging*. London: Macmillan.

Part IV

Intercountry and domestic adoption in the 'West'

Chapter 14

National bodies and the body of the child

"Completing" families through international adoption[1]

Barbara Yngvesson

Mofiz

On a trip to India in 1996 to attend a conference on international adoption, Swaran Chaudhry, Secretary of the Society for Indian Children's Welfare (SICW) in Calcutta, recounted for me what she described as a "success story." Chaudhry, a strong advocate for protecting the internationally adopted child's sense of her origins in India, had previously referred to the increasing visibility of adoptees who return to the institutions where they were cared for, and described the return visit as a process that "cements a child in its identity." Chaudhry's "success story" involved a "failed" adoption or an "almost" adoption. It involved a six-year-old boy, Sheik Mofiz, who lived with his mother in Taldi village, near the Howrah Bridge. His father drove a cycle-van in Calcutta. On July 21, 1994, Mofiz ran out of his house after being scolded by his mother and climbed onto a bus in hopes of finding his father in the city. When the bus reached the end of the line and he was still on it, the driver took him to a police station. Eventually, he was transferred to a home for abandoned children, and some months later sent to SICW, which places Indian children for adoption either domestically or overseas.

Chaudhry explains that something about Mofiz convinced her he was not "abandoned," but he could provide no details about where he came from or who his parents were and thus continued to live at SICW for several months. Then in March, 1995, a group of children from the orphanage went on a day trip to Santiniketan, outside of Calcutta. As they drove over the Howrah Bridge with its vast "flyover" of steel girders under which thousands of people live and work, Mofiz looked down and said, "There is my school." On learning of this, Chaudhry arranged to have a van take him to the area below the flyover, accompanied by social workers. She explained that it was a "terrible" area and that the social workers were afraid to enter it alone. But when they stopped near the place where Mofiz said that his school was held (it turned out to be an open-air "street school" run under the flyover for children in the area), the child jumped from the car and local residents ran to meet him, crying "Mofiz, Mofiz, you have come back!" Mofiz's mother was at work in a factory, but his father was located and eventually Mofiz was reunited with both parents. His father explained that he had lodged a complaint with the police station and with a "missing persons' squad" as soon as his son disappeared, but wherever he went he was met with indifference: "The police said it was impossible to find him."

Chaudhry, a vibrant woman in her sixties who was a successful Calcutta business-woman before becoming director of SICW two decades ago, asked me what I thought of this story, and whether I agreed that it was about "success." Was Mofiz better off living with his parents under the Howrah Bridge, or might he have had a better life in Sweden or the United States, which regularly takes older and "hard to place" Indian children in adoption through organizations such as WACAP (World Association for Children and Parents) or AIAA (Americans for International Aid and Adoption)? I agreed that Mofiz belonged in Calcutta. But the story underscores the complex issues involved in deciding what it means to "do the best for" a child, and the different visions of family – and range of interventions necessary to support different kinds of family – that must be included in child welfare policies if we are to engage seriously with what "doing the best for" a child entails.

This chapter explores these issues by focusing on the interpretation and implementation of a central tenet of contemporary international adoption practice, the child's right to grow up in a family environment. My concern is with the privileging of a particular vision of family – what Collier *et al.* (1982) describe as "The Family" – which may constrict the range of possible interventions for responding to children in need of care in Asia, Africa, Latin America, and the United States.[2] I suggest that this vision of family, favored by adoption practitioners in both sending and receiving nations, contributes to the commodification of children's bodies and their marketing abroad as national resources, even as it shapes an understanding of these bodies as belonging to the nation from which they came.[3]

Especially problematic, I suggest, is the notion, strongly endorsed by adoption and child welfare professionals, that an adoptive family placement must be both exclusive and permanent. The permanence maxim, while affirming the importance of continuity in a child's care-givers, also carries the potential for enforced *discontinuity*, when it is realized in conjunction with a modernist assumption that a "real" family is autonomous and self-contained. This assumption inscribes a bias in adoption law for dissolving prior relationships in which children may have been embedded.[4] It not only constrains the *form* of family into which adoptive children might be placed but works against efforts to reunite children with birth parents who may temporarily be unable to care for them. Staff of children's homes I visited in South America complained about parents who "dropped off" their children and expected the institution to provide for them when the parent was unable to do so, but rebuffed all efforts to terminate their rights as parents.

It is understandable that such practices pose problems both for orphanage staff and for children. At the same time, it is crucial that the drive to find a more privileged, more perfect and more permanent family for a child who is placed in temporary care not get in the way of the responsibility to provide social and economic support for needy parents and children. Guillermo Dávalos, a Bolivian lawyer and activist, noted that the effort to seek adoptive families either domestically or abroad as a solution to poverty deflects attention from the "thousands of families and populations who exist in a situation of abandonment (*estado de abandono*) because they are poor." Dávalos insisted that "We must privilege a politics that gives resources to the poor before developing policies to seek substitute families for poor children. The theme of adoption should not be associated with the theme of poverty." The dependence of orphanages and children's homes on foreign adoptive parents for needed resources, and the connection between such needs and the family permanence policy that underpins adoption practice, may stand in the way of clear thinking about a child's (and its parents') best interest.

This critique of family permanence is counterintuitive and goes strongly against accepted practice. It is important however not to conflate an ideology of *family* permanence with the need of a *child* for continuity. Continuity, as I am using this concept, refers to the *experience of the adopted child*, whose life (like that of the child who has not been abandoned or adopted) is "entangled in stories," some of which have not been recounted and have been repressed (Ricoeur 1992: 30). The permanence maxim, as it is applied to the construction of adoptive families, is conventionally interpreted in ways that privilege adoption as a "new start" that allows the adopted child to be completely absorbed into his or her new family and nation. The rationale for this approach is that only with the "complete absorption of the child into the legal and economic web of the adoptive family" will it be possible for "a lasting personal and psychological bond" to develop between the child and the adoptive parents (Hollinger 1993: 49).

I suggest however (and here I build on the work of John Triseliotis and others) that a concept of lasting personal and psychological bonds that is contingent on the termination of ties that link an adopted child (however ephemerally and problematically) to his or her pre-adoption history denies the child and the adult s/he becomes the potential for composing a narrative account of her life from the fragments of stories she has lived. It is through recountings of such stories that subjects "take charge of" their lives, drawing out of the "scattered fragments of lived stories . . . a narrative which would be at once more bearable and more intelligible" (Ricoeur 1992: 30). In this sense, paradoxically, the commitment to permanence in the adoptive family may produce the opposite effect for the adopted child and the adult s/he becomes. The mandated terminations of adoption law foreclose certain recountings of lived experience and may hinder rather than facilitate the child's capacity to create a meaningful personal identity.[5]

What would it mean to construct a policy for international adoption that does *not* focus on disembedding an adopted child so it can be placed in an autonomous family, but on re-imagining the "belonging" of a child and its adopted family in a way that promotes a more inclusive sense of connection, dependence, and responsibility? In what follows, I begin with a discussion of the ideology of family permanence in the conventions and practices of international adoption. I point to the ways that this ideology contributes to the production of inequalities in which children are sorted by kind (color, health, gender, age), families are ranked by deservingness, and nations located in a hierarchy of "givers" and "receivers." In the second half of the chapter, I draw on research in India and Latin America to discuss placement practices that complicate these hierarchies and inequalities. I conclude with interviews conducted with adult adoptees regarding their lived experiences of family to argue that current struggles and debates surrounding adoption practice are producing new understandings of belonging, with the potential to transform exclusive families and national identities.

My analysis is based on five years research with Stockholm's Adoption Centre and includes archival research, interviews, and informal exchanges with senior staff, adoptive parents, and adoptees, and travel with AC staff to sending countries (India, Colombia, Chile) that have served as key suppliers of children in the past three decades. In sending countries, I visited orphanages, hospitals, and courts, interviewed social workers, the staff of children's homes, and child welfare officials, and participated in reunions of adoptees and their parents with foster and birth families. My focus was on how the child's "object" status materializes in the practices of caretakers and staff in orphanages, maternity homes, and hospitals, where questions about the best interest of any given child are weighed on a daily basis. In spite of media coverage of adoption rings, traffic in children and other illegal practices implicated in the sale of children, and the attention given to these issues at conferences on international adoption, my research in Asia and Latin America indicates that it may be at least as important to examine what are considered to be reasonable (and legal) interpretations of best interest, the ways these interpretations "mark the operation of a master narrative of family" (Gailey 1998: 261), and the power and pervasiveness of this master narrative.

"How to manage our resources?"

A central question for delegates to the Hague Conference on Protection of Children and Co-operation in Respect of Intercountry adoption in the early 1990s was whether the increasing flow of Third World children to the overdeveloped world from the late 1950s to the 1990s was in the children's best interest. Debate on this issue, which eventually led to what Richard Carlson, a member of the US State Department Study Group on Intercountry Adoption, describes as "guarded endorsement of inter-country adoption" (Carlson 1994: 246), divided the conference roughly into two camps. Sending nations urged limits on intercountry adoptions and were successful in restricting them with language that made domestic placement (and ideally, reunification with a child's family of origin, or placement within its extended family) preferable to intercountry place-ment. Receiving nations, on the other hand, were strongly committed to intercountry placement, especially for the youngest children, who were presumed most adaptable (most adoptable) (1994: 258). For such children, they argued, a "suitable family" abroad was preferable to "local alternatives" which might include placement in a "local orphanage" (1994: 257).

What tilted the balance of opinion at the Conference in favor of intercountry adoption over such local alternatives was the discourse of a child's right to (need for) a family. As Carlson noted, "The Conference was not only an opportunity to develop confidence-building rules, it was also a forum for mutual education about the situation of children without families and the virtues of adoption." Especially important in this mutual education process was the capacity to reach agreement on a final version of the Convention which "reject[ed] arguments that preference for local placement should be absolute, by not requiring local authorities to make exhaustive and time-consuming investigation of all local adoption alternatives before an intercountry adoption is allowed. In choosing inter-country adoption, local authorities need only give due consideration to the *possibility* of local placement" (Carlson 1994: 264, emphasis added). A critique of this position is necessarily complicated. Most child welfare advocates agree that institutional care is detrimental to a child's development, and thus a process for seeking local placement that is unduly time-consuming places a child at increasing risk. From this perspective, it is of course reasonable that "authorities need only give due consideration to the possibility of local placement." This position is also (at least implicitly) of a piece with the assumption that a permanent, self-contained (nuclear) family environment is the best environment for any child. Such an assumption tends to undermine the potential of temporary institutional care or of foster placement, since neither fits the definition of a self-contained family. Representatives of adoption agencies in receiving nations, speaking at conferences and workshops I attended during the course of my research, almost uniformly opposed institutional or foster care in a child's country of origin over permanent placement abroad. I suggest that the discourse of family permanence that predominated among delegates at the Hague Conference from receiving nations, and the discourse of child as resource that predominated among representatives from sending countries are interlinked discursive formations that ultimately work – in counterintuitive ways – to privilege a narrow, nationalistic interpretation of a child's "best interest," limiting our understanding of children's needs and contributing to the commodification of their bodies.

Political theorist Göran Therborn, noting that "'the family' in public discourse has usually been a traditionalist and patriarchal concept," points out that "child policy and politics are . . . usually overshadowed by 'family policy'" (1996: 36). While feminism has been a major force in shaping a politics of the child that is not overshadowed by family politics, children's need for care is often conflated by adoption advocates with a family's "need" for children. Indeed, it is a "couple's" need for children in order to *be* "a family" and be included in civil society (Howell 1998) that provided the driving force for the growth of international adoption both in Europe and in North America in the 1960s and 1970s. The outflow of children that resulted, most notably from Asia and Latin America, fuelled concerns about the practice. Numerous conferences and workshops during the 1970s and early 1980s led to a landmark Supreme Court decision by Indian Supreme Court Justice C. J. Bhagwati in 1985, mandating that adoption should become part of a more general child welfare program. A guiding principle was to reunite abandoned children with their natal families, if possible. If not, adoptive placements were to be sought first in the child's home country, and only as a last resort should a child be placed in a substitute family abroad. These principles were subsequently incorporated into all international conventions on adoption, culminating in the 1993 Hague Convention, which was signed by all 66 participating nations.

Bhagwati's decision in *Lakshmi Kant Pandey* v. *Union of India* (1985) resulted in an aggressive program for the promotion of domestic Indian adoptions, a policy that proved successful but was challenging to implement. Building on Bhagwati's innovative concept of the abandoned child as "a supremely important national asset, a soul with a being, nature and capacities of its own" which is in need of "special protection" because "otherwise there cannot be healthy growth of the nation," Bhagwati cautioned that Indian parents would be resistant to the notion of adopting "a stranger child." If they did decide "to take such a child in adoption they prefer to adopt a boy rather than a girl and they are wholly averse to adopting a handicapped child, with the result that the majority of abandoned, destitute or orphan girls and handicapped children have very little possibility of finding adoptive parents within the country and their future lies only in adoption by foreign parents" (1985: 4–5).

Today, the directors of Indian child welfare societies report waiting lists of Indian adoptive parents, and a gradual shift in the bias against adopting girl-children. But a visit to a number of children's homes in 1997, all directed by dedicated, energetic women who are committed to fostering domestic Indian adoptions, revealed how entangled the adoption process is with the realization of an ideal vision of family in a global economy that constitutes certain children, and not others, as desirable. In India, this has meant the insistence by prospective adoptive parents on obtaining a child who is "perfect" in terms of skin color (as light as possible), the form of its eyes (as almond-shaped as possible), nose configuration, and physical health. One couple, who were adopting a newborn baby boy from SICW, arrived with the husband's mother while I was there, and became involved in a heated exchange with Swaran Chaudhry about whether the infant should be given an electrocardiogram. Chaudhry insisted that "the child has no heart problem," and advised the parents: "You are getting too tense about the whole situation. We'll get the tests that need to be done. Let the child be six weeks, we'll do all the [needed] tests."

Because of the policy that the most desirable children should be offered to Indian families (who in this way become engaged in constituting themselves, through their choice of a child, into the kind of family that will contribute to "healthy growth of the nation"), the directors of children's homes are dependent on international adoptions for the placement of older, darker, sicker children, "special needs" children, and low birth-weight babies who have been given into their care. These children are all encumbered in ways that make them undesirable for adoption in India, and orphanage staff use connections with long-term associates in Western agencies to place them in families overseas. At the same time, child welfare workers in India continue their campaign to broaden the understanding of what a family should look like for parents in India. This includes efforts to develop an effective foster parent program and encouraging more Indian parents to adopt or to foster physically challenged children, while working steadily to push the standards of adoptability among professionals and parents in receiving nations, encouraging them to accept ever older, more seriously challenged, and previously "unadoptable" children.

In this sense, an unintended consequence of the Indian Supreme Court decision in 1985 was that it *expanded* the market in children. By this I mean that it transformed more children who were "'priceless' in the full possible sense of the term" (Kopytoff 1986: 75) into precious national resources. Children who were excluded by the circumstances of their lives (abandoned in hospitals, on the streets, in orphanages, and so forth) from processes of symbolic and material exchange on which assessments of value are contingent in a market economy, became "precious" either at home or abroad as new market niches were opened through pressures from social workers, orphanage directors, agencies, adoptive parents, and the courts. This expansion of the sense in which children were valued in India also transformed the terms of the debate about adoption into a broader national exchange about abandonment and children's rights, encouraging child welfare professionals to develop a range of strategies responsive to the needs of impoverished women and children.

"You don't grab children . . ."

Andal Damodaran, Secretary of the Tamilnadu Council on Child Welfare and a powerful advocate for children's rights in India, argues that given the massive problems of poverty in India, the key questions are not so much about which kind of adoption (domestic or international) should be sought for an abandoned child, but rather:

> How do you prevent abandonment? How do you prevent destitution? I feel all agencies – both placement agencies in India and

receiving agencies abroad – have a responsibility to stop abandonment if it's possible. I'm not saying it's possible in every case. It
brings me to a very basic thing: You don't grab children just because
you want children. And I don't think placement agencies in India
should keep finding children because they've got families and they
can't run without doing a quota of intercountry adoptions.

(Interview, November, 1995)

Damodaran describes the 1985 Indian Supreme Court judgment as a
turning point, when "we started looking at things in another way. We
found so many cases of children being offered for adoption because
people would – couples would – abandon them due to poverty. And I
think that's unfair and unjust. Had the couple been told about what other
options were available, or did the placement agency just take the child
because it's one more kid?"

For Damodaran and others, birth mothers are at the center of a reform
program oriented towards what she describes as "the much wider issue
of empowerment and of rights," an issue that includes but goes beyond
the problems that surround child adoption. One of the most innovative
and successful programs of this kind is the mother and child welfare
project of Usilampatti in Madurai District, Tamilnadu. Partially funded
by Sweden's international development agency (SIDA), its aim is to
counsel pregnant women so as to prevent patterns of female infanticide,
which are widespread in the Usilampatti area. The program operates in
288 villages, by 1995 had counseled 1,500 pregnant women, and claims
to have stopped the practice of infanticide entirely in twenty-three of
the villages. The program works by establishing Grameen-style credit
unions for local women as a way of engaging them in collective economic
projects that will improve their conditions of life. But Damodaran empha-
sizes that the program has made possible "things which were much wider
than . . . saving a girl-child or just counseling the mothers. It's helped us
to organize, to get staff trained."

Empowerment is also a central concern for Nomita Chandy, Secretary
of Ashraya Children's Home in Bangalore. Chandy is the niece of Tara
Ali Baig, a legendary figure in Indian child welfare activism who was close
to Indira Gandhi. A strong, outspoken advocate for the rights of Indian
women and children, she describes herself as "looking like a nice, gentle,
pliable, malleable kind of person, which a lot of people mistake me for"
(interview, September, 1997), but if this is the initial impression she
creates, it is quickly dispelled. Chandy is a visionary, but one whose
feet are firmly on the ground. She was recruited in the 1970s by a local

representative of Stockholm's Adoption Centre in Delhi to help further
the adoption of Indian children to Sweden. Uncomfortable in this role
and critical of the ways adoptions were handled, Chandy persuaded
Adoption Centre to provide her with support to establish the Ashraya
Children's Home in Bangalore, where she developed a more broadly
based child welfare program in which foreign adoptions were only one
of many options for children.

Today, Ashraya is considered a model child welfare organization by
agencies in the West. It includes a program of temporary care for children
whose families need assistance, a strong domestic adoption program,
a program of "creches" which provide day care for over three hundred
children in the Bangalore area, and a foreign adoption program that
specializes in hard-to-place children (older, handicapped, sibling pairs,
and so forth). While Chandy is not opposed to international adoption,
she does not think that it should be the first option for children in need:
"I support multiple services for children, including international adoption." And while she continues to work closely with Adoption Centre
in Sweden, which has underwritten a number of her projects for
women and children, she is an outspoken critic of AC's refusal to accept
older and other types of special needs children, the children she considers
most appropriate for adoption abroad.

I also visited Chandy's newest project, a residential center for "dis-
tressed" mothers and their children (women who have been victims
of domestic abuse, who have been abandoned by their husbands, who
are unwed mothers, and so forth) located on the outskirts of Bangalore.
Designed like a village, the center has twenty-three units, built in small
clusters "so women can be by themselves for a while and when they feel
stronger can come out to the courtyard." Each cluster has a community
kitchen. The entire complex is served by a health care program, a program
for unwed mothers, a day care center, and a training area. Chandy explains
that she began planning the center, named Tara in honor of her aunt, in
1993 because "every time a mother came to us [at Ashraya] with a child
she could not care for, we felt we had to provide her with other options,
not just adoption."

Ashraya and Tara are only two of many programs developed in the
past two decades for the support of impoverished Indian women and
their children. Each contributes to the prevention of child abandonment
by providing alternatives (temporary institutional care for children,
temporary residential services for mothers with children) for women
whose children might otherwise be placed in substitute families in India
or overseas.

Unequal families

The value placed by international adoption law on the benefits of a "complete" or whole family for every child underpins practices that tacitly or explicitly encourage child abandonment by poor parents in the "sending" countries of the developing world. In an article that examines the parenting of middle- and upper-class New York children by West Indian childcare workers, Shellee Colen (1995) illustrates the different norms that shape motherhood across class and hints at the ways that state policy (in its failure to provide adequate resources for low-income women and their children) forces them to leave their children or "place them out," in this way contributing to practices that produce or may be interpreted as child abandonment by state officials or staff at children's homes (see also Fonseca 2003). Other research documents the ways in which poor, unmarried women are encouraged to relinquish their children in adoption on the premise (shared by the directors and staff of children's homes in a number of sending nations) that the child of a single mother or of parents living below the poverty line will be better off in an adoptive family abroad (Hoelgaard 1998).

As internationally adopted teenagers and adults return to visit the orphanages, families, and nations where they spent their first months or years, they are beginning to raise questions about these assumptions and to explore the possibilities for establishing ongoing relations with people they experience as kin in their countries of birth (Aronson 1997; Liem 2000; Kim 2003). Inevitably, these relations are extremely complicated, and it is unclear what import they will have for adoption policy and practice in the coming decades. For adoptees, they may help in answering the questions, "Who am I?" and "Why was I abandoned?", while opening up other disturbing questions about the inclusions and exclusions of international adoption practice.

Anna Chuchu Petersson, adopted from Ethiopia by Swedish parents when she was two, returned in 1997 on a visit in which she searched for and found her birth family, found the experience of having two families, especially "two mothers," initially unsettling. When she was in Ethiopia, she said,

> I couldn't afford to have any feelings, because it was too overwhelming. And when I came home to Sweden, I felt terrible. It was partly because I was physically sick, but I was put in the hospital. I think a lot of it was psychological, actually. But it felt so good to lie there in the hospital when I came home, in a completely white room,

no impressions, nothing, and it was completely quiet. Then I could begin to think a little. So I lay and cried for maybe two days. I hadn't been able to handle any feelings down there, it was too much for me. My mamma Ulla here at home handled it really well. I mean she did not become anxious. When I lay in the hospital she just came and lay next to me in the bed, without speaking. She didn't attempt to ask me a lot of things. She did not try to come to conclusions about what had happened. Others were very curious and kept asking how my mother felt. But she herself was not, it didn't feel that way.

(Interview, August 22, 1999)

Chuchu returned to Ethiopia in 1999 with her friend Amanda, who was also adopted from there, and they spent a month with their respective birth families – two weeks with each. This time, Chuchu said, the return to Sweden was less traumatic.

The most important thing for me when we were in Addis was that we spent a lot of time with my family and with my brothers and sister. I have ten brothers and a sister, and they have children. And my mother and my father – they are divorced and both are eager when I come to be together with me. . . . But the biggest thing for me was when we went to their village and slept over at my mother's house. . . . To wake up in her bed, and that she tucked me in at night, and caressed my cheek. That was a big thing for me (*jättestort*). Amanda and I slept in the same bed, so she tucked us both in. They treated us like sisters the whole time. My mother said: "That is my child, too. I will take care of her."

After a third trip to Addis, in 2002, Chuchu described herself as feeling "more relaxed" because of the time she has now spent with her Ethiopian family:

I feel that I have tried and I have given what I can. I haven't been able to move there and I haven't wanted to live there permanently. But I have been able to travel there and stay for longer periods, and that has perhaps given me a certain distance. It has made me feel calmer. . . . At the same time, it has become clear to me how close these people are to me. They are incredibly important to me, and will always be so. And that is why I perhaps don't need to pursue them quite so much any more. . . . That is, I don't have to search for that part of myself in the same way.

I feel as though I have gathered together what I can. I can't reverse time. There are those two years before I came to Sweden. I have done what I can to assemble a kind of tote-bag, something I always carry with me that contains my Ethiopia. It is not the Ethiopia that many immigrants talk about, but it is the one I share with Amanda and Sara and Hanna, I think.

Chuchu's friend Amanda, describing her own reunion with her parents and six siblings in Ethiopia several years ago, explained:

What I felt so powerfully and have more or less understood intellectually, is that one is their child, that is just the way it is. . . . And that can be difficult because it sometimes means that there are expectations, with regard to money and helping them. But for my part, I feel really good about that.

Chuchu noted that "here in Sweden, there is no one who supports one in that feeling. Here it is something that scares people."

The experiences of these adoptees are in some senses unique, growing out of specific situations, the time when they were adopted, and the nation in which they were raised. At the same time, their stories resonate with those of others of their generation in Sweden and elsewhere and may lead to a radical rethinking of what the practice of international adoption should become in the twenty-first century.[6] Rather than a cut-off from the past, adoption is increasingly bringing the past into the present in a multitude of ways, through roots trips to the birth country, reunions between adoptees and their birth families, culture camps and language classes for adoptees, and other practices that acknowledge the birth "identity" of the adopted child.

It remains to be seen to what extent these practices will have an impact on state and international adoption policies. In some sense, the fascination with a child's birth culture and the insistence on the need for the child to "return" in order to become whole is simply one more re-enactment of commodity thinking and the longing for exclusive belongings to which this gives rise. As Adoption Centre's Gunilla Andersson suggests, fascination with the "wonderful birth culture" of a child may stand in the way of coming to terms with the tragedy that underlies her adoption. The enforced cut-off of this child from her "past" and the assumptions about family and individual "completeness" in which such cut-offs are entangled, complicate the lived experiences of *in*completeness with which we all struggle, compelling us in a search for "integration, culmination and closure" (Ricoeur 1992: 22). The fiction of closure in adoption law is in ironic contrast to the mother tending to the child who is not "hers" and whose capacity to say, "This is my child, too. I will take care of her," reminds us of how dependent we are on others for the sense that we have become "complete" in ourselves.

Notes

1 Research on which this article is based was supported by the National Science Foundation (grant #SBR-9511937) and by faculty development grants from Hampshire College. My research would not have been possible without the generosity and participation of women in India, Sweden, Colombia, and Chile who are engaged in finding homes for homeless children, and without the cooperation and generosity of adult adoptees who participated in my project. I thank Nina Payne, Nomita Chandy, Claudia Fonseca, and Kay Johnson for their helpful comments on earlier drafts.

2 For a critique of modernist conceptions of childhood and family, and the problems of such conceptions for the welfare of children, see Zelizer (1985), Stephens (1995), and Gailey (1998).

3 My understanding of "commodity" follows Strathern (1997), who argues that commodities are "free-standing entities," anonymously produced so that they can become "part of a store on which others draw." The strong preference expressed in the Hague Convention and in receiving nations for plenary adoptions – adoptions that terminate the existing legal relationships that link a child to her natal kin – transform the child into a commodity in Strathern's sense. That is, they render the child into a freestanding entity by dissolving the links between the child and the network of persons into which it was born. As this suggests, commodification is not simply about the sale of children, a practice that is universally condemned. Commodification is a consequence of cutting off a child, construing her as "anonymously-produced" (1997: 302), the child of no one, so that s/he can be given or placed in a new family or nation.

4 Duncan (1993: 53), commenting on the widely held view among delegates at the Hague Conference on Intercountry Adoption that "adoption which completely severs ties with the biological family is the most appropriate model for intercountry adoption," notes that "there is a certain irony in this at a time when on the domestic front a number of countries are reassessing the value for the adopted child of retaining links with biological parents."

5 Triseliotis (1991: 412) notes that studies of contact between adoptive children and their birth kin indicate that "maintenance of meaningful links with the birth family appear to be beneficial to children, to their sense of identity and self esteem and for gaining a better understanding of their genealogical background and adoption circumstances," provided that there is a framework of legal security with the adoptive family. While Triseliotis focuses particularly (although not exclusively) on older child adoptions, other studies support his claim that contact between birth and adoptive kin do not disrupt adoptive placements and may facilitate them. See McRoy et al. (1994).

6   See, for example, Trotzig (1996), Aronson (1997), von Melen (1998), and the documentary film *First Person Plural* (Liem 2000).

References

Aronson, J. C. 1997. Not My Homeland, Senior thesis, Hampshire College, Amherst, Massachusetts.

Carlson, R. R. 1994. The Emerging Law of Intercountry Adoptions: An Analysis of the Hague Conference on Intercountry Adoption. *Tulsa Law Journal* 30, 243–304.

Colen, S. 1995. "Like a Mother to Them": Stratified Reproduction and West Indian Childcare Workers and Employers in New York. In *Conceiving the New World Order* (eds) F. D. Ginsburg and R. Rapp. Berkeley: University of California Press.

Collier, J., M. Z. Rosaldo, and S. Yanagisako 1982. Is There a Family? New Anthropological Views. In *Rethinking the Family* (eds) B. Thorne and M. Yalom. New York and London: Longman.

Duncan, W. 1993. Regulating Intercountry Adoption – an International Perspective. In *Frontiers of Family Law* (eds) A. Bainham and D. S. Pearl. London: John Wiley & Sons.

Fonseca, C. 2003. Patterns of Shared Parenthood among the Brazilian Poor. *Social Text* 21, 111–127.

Gailey, C. 1998. Making Kinship in the Wake of History: Gendered Violence and Older Child Adoption. *Identities* 5, 249–292.

Hague Convention on Protection of Children and Co-operation in Respect of Intercountry Adoption 1993. Hague Conference on Private International Law, Final Act of the 17th Session, May 29, 1993, 32 I.L.M. 1134.

Hoelgaard, S. 1998. Cultural Determinants of Adoption Policy: A Colombian Case Study. *International Journal of Law, Policy and the Family* 12, 202–241.

Hollinger, J. H. 1993. Adoption Law. *The Future of Children* 3, 43–61.

Howell, S. 1998. Self-Conscious Kinship: Some Contested Values in Norwegian Transnational Adoption. Paper delivered at the 97th Annual Meeting of the American Anthropological Association, Philadelphia, 2–6 December.

Kim, E. 2003. Wedding Citizenship and Culture, *Social Text* 21, 57–81.

Kopytoff, I. 1986. The Cultural Biography of Things. In *The Social Life of Things* (ed.) A. Appadurai. Cambridge: Cambridge University Press.

Lakshmi Kant Pandey v. Union of India 1985. Writ Petition Crl. No. 1171 of 1982. Decided 27 September 1985.

Liem, D. B. 2000. *First Person Plural*. Ho-Ho-Kus, N.J.: Mu Films.

McRoy, R., H. D. Grotevant, and S. Ayers-Lopez 1994. *Changing Practices in Adoption*. Austin, Texas: Hogg Foundation for Mental Health.

Ricoeur, P. 1992. Life in Quest of Narrative. In *On Paul Ricoeur* (ed.) David Wood. London: Routledge.

Stephens, S. 1995. Children and the Politics of Culture in "Late Capitalism." In

Children and the Politics of Culture (ed.) S. Stephens. Princeton: Princeton University Press.

Strathern, M. 1997. Partners and Consumers: Making Relations Visible. In *The Logic of the Gift* (ed.) A. D. Schrift. New York: Routledge.

Therborn, G. 1996. Child Politics: Dimensions and Perspectives. *Childhood* 3, 29–44.

Triseliotis, J. 1991. Maintaining the Links in Adoption. *British Journal of Social Welfare* 21, 401–414.

Trotzig, A. 1996. *Blod är tjockare än vatten*. Stockholm: Bonniers.

Von Melen, A. 1998. *Samtal med vuxna adopterade*. Stockholm: Raben Prisma.

Yngvesson, B. 2003. Going "Home": Adoption, Loss of Bearings, and the Mythology of Roots. *Social Text* 21, 7–27.

Zelizer, V. 1985. *Pricing the Priceless Child*. Princeton: Princeton University Press.

Chapter 15

The backpackers that come to stay

New challenges to Norwegian transnational adoptive families[1]

Signe Howell

> Transnationally adopted children are *not* born at the airport.
>
> (Leader of the Association for Adoptive Parents)

Involuntary infertility is never a happy condition. Involuntary infertility represents a rupture – personal, social and historical – of the flow of life for the couples concerned, their relatives and their friends. In a country such as Norway, in which a comparatively high proportion of women give birth,[2] where values placed on kinned relations predominate over most social relations, and where couples tend to interact with their contemporaries as families, not to have children becomes a heavy burden for involuntary childless couples (Howell 2001). Contemporary cultural expectations hold that a woman, and increasingly a man, cannot fulfil themselves without embracing parenthood. In a certain sense they are incomplete social beings. Those who want children, but are unable to reproduce themselves biologically, therefore have to turn to alternative methods of procreation. Available options fall into two separate, but related, kinds: the various forms of new reproductive technologies (NRT), and adoption. Domestic adoption is virtually non-existent in Norway. A combination of medical provision, cultural attitudes and economic provision enable a pregnant woman to decide whether or not to have the child. Abortion on demand has been available since 1975. Single mothers are not stigmatised and they receive sufficient financial support to enable them to bring up children on their own. These factors have led to few unwanted babies being born and, hence, few Norwegian-born babies available for adoption. It is not surprising therefore that many Norwegian involuntarily infertile couples have embraced transnational adoption as the solution to their dilemma.

My studies have shown that between half and two-thirds of those who have adopted in the past ten years have first tried some form of NRT. This is experienced by most as extremely distressing and stressful. My studies also show that after they have obtained a child through adoption, most couples express regret concerning the time wasted on techniques of assisted conception. Had they known what they know now, they say, they would have gone straight for adoption. "Adoption is the natural way for us to have children" one adoptive father of two children from Korea told me.

Franklin and Ragoné argue that "an important genealogy of modern anthropology can readily be traced through its relationship to a core set of ideas related to reproduction" (1998: 2). Indeed, the early founders of the discipline made a comparative study of ideas of procreation and kinship their starting point for analysing social organisation. Although these theoreticians were at pains to declare that kinship should be studied as a classification system of significant others, they nevertheless unquestionably maintained a biological model of procreation and kinship as their point of reference. Social practices that seemed to emphasise different criteria for relatedness emerged as highly problematic[3] or were dismissed as "fictive kinship" (cf. Schneider 1984). Research on adoption is particularly well placed to examine these basic assumptions. My research on transnational adoption in Norway has convinced me of two related facts: first that biology remains the model by which most people approach kinned relatedness, and second that adoptive parents do not regard their relationship with their adopted children as in any sense fictive; rather it results in a kinship that is highly self-conscious. I have argued elsewhere (Howell 1999) that a pattern of fluctuating between foregrounding and backgrounding biology and sociality according to context is observable amongst adoptive parents.

In this chapter I want to explore some aspects of the adoption process as it has been, and currently is, perceived and evaluated in Norwegian society. I shall focus on some of the implications of the statement quoted at the outset, namely that transnationally adopted children are *not* born at the airport in Norway when their adoptive parents first meet them.[4] I am particularly interested in identifying changes that may be observed in cultural attitudes regarding the importance attributed to the child's circumstances before arriving in Norway. From being a topic of very little interest to those concerned, it has obtained great significance in the eyes of adoption agencies and, by extension, the adoptive parents. It is receiving particular attention in those cases when the adopted children fail to settle down in their new circumstances and challenge their parents with unforeseen problems of various kinds.

Transnational adoption the Norwegian way

Transnational adoption took off in Norway in the late 1960s and has been increasing in volume ever since. Approximately six hundred children from about twenty different countries arrive each year to new parents. This figure represents slightly more than 1 per cent of the annual birth rate and makes Norway the largest recipient *per capita* of any country of children from overseas for adoption. In stating that these children are *not* born at the airport, the speaker highlighted important changes in attitude. She challenges frequently heard claims, even if made in jest, that an adopted child was indeed born at the airport. This she wished to debunk as not only incorrect but, in light of recent experiences, damaging. However, as far as the adoptive parents are concerned, the child became a living reality to them at the moment of the first encounter. From this moment they engage in a meaningful relationship. Henceforth, the child is indisputably *their* child, and they have been transformed into a normal family. Upon arrival in Norway the child receives a new birth certificate, new nationality, new names, new language and new kin. A new social birth has been effected. But the child was, of course, already born. It was born by unknown (to the adoptive family) biological parents in an unknown country where unknown people had been engaged in its becoming a person. The language of "coming home" helps disguise this fact. The adoption agencies list the number of children who have "come home" each year from different countries with whom they have an arrangement. Parents send photos to be published in the agencies' magazines of children who have "come home".

Implicitly the transnationally adopted child has been regarded as *tabula rasa* by parents and authorities alike. Whereas all concerned assumed that they would effortlessly become Norwegian children, a noticeable shift in attitudes can be observed in recent years. Today, one increasingly hears that children arrive with a "backpack" full of past experiences. Although the amount of "baggage" in the backpack varies with each child, the implicit message of this metaphor is that the past, however brief, has consequences for the child's development in its new circumstances. The pre-Norwegian past can no longer be ignored. It is increasingly taken to have been formative in the development of the child's personality and identity. As a result of this shift in understanding, many parents are developing a new-found interest in the period before the child came to them.

This shift in explanatory models can be linked to earlier nature/ nurture debates in understanding child development. Changes in intel- lectual fashion regarding these issues affect those involved professionally with adoption as well as adoptive parents, with a noticeable shift in the relative weighting given to biological as opposed to social factors. This is exemplified most crudely in a talk given by a social worker to an audience of adoptive parents at which she stated, "when I first began in this business [adoption] more than thirty years ago, we believed that personality and identity was a question of 70 per cent environmental factors and 30 per cent biological ones. Today, research has shown that these figures should be reversed". This statement demonstrates what I have called elsewhere an increasing biologization of discourses of personhood and identity in much of the modern Western world. Recent research in medicine and genetics is probably a major contributory factor in this biologization, and it is interesting to observe the effects on adoption discourses. I wish to suggest that there is a trickle-down effect from medical research, through psychology to social workers and adoption agencies, ending up with the adoptive parents.

The roles of the adoption agencies

Scandinavian adoption agencies, unlike those in the USA and parts of Europe, are non-profit-making NGOs. In Norway there are three agencies and they are under ministerial surveillance. They link children in orphanages in about twenty different countries to couples already approved by local government social services bureaucracies as well as by a national adoption bureau. However, these agencies are much more than providers of children and the scope of their roles is ever-increasing. Today they are major disseminators of knowledge about the adoption process itself and values attached to it. It would not be too far-fetched to claim that the agencies are the prime source of parental attitudes. They organise courses in preparatory parenthood for groups of waiting parents, they publish books and pamphlets on practical and theoretical issues pertaining to adopting children from overseas, they transmit information about the donating countries and cultures, they organise seminars, talks, and conferences on various topics held to be of interest and relevance to adoptive families, and they publish regular magazines for their members that contain increasingly sophisticated articles on psychological, medical, educational and social issues pertaining to transnational adoption.

The effects attributed to the quality of environmental and nurturing factors in early infancy were strongly argued during the 1960s and 1970s by influential psychologists. The statement by the Norwegian social worker cited above confirms its orthodoxy. The influential psychologist John Bowlby, for example, concluded that if a child was repeatedly separated from its mother during its first year, this affected its personality development detrimentally. Such children tended to go through a process from anger to despair to apathy. Similarly, the famous paediatrician and psychoanalyst D. W. Winnicot argued that there is no such creature as "a baby", there are only "mother and child couples", or "social environment and child couples" (Kats 1990: 18, 28). While these ideas were broadly speaking taken up in Norwegian psychological circles, it is curious that they were not brought to bear on the situation of the transnationally adopted children. Or rather they were applied only to the time after arrival in Norway. In the early days of transnational adoption it was more or less taken for granted that once the children arrived "home" to their adoptive parents they would rapidly become Norwegian. The pre-Norwegian situation of the children was hardly taken into account. Although the fact of adoption could not be hidden since the children look quite different from their parents, it was largely ignored as a topic for discussion. Instead everyone focused on the speed with which the children seemed to adjust to their new lives. Letters to the journal expressed how fast the children put on weight and grew, how quickly they learnt the language, how affectionate they were towards their parents and other relatives and so on. The discourse reflected the feelings of delighted couples whose dream of becoming a normal family was being fulfilled. Every effort was made to transform the children into happy, normal Norwegian children. Such was the aim. Its success was confirmed again and again in reports in the agencies' magazines.

The majority of adoptions are successful. Most adoptees adjust well to their new circumstances, however, some do not, and we are witnessing an increasing willingness to confront the fact that some adoptions provide serious challenges to all concerned. The publication of an account by an adoptive father of the extremely distressing experience of living with his two children adopted from a Latin American country provoked much debate (Øhren 1995). It was one of many contributing factors that led to the emergence of a serious concern with the significance of roots, of genes, of original culture in influential adoptive circles – as well as in the Norwegian social climate more generally. This renders the process of easy transformation more problematic. Today the question of whether one should aim for a complete transformation of the self (as earlier was taken for granted) or deliberately foster a dual attitude to identity in the children (for instance, Norwegian *and* Korean) has become important for many.

The kinning of adopted children

Perhaps because of the time and effort, both practical and emotional, they have invested in becoming a family, adoptive parents as a group are noticeably more actively engaged in child-centred activities than are biological parents. It is my impression that adoptive parents of the past, as well as of today, are more eager than most parents to replicate "normal family life". So much of what is taken for granted by biological parents becomes a matter for deliberate achievement for adoptive ones. In this quest, any detrimental implications of the fact of adoption are, not surprisingly, downplayed. Thus adoptive parents work hard at "kinning" their children (Howell 2003). Becoming a son or daughter, grandchild, niece or nephew is never an automatic process – although it very often is thought of as such. What I wish to argue is that parents (and/or other significant kin) everywhere engage in their children's subjectivation, and that they do so in the idiom of kinship. Kinship may thus be regarded as fixing the self in relation to significant others (Faubion 2001). Through rituals of various kinds, through exchanges between kin and affines, and through acknowledging each other as kin, meaningful relatedness is established. However, precisely because kinning is obviously not automatic where adoption is concerned, the activities engaged in by adoptive parents highlight the kind of kinning work that is engaged in with regard to children elsewhere in society. In Norway, where flesh and blood are central metaphors for relatedness across generations, adopted children represent a contradiction. In transforming adopted children into kin, the parents have to negotiate a challenging path where sociality and biology fight for precedence.

In light of all these uncomfortable challenges it was very convenient to maintain the fiction that one's child was born at the airport, and to ignore the implications of the child's unknown biological origins and the content of their past life and experiences. Recent changes in parents' attitudes necessarily affect those of the children. Their self-perceptions are influenced by debates on such topics and I wish to explore some implications of these changes in the rest of this chapter.

The birthing of the adopted child

There is a liminal phase between the stripping of a child's original social identity and obtaining a new one. This is a period that corresponds to what I have called the birthing of the adopted child (Howell 1999, 2002). In temporal terms it coincides with the moment when a child is allocated by the donor organisation (usually an orphanage) to its prospective parents, and ends with the actual handing-over from the donor to the recipient. This birthing period lasts from anything from four months to several years. From the adoptive parents' point of view this period can be used to start the kinning process, and strong emotional bonds are forged immediately information is received about the allocated child. They are sent a photograph and brief biographical data of the child that is being "born" to them. Although given the option to decline the offer of a particular child, my material shows that this happens very rarely, even if sex and age are not what had been stipulated. It is as if the expectant parents accept what is given them much as biological parents must accept whatever child is born to them. Indeed, parents seem to believe that fate somehow plays a part. Many are of the opinion that the administrators at the orphanage spend much time and effort in matching the characteristics of a child with those provided by the Norwegian agency about each couple. Upon the child's arrival, parents tend to look for similarities between themselves and the child. Of course, they know perfectly well that these can arise only by pure chance, but it is noticeable that adoptive parents identify personality traits in common with their children as they grow up. This may even extend to physical characteristics. I once expressed my surprise at the curly hair of an adopted girl from Thailand. The mother exclaimed, "but of course she has curly hair, just look at my hair!" Although said jokingly, there were serious undertones to the statement.

The bonding that occurs upon allocation is strong and forms the basis for the future relationship. The waiting parents distribute the child's photograph to their kin and friends. The child is given a Norwegian name – a name which is put on the subsequent new birth certificate and which will signal its new identity as a family member. Formerly a Norwegian name replaced the original foreign one, whereas now adoption agencies advise parents to keep one original name as a middle name. This is because, it is claimed, it will help to integrate the two sides of the child's identity, deriving from its country of origin and from Norway.

During this liminal period the child is talked about a lot and preparations are made for his or her arrival. The depth of the attachment is demonstrated by a case in which the allocated child died before arriving in Norway. The parents wrote an article about this for the adoption agency magazine in which they describe their grief and the ceremony that they organized for her in the local church (*Adopsjonsforum* No. 1, 1999). It was a funeral service without a body. A memorial plaque was erected in the churchyard and the service was attended by various categories of kin.

The birthing period ends when the child is united with its waiting parents; when it has "come home". Now the child is experienced as a real human being with needs and desires, and the intersubjective kinning process between child and parents can start.

Ambiguities of the law

A number of ambiguities concerning the identity of adopted children and adoptive parents may be observed in Norwegian thinking and cultural practices. This comes out particularly clearly in the legal provisions. An historic overview of the various white papers, acts and amendments to the acts gives insight into changing cultural values regarding the meaning and quality of an adoptive relationship. The first Adoption Act was passed in 1917. It was one of the earliest in Europe. Its formulations reveal that biological connectedness was unquestionably regarded as being of overriding importance. Unless otherwise stated, adopted children inherited from their biological parents, not from their adoptive ones. Biological and adopted children did not have equal rights in their parents and adoption was engaged in for the benefit of the parents, usually in order to provide an heir. At that time few attempts were made to hide the nature of the relationship. Adoptions might even be dissolved if the adoptive parents were dissatisfied. Amendments to the act during the 1950s demonstrate changing attitudes. While biology was still the reigning metaphor, reasons for wishing to adopt were less pragmatic and more driven by psychological motivations. Adoption had become an issue that concerned the involuntarily childless couple alone and the practice had become shrouded in secrecy. There was no legal requirement for parents to inform their adopted children about the state of their relatedness, and many chose not to.

A major shift occurs again with the Adoption Act of 1986 in which it is stated unequivocally that adoption must be in the best interest of the child. Adopted children become in every way equal to biological children and they have equal rights of inheritance. Adoption is permanent and indissoluble. Although this was not included in the final Act, the White Paper preceding it made a distinction between what it called biological kinship and social kinship, stating that in practice no differences exist. However, the law changed the standard expressions from "own children" and "real parents" to "biological children" and "original parents" (Ingvaldsen 1996). Nevertheless, having firmly established the equality between biological and adopted children, the law goes on to state the right of adopted children to be told about their biological origins upon reaching legal maturity. An underlying theme runs through all debates and hearings in connection with the Act, namely that the desire to know about biological origins is a powerful and natural one and, as such, has to be accommodated. A question that immediately arises in the mind of the analyst is to what extent and by whom, adopted children are thought of as equal to, or different from, biological children. My argument is that this will vary according to context.

The end of the idyll

There has been a tendency in Norway to focus upon the idyllic aspects of adoption. The magazines of the adoption agencies are full of sunshine stories. Photos of children newly arrived "home", the first day at school, confirmation and, increasingly, wedding photographs are appearing. The fact that not all children adjust equally well to their new circumstances has, until recently, been ignored by all but the involved parties, who have tended to keep it to themselves. What is becoming clear is that the parents whose children failed to settle down and who developed serious behavioural problems have experienced a massive destruction of the dream of becoming a normal family. To make matters worse, most have had no one to talk to. Many parents with children who have experienced extreme difficulties in coping with life in Norway feel bitter about the lack of warning they were given concerning the significance of early history upon later development. The emphasis placed on environment as the determining factor led many parents who adopted older children to believe that entering a loving and well-appointed home would negate whatever unhappy experiences the child might have had. When this turned out not to be the case, they felt bewildered and betrayed, and many experienced guilt-related reactions. Norwegian social services are predominantly geared towards giving assistance to families where the parents in some way fail. Their theoretical apparatus is little suited to dealing with families which are severely challenged because of problems arising out of the child rather than the parents. In line with this, many parents perceive themselves as failing and this can produce a powerful sense of guilt. It is not uncommon for them to be told by social workers that it was their choice to adopt from overseas and they must take the consequences when things don't turn out the way they had hoped.

In light of this situation, the recently formed Association for Adoptive Parents (AAP), whose leader is quoted at the outset of this chapter, have filled a need. The members of the association have been able to voice their anxieties, frustrations, unhappiness and feelings of guilt for the first time in a forum of equals. At the same time the adoption agencies have begun to take up issues connected to adoptions that somehow went wrong. The adoptee with a "backpack" filled with early experiences is increasingly appearing in the literature and discussions. One agency arranged in 1998 its first course intended for parents with adopted children in, or about to reach, puberty. Puberty is presented as a period when adopted children begin to question their identity and rebel against their situation. This coincides with a view of puberty as a period in people's life when tumultuous physiological and biological changes take place which somehow result in existential questionings and rebellion against authority – particularly parents. Adopted children are thought to experience puberty more intensely than other young people, and there is some evidence to support such claims. In a recent study of children receiving some kind of assistance from child care services in Norway there are virtually no transnationally adopted children below the age of twelve, whereas between fifteen and nineteen they supersede the Norwegian-born. A peak is reached at sixteen when 4.7 per cent of transnationally adopted children (or their families) receive support of some kind, as opposed to 2.7 per cent of Norwegian-born children (Kalve 1999: 14). While these figures represent the extreme end of the situation, it is nevertheless indicative of the difficulties experienced during puberty by some transnationally adopted children.[5]

In trying to handle this situation, we again encounter an ambiguous and ambivalent attitude among professionals and parents. The explanatory pendulum swings from biology to sociality and back and the child now stands forth as anything but a *tabula rasa*. Rather, the child is presented as having a backpack full of unpleasant experiences, both physical and psychological, which are thought to have affected emotional and psychological stability. Many scientific terms are bandied about. A particularly well-received term is "early emotional damage". An article about this phenomenon was published in one of the agencies' magazines by a psychologist – himself the father of a transnationally adopted child, who has made a special study of these children. Basing his argument on ideas of psycho-social development by the psychologist E. H. Erikson, he suggests that children develop during their first year a basis-feeling made up of trust versus mistrust. People go through life reproducing the particular basis-feeling created during early relationships in their subsequent relationships. With a background of frequent ruptures in the identity of their main nurturer, the primary experience of adopted children is one of unpredictability, disturbance and chaos. This may be interpreted by the infant as rejection and lead to a general distrust of adults. It is this experience which forms the basis-feeling of these children who, in later life, seek to reproduce it. The child does this in order to re-create a sense of security, perversely derived from an experience of rejection. It is this that is termed early emotional damage and which is held to affect the adopted child's behaviour. Unconsciously, the child's behaviour becomes dictated by rejection, which it then reinforces in its new relationships. This may manifest itself in a self-destructive rejection of others, and "[they] act almost on principle 'against' in order to recreate their sense of security" (Haarklou 1998: 5).

What we see here is a return to the ideas of Bowlby and others but now applied to the transnationally adopted child. The author was subsequently invited to speak at a members meeting of the AAP to which a large number of people turned up. They expressed immense satisfaction with someone not only putting into words what they had experienced in their own families, but also with providing sensible explanations for it. At such meetings a rational (but not emotional) distancing of the child is observable on the part of the parents. They acknowledge the child's different origins and identity, which become distinct from their own in ways they had earlier sought to negate. They now have to confront the differences and their own inability to cope with them. The backpack idiom becomes a helpful metaphor for understanding, for forgiving and for reducing the pain and guilt. New bonds are forged between adoptive parents whose dreams of happy families have been shattered. The relationships that people from otherwise divergent socio-economic backgrounds create strikes deep chords, and the shared painful life situation overrides other differences. In this forum of unhappiness, an analytical focus on environmental factors reigns. It is the early experiences of the child that are made relevant for its personality and identity development when these show signs of maladjustment, not the child's genetic make-up. Interestingly, despite the increasing preoccupation with biology in society at large, the adoptive parents rarely attribute the difficulties to genetic factors. The Association of Adoptive Parents fights for a public recognition of the special situation of their children and demand that the public social and health services take account of their child's backpack with its possible negative consequences, rather than placing all the responsibilities on the parents.

The significance of roots

This focus on the adopted children's past is related to a new concern in adoption circles with "roots". The two largest adoption agencies have members of staff whose jobs are in part to deal with this question. Articles appear regularly about adopted children who return to their country of origin in order to search for biological family members. Those whose aims are less ambitious visit the orphanage where they lived before coming to Norway and hope to meet any staff who knew them. Parents are strongly encouraged to take their children on one of the increasingly popular "roots" or "motherland tours" to their country of origin. There are several reasons proffered. The most frequently heard are that the children should be instilled with a sense of pride in their "original culture", and that a visit will assist them in handling the dual aspect of their identities. Such views are somewhat vaguely linked to an assumed universal and natural desire to find out about one's origins (see Howell 2002).

Somewhat different reasons for undertaking return visits can be detected in the families who experience real difficulties from those for whom life is relatively unproblematic. In so far as the "unsuccessful" families become preoccupied with roots, it is primarily in order to fill in concrete gaps in the knowledge of the child's early life in order to understand and explain the difficulties they have been going through. "The differences between our children and Norwegian-born children is not the colour of their skin, or the country of origin, but the fact that they have had very different early childhoods," stated one adoptive mother at an AAP gathering. The journey to the country of origin for these families often becomes one that deliberately seeks to confront the unhappy past. The ultimate aim is to drive out the effects of the bad memories contained in the backpack.[6] The preoccupation of these parents with the content of their children's early past is thus a very different search for roots than that which other adoptive parents (and children) engage in. The latter usually express an open-ended desire to link up with the country, the culture, the places and people in order to gain an understanding about their children's origins. They search for pieces in the jigsaw puzzle for the sake of completeness rather than as a source of explanation. The children are happy "to see for themselves" what the country and the people look like, and for most it is little more than an exciting holiday. It is in keeping with a general Norwegian preoccupation with place of origin (Howell 2002).

Conclusion

The kinning process of the adopted child who fails to adapt is no different from that engaged in by the adoptive parents of the child who adapts easily. The anticipation, the preparation, the joy of finally becoming parents are shared by all. The activities directed at symbolically planting the child in the kinned soil of its parents and connecting it to their own kinned places are engaged in by all adoptive parents and serve to incorporate the child into its parents' families and kin (Howell 2003). For example, adopted children visit their grandparents more frequently than do biological grandchildren (Botvar 1994). The early days of having an adopted child are, in most cases, characterized by ignoring the child's alien origins and by emphasizing the quality of the new sociality being forged with parents and kin. There is little, if any, direct interest in the child's origins; everyone looks towards the future. Unequivocally, the child becomes its adoptive parents' child. In light of this, I find the concept of fictive kinship (see Schneider 1984) inappropriate. In my view, the situation is better characterized by a notion of self-conscious kinship. It is characteristically a period of excited optimism. The dream of becoming a normal family is energetically pursued. The vast majority of families achieve their dream, but for the minority whose children fail to settle down, the disappointment becomes hard to cope with. However, I have not come across a single parent who wished to sever their relationship with their child, however difficult the relationship might be. Their love and loyalty and willingness to work on their child's behalf is as strong as if the child were born to them. Perhaps precisely because of the dream, the effort spent in obtaining a child, and the intense kinning engaged in at the outset, the fact of profound connectedness is never questioned. There are, however, a rapidly increasing number of complaints about faulty or incomplete information prior to adoption, and the failure of the social services to provide relevant help when things take a bad turn.[7] A much more serious attitude may be observed with regard to information about the children's lives before they were sent to their new homes. The earlier *tabula rasa* attitude is replaced with a belief that much has already happened to shape a child's identity during its first months and years in its country of origin, resulting in an increasing reluctance to allow adoption of older children.

Despite a biologization of discourses about human nature, personhood and health in contemporary Norway, discourses emphasizing sociality continue to exist in parallel. This is particularly noticeable in adoption circles with an oscillation between the two discourses according to context (Howell 1999, 2001). Thus, biology is foregrounded at times of trying to become pregnant as well as during puberty. Sociality is foregrounded in matters pertaining to development of personality and identity. I have argued that environmental factors before a child arrives in Norway increasingly constitute an explanatory model of personality development. This model becomes particularly relevant when the child fails to adapt successfully to the new life on offer. Directly related to this shift in focus, I argue, is the importance attributed to the baggage that the children carry with them in their backpacks as they leave their countries of origin.

Notes

1   The research this chapter is based on began in 1997 and is part of a larger project entitled "the meanings of kinship in Norway", partly funded by the Norwegian Research Council. I have received much assistance from the three adoption agencies: Verdens barn, Adopsjonsforum and Inoradopt and am very grateful for their interest. I particularly wish to thank the many adoptive parents who have shared with me their experiences and thoughts.

2   Between 92 and 94 per cent of women in Norway have given birth before they are forty. This is a higher proportion than in other Western countries (Sundby and Schei 1996).

3   For a thorough critical review of the "virgin birth" debate, see Franklin 1999.

4   The statement about the airport is to be taken metaphorically to stand for first encounter. With the exception of some Latin American countries who always insist on adoptive parents collecting their children themselves, until recently most children met their new parents at the airport escorted by an employee of the adoption agency. Today, however, most adoptive parents choose to travel to donor countries in order to bring the child home themselves.

5   Due to the virtual non-existence of Norwegian-born adoptees, this category is not included in the study.

6   The healing effects attributed to such visits is manifest in the case of a local authority which, on the advice of a psychologist, paid for an adolescent girl who had exhausted other means of assistance to visit to her country of origin, together with a social worker and distant relative.

7   The fate of the adopted children is clearly not one of either total acceptance or rejection of their circumstances. Like all children, adoptees experience varying degrees of contentment. Transnationally adopted children do not receive any special attention from the social services once they have arrived. Some parents are beginning to demand a follow-up service on par with that provided for domestic adoption or fostering.

References

Botvar, P.K. 1994 *Ny sjanse i Norge: Utelandsadoptertes oppvekst og levekår*, Oslo: Diaforsk Research report.

Faubion, J. 2001 *The Ethic of Kinship*, Lanham: Rowman & Littlefield.

Franklin, S. 1999 *Embodied Progress: A Cultural Account of Assisted Conception*, London: Routledge.

Franklin, S. and Ragoné, H. 1998 *Reproducing Reproduction*, Philadelphia: University of Pennsylvania Press.

Haarklou, J. 1998 "Adopotivbarn med tidlig følelsesmessig skade" *Verdens Barn* 10 (2): 4–7.

Howell, S. 1999 "Biologizing and de-biologizing kinship: Some paradoxes in Norwegian transnational adoption". In Rygvold, A.-L., M. Dalen and B. Sætersdal (eds) *Mine, Yours, Ours and Theirs*, Oslo: University of Oslo Press.

—— 2001 "Self-conscious kinship: Some contested values in Norwegian transnational adoption". In Franklin, S. and S. McKinnon (eds) *Relative Values*, Philadelphia: University of Pennsylvania Press.

—— 2002 "Community beyond place: Adoptive families in Norway". In Amit, V. (ed.) *Realizing Community*, London: Routledge.

—— 2003 "Kinning: the creation of life trajectories in transnational adoptive families" *Journal of the Royal Anthropological Institute* (incorporating *Man*) 9 (3): 465–484.

Ingvaldsen, S. 1996 "Rette foreldre og virkelige barn", unpublished M.Phil. thesis in History, University of Bergen.

Kalve, T. 1999 "Utenlandsadopterte barn sjelden i barnevernet" *Verdens Barn* 11 (1): 12–16.

Kats, M. 1990 *Adoptivbarent vokser opp*, Copenhagen: Fremad.

Øhren, A. 1995 *Consuelo: En adopsjons historie*, Oslo: Gyldendal.

Schneider, D. M. 1984 *A Critique of the Study of Kinship*, Ann Arbor: University of Michigan Press.

Sundby, J. and B. Schei 1996 "Infertility in a sample of women aged 40–45" *Acta Obstet. Gynecologica Scandinavia* 1996: 832–837.

Chapter 16

Partial to completeness

Gender, peril and agency in Australian adoption

Jon Telfer

In Australia, a range of practices associated with adoption provide contexts for persons to experience 'kinship' and 'family' in rich, but often contingent ways. Relations between persons that are shaped by adoption can be ambiguous, fragile or subject to transformation. While kinship in Australia is homologous in many respects with Western or 'Euro-American' kinship, some research has pointed to distinctive characteristics. Stivens has noted a predilection for geographical clustering by mothers, daughters and other female relatives in suburban Australia and a marked difference in the constitution of kinship and family for and by men and women. Women are 'the custodians of kinship' (1985: 31). Wearing's (1984) study of Sydney suburban mothers suggests that the ideology of motherhood is pervasive for Australian women, and plays a central role in their lives. Such cultural patterns raise questions about precisely how experiences of affiliation, exclusion and kinship might proceed through a myriad of circumstances that pivot on adoption.

Being partial

People whose lives have been profoundly affected by adoption may experience their senses of identity and kinship affiliation as incomplete or partial. Prospective adoptive parents, adoptees, relinquishing parents (the 'adoption triangle') and others experience relational 'gaps' in their identity and sense of belonging. For adoptees, the question of their individual identity can be problematic, since they may not have biogenetically founded, biographical social moorings. But the picture does not end there. Relinquishing parents can also be un-rounded or incomplete, stemming from the fact that their child, their 'issue', is absent (Weinreb and Konstam 1995). Not only is the child absent in bodily form, but information about the 'child' (including well into adulthood) is often missing. Relinquishing parents typically experience such incompleteness persistently (but not evenly) over time as a 'gap'. The incompleteness is often described by relinquishing mothers as being a traumatic, personally devastating and acerbic form of loss (Weinreb and Konstam 1995; Logan 1996). As one woman put it: 'there's this hole in you, right in here, that just never goes away.' Incompleteness is embodied, contained within, but at the same time it is constructed on the premise of relatedness, both in and by the individual.

Adoptive parents also typically experience and verbalise a sense of incompleteness in their lives prior to adoption. Very often, although not necessarily, this incompleteness or lived partiality emanates from infertility (see Albury 1999; Franklin 1997). My fieldwork in Adelaide[1] included individuals and couples who had adopted children, were in the process of adopting, or hoped to adopt a child. These included 'stranger' adoptions ('local' and 'intercountry') and step-parent adoptions. Some couples already had 'biological' children and wished to adopt from overseas as a humanitarian gesture. For other couples, the marriage was a second one, and with one or both partners bringing children to the marriage, the couple sought to adopt a child from overseas so as to produce a procreative effect to their marriage; to complete their union.

Mike and Chris have been married for sixteen years. Mike, a secondary school teacher and Chris, the manager of a child care centre, live in a southern suburb of Adelaide with their locally adopted son Andrew, aged four. The decisions to pursue adoption and the entire protracted journey to parenthood were marked by emotional stress, tension and uncertainty. Mike and Chris 'suffered in silence' for years during IVF treatment since they felt ambivalent about discussing their attempts at parenthood with their respective families. Breaking the news of adoption later rather than earlier, Mike and Chris's experience highlights the singularity of purpose needed to not merely survive the demands of the Quest, but to emerge as an intact couple. Chris describes how they came to pursue adoption:

we were married 16 years ago last December, and we'd been trying to have a child naturally for 11 or 12 years, we were unsuccessful, we went through the mill on the IVF program but we didn't tell a lot of people about that, you don't tell that to everyone . . . anyway, we put in our Expression of Interest, and we told not a lot of people, we thought we'd just go and find out . . . we, *or at least I*, thought 'IVF *will* work and we won't need adoption', . . . I basically got to the point where I said to myself 'if I can't have one of my own, I won't have children at all', I remember this very clearly because it was exactly when my sister moved into their new house and I told her exactly how I felt and she said 'don't be silly' . . . then in March 1988 we were put on the Prospective Adoptive Parents Register, . . . we had to complete the papers by July 89 . . . this is where the emotional bit fits in, Mike just goes with the flow, he doesn't have to make the decisions, I make them . . . the question arises when to give up on IVF, . . . really our area is adoption now, I think . . . the miscarriage I had, without Andrew (adopted son) that would have been more devastating.

Chris's comment 'I make them' (decisions), while perhaps more direct than comments from other prospective adoptive parents, was by no means atypical amongst the ranks of couples seeking to achieve (or extend) experiences of parenthood through adoption.[2] This tendency raises a number of questions, not only concerning momentous decisions by adopters, but also about the predicaments of others who seek transformations of identity through practices associated with adoption, such as birth parents and adoptees. How do couples and individuals seek to make themselves (and others) whole, through various 'proactive' or 'creative' endeavours that characterise adoption? What kinds of experiences are entailed in these strenuous endeavours? What kinds of agency are exerted in the process?

Cohen has questioned whether the dynamics of personal identity are fixed and certain, arguing instead for a rich and problematic version of agency that is active and creative, to be exercised by the 'multidimensional self' (1994: 7, 115). Strathern notes similarly: 'all human agents are inventors (creators) in a modern, Euro-American sense: the person is substance plus the animating self-inventiveness of agency, a combination of distinct elements' (1996: 531). By embarking on quests for whole identities, people render visible the contours and limitations of agency itself in a specific context – not only in relation to the individual, but also in relation to the marital couple as a cultural unit. In adoption, Quests for wholeness occur within a field that is politicised and contested as much as it is removed from the public gaze, intensifying and problematising the experience for those concerned. The predicaments of individuals and couples within this politicised field tend to be discussed in various adoption organisations within a rhetoric of 'rights', usually contextualised within naturalised understandings of the (oppositionally constituted) adoption triangle. The continuously altering configuration of forces simultaneously sharpens senses of jeopardy and hope for any given 'agent' at any given time. Rights are not only critically implicated in states of incompleteness, but also in processes of imagining, dreaming and fearing which imbue the anticipation of completeness.

Quests for wholeness

Agents' predicaments can be addressed by examining two kinds of epic journeys or 'Quests' (Natanson 1970), which people undertake in order to alter the incompleteness and so transform, preserve or reappraise their own identity. One man characterised his search (which had filled some five years) as a 'pilgrimage', articulating its importance in his life and the single-mindedness with which it had been pursued; a description reminiscent of Turner's analysis of pilgrimage as 'lifelong drama of salvation or damnation, hinging on individual choice' (1979: 129).

Laura is a twenty-five-year-old adoptee who works as a receptionist in a real estate agent office and lives alone. She grew up knowing she was adopted, with an adopted brother four years her junior. Although Laura's sense of identity was 'OK on the surface', she felt a particularly keen sense of aloneness and emptiness as she grew up. Laura was prompted to search immediately after her twenty-fourth birthday because turning twenty-four was instrumental in her realisation that 'I wasn't a kid any more; that's how old my mother was when she had me'. Laura's Quest was facilitated by initial advice from an adoption support group that Laura contacted through the telephone book, after applying for and receiving her identifying information. Having been provided with some advice about practical aspects of searching the Electoral Rolls, Laura proceeded with the search, with an immediate, positive outcome:

> When I started searching, I was basically looking for my mother but was on the lookout for *anyone* I was related to; I knew it was likely my mother would hold the answers . . . my father was described, but not named[3] in the identifying information . . . I found my mother in Gosford [New South Wales] . . . talking to my mother on the phone the first time it was really scary, our first conversation lasted for three and a half hours, she said to me 'do you have any questions?' and I said 'who's my father?' and she said 'Matt, my husband, do you want to speak to him?' and I said 'yes' and when he came on the phone he said 'you sound delightful' . . . then I found out I have two full sisters and three full brothers, I really hit the jackpot . . . my mum and dad and my adoptive brother are resentful of me finding my other family, they think I should have just left it alone . . . it's really weird having Jill and Matt and my brothers and sisters, when

I was in Gosford with them someone had dropped in and as they left they told my sister they thought I was a visitor and Rachel (biological sister) and I talked about this afterwards and we said exactly the same thing, 'no, not a visitor, like someone I've known before who's been away and come back'.

Laura's experience illustrates elements of Turner's social drama; the emptiness of the breach in identity, the emerging plot over whether and when to search, the prospect of reintegration of identity following a successful search and the performative nature of the journey-as-process which the agents undertook (1987). Laura's narration is also reminiscent of Turner's regard for 'what Dilthey calls the "riddle of life" . . . the mysteries and paradoxes that surround the great crises of birth, mating and death . . . and its perils' (Turner 1987: 85).

Yet Laura's experience also highlights the importance of concentrating on the quality of people's *experience*. Laura's quest for consanguines is a profoundly risky undertaking in terms of result, outcome and identity – not only of the searcher, but also of the searched and significant others. Here I follow Turner's association between jeopardy or 'peril' and human experience (Turner 1982). The perilous nature of the epic journeys undertaken by people whose lives are affected by adoption is acute and saturates the entire field. The presence of jeopardy throughout these epic journeys is signalled by the distinct possibility that 'completeness' might never arrive. The perilous cast of the Quest sharpens the problematic quality of agency in this setting, at the same time as it impels agents as 'architects of action' to creative authorial pursuits (Cohen 1994: 21). In striving for completeness, people struggle, suffer and risk not only their own redemption, but the redemption or completeness of others as well. That no guarantee applies to sought identities and affiliations renders peoples' experiences vivid, extraordinarily taxing and emotionally charged. Epic Quests in adoption constitute sites for imagining the culmination of life-long dreams, fantasies and the manifestation of hope amidst jeopardy. Inescapably, Quests also demand confrontations with the possibility of failure and the acuity of unremitting incompleteness and partiality.

A feminised field

Many facets of fieldwork underlined the cultural weight of the feminine in realms of kinship and identity. One example concerns Brenda and Bob, now in their early forties. They have two adopted children from the

Philippines, a boy (nine) and a girl (seven), thought to be biological siblings. Brenda and Bob pursued adoption after 'many years of trying to have children' and 'nineteen failed attempts on IVF'. Brenda told me how Bob was 'supportive during all those years on IVF' but that he 'didn't really feel involved . . . when we put the adoption application in, Bob told me '"*now* I feel involved!"'

During one evening conversation Brenda, Bob, and their children were discussing their adoption experiences and 'going through the photo books' with me in their lounge. After the children had gone to bed, Bob explained to me that he 'didn't mind' which country the child came from; 'when we were filling in the forms I said to Brenda "just put down *anything*, boy, girl, twins, siblings, Martians, *anything*".' In the course of conversation they described the process of meeting their children for the first time: (Bob) 'the social worker said, as we were just standing there waiting (at the orphanage) "here they come" and it was a bit awkward, you don't know what to do, so we were just casual, it wasn't emotional or anything.' Brenda went into the kitchen for a few minutes to make coffee. Bob told me in a lowered voice that as I would 'know', while adoption is important to both members of the couple, it's 'really important for the woman . . . it's different for them than it is for us'.[4]

Upon her return Brenda described the surprise and the 'utter bliss' of becoming an adoptive mother;

> (at the orphanage, expecting first of a series of visits with children) and they put these papers in front of us and said 'sign here' and so I said 'why am I signing these?' and she said 'take children today' . . . I was in a state of shock, but once I got them, they were ours . . . I remember thinking 'I don't know if I'm ready for this!', then I saw them walking towards me and that was it . . . that first day I couldn't eat, I was too nervous . . . later that day, in the hotel room, the kids were asleep and we had a beer and I said to Bob 'let anyone try and get them off me now, they're *my* children'. I remember thinking 'this is it, there's no going back now.'

It is Brenda who is foregrounded as both the prime mover and the most immediate beneficiary of the Quest. Indeed, matricentricity has been a prominent factor in Brenda and Bob's pursuit, attainment and experience of parenthood. They regard this state of affairs as entirely 'natural'. Matricentricity has been crucial in the transformation of their personal and collective identities from an 'infertile couple' to 'adoptive parents'. Further, matricentricity has been pivotal in the articulation of agency; the 'authorial' aspects of selfhood for this couple are hinged upon a particularly feminine authorial self.

The anthropological literature addresses matrifocality (rather than matricentricity), but it is rendered conceptually as a consequence of absent patrifocality. In the process, matrifocality is systematically (if inadvertently) theorised as a state of marked incompleteness. It is perhaps ironic that Firth noted in 1956 of the 'English kinship system' that 'there is in the ordinary social field a strong matrilineal bias with particular emotional significance' (1956: 18).

The field of adoption is equally describable as female-centred, female-dominated and female-oriented. The feminised cast of the field is evidenced in a paradox. While relinquishing mothers are often considered to be the agents most needing or desiring to search for their 'child', they are typically understood to be extremely reluctant to do so, through fear of disrupting a harmonious (adoptive) family environment. Naturalised maternal love simultaneously explains the pain of an absence and a sacrificial reluctance to act. Further, the vast majority of workers in this field, both paid and voluntary, are women. Support group activities are arranged, conducted and attended by more women than men. Voluntary and paid workers 'know' that women are far more active and involved in any kind of adoption-associated activity. Women were assumed to 'know' more about many aspects of adoption and kinship, to be generally more competent at tasks and events centring on adoption and kinship, and to be 'naturally' more interested in such matters, with men assuming a subsidiary or supportive role in the Quest. While persistent, this pattern was also largely unrecognised by those involved.

Not only does this perspective on the data problematise 'egalitarian individualism' as a uniform, homogenising gloss on Australian sociality (B. Kapferer 1988; J. Kapferer 1996), it also helps explain the persistent, accentuated flavours of contemporary popular Australian literature concerning masculinities and fatherhood, which pivot, above all else, upon the need for men as partners, husbands and fathers to be '*supportive*'; putative remedies to 'the flight of men from commitment' (Silva 1996: 31). Urgings to involvement, encouragements to take on responsibility, calls for consistency are all predicated upon the generalised notion that men lack, or at least minimally express, such qualities to begin with, with the potential or promise, through enhanced relatedness, to make a man 'whole'.

Experiencing the feminised field: step-parent adoptions

Step-parent adoptions not only feature matricentricity, but are an exemplar[5] of it. There are several reasons for this. The domain of step-parent adoptions constitutes a sphere of activity which is, in practical terms, separated from the complex web of associations, allegiances and discord which typifies much of the field. Step-parent adoptions are assessed and administered as a different enterprise from 'stranger' adoptions. Any discernible trend towards patricentricity or matricentricity in step-parent adoptions thus provides a useful counterpoint to the data obtained from the rest of the field. Step-parent adoptions also present a scenario in which one parent is the biological and social parent of the children, with a spouse seeking to adopt the children so as to become their legal and social parent (Webber 1991). The social and the biological are therefore positioned in unusual yet visible postures.

In step-parent adoptions, men seek to adopt the children of the women they have married, so that several versions of completeness ensue for different agents. Yet the dynamics infusing social paternity here do not pertain to social maternity. A social worker who has worked in the area for some years was hard pressed to remember the last time a woman sought to adopt the children of the man she had married. In addition to this plain bias, two other aspects of step-parent adoption are important; the surrendering of paternity and the nuances of the negotiations which occur between mother, children and step-father.

In order for a step-parent adoption to proceed, the biological father is required to sign a document waiving his paternity in full. He becomes, literally, an ex-father. Negotiations towards the signing of this document are frequently undertaken by the woman who has remarried, thus placing her in a mediating position between her children and their biological father. While some children seem to maintain or later establish contact with their 'ex-father', the genitor–child relationship is constructed along altogether different axes from the genetrix–child relationship. The act of paternal capitulation in step-parent adoptions bears a striking resemblance, at least on the face of it, to the act of relinquishment in stranger adoptions when a mother agrees to the adoption of her child; after all, both constitute 'irrevocably transferring legal parentage' (Murch *et al.* 1993: 248). Yet with relinquishing mothers, the act of relinquishment does not create, for mother or child, the social or legal category *or* epithet 'ex-mother'. Backett (1982) contrasts discretionary social fathering with non-negotiable responsibilities of social mothering. Step-parent adoptions corroborate such patterns, but simultaneously highlight biogenetic connections between genitor and offspring as ultimately extinguishable. Shared substance between genitor and offspring on one hand and between genetrix and offspring on the other hand is not homogeneous, but gendered through various social practices (Uhlmann 2000).

Participants' accounts of how step-parent adoptions unfolded typically positioned the mother as the mediator, negotiator and, at times, instigator of step-parent adoptions. This pattern was especially notable, although not restricted to, households featuring boys.[6] One step-father described the process of negotiating his relationship with his wife's sons as follows:

> well, I was very shy and it was very like proposing marriage . . . I wanted to find out how they felt about it . . . we'd talked about it for five years, . . . it was very rough on the kids when they lost their natural father . . . and then we formed a relationship . . . I guess you could say with me and the boys there was a long engagement!

The parallel, perceived by participants and otherwise, between adoption and marriage[7] is significant; indeed, experienced agents will sometimes speak of adoption as a 'marriage of needs'. Adoption and marriage are also the two social vehicles in this cultural context for the routine changing of name; surname, given name, or a complete change of name.

Completeness and knowledge

Knowledge is produced, sought and restricted in this field in very particular, diverse ways. The production and management of knowledge are significant factors for potential adopters, but the locus of control over such knowledge often lies outside the individual or couple; namely, with social workers, counsellors or voluntary support group workers. Such counsellors are often perceived to exercise control over information that may ultimately determine whether agents achieved completeness or remained forever incomplete.[8]

Adoptees and birth mothers seeking consanguines often approach adoption-related organisations for assistance. These organisations are likely to strongly recommend that an intermediary be utilised to contact the other person. While this is appealing to the searcher since it appears to increase the chances of 'success', it involves the perilous act of placing control over one's destiny in the hands of another. The person so recommending and the person recommended are usually, although not invariably, women. The imperative of an intermediary's involvement is typically explained in terms of the acute delicacy of the crucial initial approach to the sought relative.

The searching process is part of a social drama for those who initiate the search. The search often also triggers a position in the social drama for the person sought, typically the biological mother. The person 'found' is quickly presented with a breach (of silence, of secrecy) which may occasion joy or despair, a crisis (of how to respond), a redress (negotiated terms of any contact) and reintegration (either an ongoing relationship or a resumption of an altered *status quo*) or schism.

Knowledge and completeness are also closely connected in the compulsory 'education' activities which prospective adoptive parents must participate in, both 'pre' and 'post' placement of the child (Berkowska and Migaszewska-Majewicz 1991). By and large, women participated actively in parent education groups, with men's attentiveness more discretionary. For the women attending these groups, (adoptive) motherhood was an emotionally intense, vital experience, of which imagined motherhood was but a part. Imagined (adoptive) fatherhood was not as compelling or engaging for most of the men concerned. An important feature of the courses is the gradual accumulation of knowledge about parenting which directly accompanies the approach in time of placement of a child, mediated and enabled by the respective adoption agency that is embodied in the female educator/facilitator.

The allocation of a child to a couple critically links knowledge to completeness, but along a different relational axis from 'education groups'. Typically, with intercountry adoptions, a report of several pages arrives at the adoption agency with a photograph of the child. The couple is advised by phone that they 'have had an allocation' and usually go to the adoption agency office that day or the next to be handed the report and the photograph. This point of allocation is one of great emotional import. What is of most relevance here is the coincidence between knowledge (about the child to become the couple's adoptive child) and completeness. Many couples, especially the adoptive mother, experience and relate a profound awareness of 'the gap having been filled', of having become complete at this precise point. Completeness occurs not with the corporeal presence of a child, but with information and a photograph of a child. Completeness arrives, in a sense, without the presence of a body (Telfer 2000).

In South Australia, adoptees and relinquishing parents can apply for and receive 'identifying information' about themselves or the child they relinquished once the child attains eighteen, provided there is no 'veto' in place. Legislative requirements include that the adoptee or relinquisher 'be counselled' prior to receipt of the information by a social worker from the Family Information Service. Relinquishing mothers and adoptees attending the Family Information Service often did so without the knowledge of significant others in their life. The counselling associated with the receipt of identifying information is frequently effected via a half-day group counselling session involving a (female) social worker and approximately six participants (McPhee 1993). During the first half of the session, the social worker would explain the 'rights' of different parties, the advisability of using a mediator in searching and (especially) in negotiating 'contact', and the likely personal and emotional impact of the information they were about to receive.

These sessions constitute dramatic performances; by participating in such sessions and helping to constitute such processes, people were subjecting themselves to extraordinarily perilous forces. For adoptees, such peril could entail the knowledge that they had been conceived as a result of a rape or an incestuous relationship. But, as one adoptee advised, however perilous this course is, it is less perilous than living in ignorance, 'you know, *not* knowing is much worse than *knowing*'. For relinquishing mothers, such peril entails entertaining the dreaded possibility that their child had experienced a life of misery at the hands of the adoptive parents. Such horrific discoveries were often imagined by participants, and their fears were occasionally intensified by comments by workers or experienced voluntary co-ordinators that 'such things do happen'. What was imagined by one had actually been experienced by others.

After a coffee break, which was usually saturated with an atmosphere of anticipation, silence and occasional snippets of conversation, the social worker would announce that she was about to 'hand out the brown envelopes'. She would emphasise in solemn tones that these envelopes had been sealed and stored in a public record office since the day of the person's adoption in court 'all those years ago'. The social worker would then proceed around the circle formed by the seating arrangement. This meant that each could all see the reactions of the others. The movements and the passage of the social worker were deliberate, slow and momentous. Clearly, the contents of each envelope were awesome, either to be treasured or feared. The social worker would check the name of each person before carefully handing the brown envelope to them. Some sat and simply stared at the envelope on their lap. Some cried. Others began tearing the envelope open as soon as they had grasped it. A myriad of actions and reactions followed. Some spontaneously declared their 'origins', either in terms of 'original' name, ethnicity or nationality of their birth mother, or 'wow, my father's name is here too!' and 'I've got a sister!' One woman in her mid-twenties sat very still, her face wet with tears, smiling. She looked at the social worker and said quietly 'I've got a mother'.

Agents related a pronounced sense of closure from receiving the identifying information. While for some this sense of closure was a gratifying, peaceful sensation, for others it was unsettling or disturbing, but no less a closure because of it. Completeness is thus resonant with closure as well as knowledge. The ceremonious receipt of identifying information had the same manner of effecting completeness both in relation to receiving information about *oneself* and in relation to receiving information about *another*, one's relinquished child. One entails knowledge from the past in order to bring completeness to the present and perhaps the future. The other entails knowledge from the present to bring a sense of completeness to the past and perhaps the future. The feminised quality of the field is marked here. Searchers, and the custodians and conveyors of the precious information, are primarily women. Completeness for adoptees hinges upon knowledge concerning, first and foremost, the biological mother. Completeness for relinquishing 'parents' almost invariably implies a quest by relinquishing mothers. A sharper indication of a feminised field is difficult to imagine.

However, in some situations incompleteness/completeness and knowledge also interrelate in ways which constitute the inverse of the above examples. Here an existing or assumed aura of completeness is fractured and replaced by a penetrating, sudden sense of incompleteness. Two types of revelation occur; some people make the shocking discovery in adulthood that they are adopted and some women are exposed as having borne and relinquished a child long ago. Here we find, in Turner's terms, 'experiences that erupt from or disrupt routinised, repetitive behaviour begin with shocks of pain or pleasure' (Turner 1986: 35). The ability of knowledge acquisition to undo a state of completeness indicates the potency of the alliance between knowledge and completeness as much as its inverse. Many adoptees who discover their adoptive status in adulthood feel most angry, confused or hurt not simply by the fact of their adoption, but by the deceit attributed to their adoptive parents, most especially to their adoptive mother. Where adoptive parents or adoptees fear an unwanted approach by the relinquishing mother, knowledge fragments completeness through the anticipation of feminised action. Here the possession of knowledge (information about the adoptee and the adoptive family) by the relinquishing mother is framed as potentially dangerous, unpredictable and perilous by some adoptive parents.

The same process occurs (and is feared) in the case of an adoptee approaching her or his biological mother who has kept secret the birth of her child from her spouse and other children. Such approaches may come from sons or daughters, but given the perception that women are more likely to search for their biological mothers than men, the agent who brings about a disaggregation of completeness is typified as female. The spouse and other children of a relinquishing mother so approached would, of course, be likely to have had their sense of completeness shattered not only by the adoptee but by the deceit of the mother as well.

The hope of completeness for the relinquishing mother is framed as the anticipated fracture of completeness for the adoptive parents or the adoptee. The fear of such schism in a state of completeness arises primarily from two apprehensions. The first is a generalised distrust and uneasiness, so that irrespective of the personal qualities or circumstances of the relinquishing mother, any intrusion by her is feared because of the disruption she would bring. The (anonymous) relinquishing mother, cast as the custodian of secret, dangerous knowledge, becomes an artifice of disaggregation. Such typifications of biological fathers are rare. It is the biological *mother* who constitutes the focus of distress and foreboding.

Conclusion

The experience of adoption in Australia repeatedly signals the pivotal quality of the feminine in personal and marital quests for senses of wholeness. As well as risking unremitting incompleteness, those who pursue longed for realms of wholeness render the contours, capacity and limitations of human agency visible. In the process of pursuing such quests, peoples' experiences also remind us of the fragilities and complexities that imbue orientations to and understandings of kin affiliation and identity. For those whose lives have been profoundly affected by adoption in this setting, the creativity inherent in self-authorisation is constituted as much by peril as it is by the anticipation of closure.

Notes

1   From February 1994 to May 1995, encompassing a variety of adoption-oriented organisations, networks and bureaucratic processes.
2   This aspect of the couple's experience is consistent with Franklin's analysis of infertility treatment in Britain, which concerns couples but which is primarily focused on the experiences of women (1997).
3   It is common for adoptees receiving their identifying information to find that their biological father is not named on the original birth certificate. For many,

access to and through the biological mother is the only avenue to information concerning the identity of the biological father.

4   In apparent contrast with the adoption of Chinese girls into the USA, where 'decisions to adopt are just as likely to involve men as women, and many of the practices and attitudes I will be discussing are equally applicable to American men as women' (Riley 1997: 93).

5   Kristeva's observation that 'Christ, the Son of man, when all is said and done, is "human" only through his mother' points to what might be taken as the *sine qua non* of matricentricity (1997: 304).

6   The positioning of wife-mother as mediating between husband-father and children in Australian households has been identified as a significant pattern elsewhere (Ernst 1990).

7   In both adoption and marriage, one person changes their name. While in divorce, the woman often reverts to her 'maiden name', thus reversing the name change (Simpson 1994: 837). Both divorce and the receipt of identifying information involve a 'return' to aspects of the past which have purchase in the future; the nominal dimensions of both divorce and identifying information frequently pivot on biogenetic 'origins', thus underlining the profoundly *social* cast of both marriage and adoption.

8   A position which is reminiscent of Bourdieu's observation that 'the family is indeed a fiction, a social artifact, an illusion in the most ordinary sense of the word, but a "well-founded illusion," because, being produced and reproduced with the guarantee of the state, it receives from the state at every moment the means to exist and persist' (1998: 73).

References

Albury, R. M. 1999. *The Politics of Reproduction*. St Leonards, New South Wales: Allen & Unwin.

Backett, K. C. 1982. *Mothers and Fathers*. New York: St Martin's Press.

Berkowska, M. and J. Migaszewska-Majewicz 1991. Preadoption parent education. In *Adoption: International Perspectives* (ed.) E. Hibbs. Connecticut: International Universities Press.

Bourdieu, P. 1998. *Practical Reason*. Cambridge: Cambridge University Press.

Cohen, A. P. 1994. *Self Consciousness*. London: Routledge.

Ernst, T. 1990. Mates, wives and children. *Social Analysis* 27: 110–118.

Firth, R. 1956. Introduction. In *Two Studies of Kinship in London* (ed.) R. Firth. London: Athlone Press.

Franklin, S. 1997. *Embodied Progress*. London: Routledge.

Kapferer, B. 1988. *Legends of People, Myths of State*. Washington: Smithsonian Institute Press.

Kapferer, J. 1996. *Being all Equal*. Oxford: Berg.

Kristeva, J. 1997. *Sabat mater*. In *Feminist Social Thought: A Reader* (ed.) D. T. Meyers. London: Routledge.

Logan, J. 1996. Birth mothers and their mental health: unchartered territory. *British Journal of Social Work* 26: 609–625.

McPhee, G. 1993. Exposing adoption myths: access to information about origins in Victoria. *Australian Journal of Social Issues* 28 (2): 142–157.

Murch, M., N. Lowe, M. Borkowski, R. Copner and K. Griew 1993. *Pathways to Adoption: Research Project*. Bristol: Socio-Legal Centre for Family Studies, University of Bristol.

Natanson, M. 1970. *The Journeying Self.* Manila: Addison-Wesley.

Riley, N. E. 1997. American adoptions of Chinese girls: the socio-political matrices of individual decisions. *Women's Studies International Forum* 20 (1): 87–102.

Silva, E. B. 1996. The transformation of mothering. In *Good Enough Mothering? Feminist Perspectives on Lone Motherhood* (ed.) E. B. Silva. London: Routledge.

Simpson, B. 1994. Bringing the 'unclear' nuclear family into focus: divorce and re-marriage in contemporary Britain. *Man* 29 (4): 831–851.

Stivens, M. 1985. The private life of the extended family: family, kinship and class in a middle class suburb of Sydney. In *Australian Ways* (ed.) L. Manderson. Sydney: Allen & Unwin.

Strathern, M. 1996. Cutting the network. *Journal of the Royal Anthropological Institute* 2: 517–535.

Telfer, J. R. 2000. Relationships with no body? – 'Adoption' photographs, intuition and emotion. *Social Analysis* 43 (3): 144–158.

Turner, V. W. 1979. *Process, Performance and Pilgrimage*. New Delhi: Concept Publishing Company.

—— 1982. Dramatic ritual/ritual drama: performance and reflexive anthropology. In *A Crack in the Mirror* (ed.) J. Ruby. Philadelphia: University of Pennsylvania Press.

—— 1986. Dewey, Dilthey, and drama: an essay in the anthropology of experience. In *The Anthropology of Experience* (eds) V. W. Turner and E. M. Bruner. Chicago: University of Illinois Press.

—— 1987. *The Anthropology of Performance*. New York: PAJ Publications.

Uhlmann, A. 2000. Incorporating masculine domination: theoretical and ethnographic elaborations. *Social Analysis* 44 (1): 142–161.

Wearing, B. M. 1984. *The Ideology of Motherhood*. Sydney: George Allen & Unwin.

Webber, R. 1991. Life in step-families: conceptions and misconceptions. In *Images of Australian Families* (ed.) K. Funder. Melbourne: Longman Cheshire Australian Institute of Family Studies.

Weinreb, M. and V. Konstam 1995. Birthmothers: silent relationships. *Affilia* 10 (3): 315–327.

Chapter 17

Adoption
A cure for (too) many ills?

Peter Selman

Introduction

In Britain and the United States today, adoption is seen as a service for children and there are calls in both countries for an increase in the number of adoptions to provide families for cared-for children. But this ignores two important features of legal adoption in the two countries:

- that over its brief history legal adoption has come to serve a number of very different goals and it should not be assumed that all are equally successful
- that, whatever the rhetoric, adoption affects all three members of the 'adoption triangle' and benefits for one may be at the expense of the others.

This chapter looks at changes in legal adoption in Western countries over the past fifty years and considers the argument that it has been seen as a cure for (too) many ills. I shall be starting from a consideration of patterns in Britain and the United States, but shall refer wherever possible to other European countries and also to states of origin in relation to intercountry adoption. I also look at a range of personal and social problems which adoption has been seen as resolving:

- involuntary childlessness
- children without parents – the orphan
- the 'shame' of illegitimate birth
- custody issues in reconstituted families
- the high number of children in public care
- problems of ethnic minorities
- consequences of war and famine
- overpopulation and poverty.

I also look at a number of ethical issues (cf. Freundlich 2000): is adoption now a 'market'? How do we justify adoption without parental consent? How do we stop abuse in intercountry adoption? Should birth mothers have a right to information about the children they relinquished?

Adoption as a cure for many ills

Legal adoption in the West today

In the introduction to her book, *The Character of Adoption*, Benet (1976: 11) wrote that: 'In the West today, adoption is accepted as the neat and sensible solution to the problem of two groups of people: childless couples and children without families.' A year later Tizard (1977: 1) wrote that:

> the essence of adoption is that a child not born to you is incorporated into your family as though he was your own. . . . The primary purpose of adoption is seen as the satisfaction of the desire of a married couple to rear a child: at the same time, a home is provided for a child whose natural parents are unable to rear it.

Both statements place the adoptive parents first and the adopted child second, with scant reference to the third party in the so-called adoption triangle – the birth parent(s), but it is assumed that their interests are also met by being relieved of the obligation to care for a child and the stigma traditionally associated with unmarried parenthood.

Benet stresses that what we usually mean by 'adoption' is the adoption of a non-related child by a childless couple through an agency or go-between. Yet by the 1970s the primary form of adoption in the UK had become step-parent adoption, where the needs being met included those of a step-parent, where the child was not 'without a family' and no third party was involved (Potts and Selman 1979).

The best interests of the child

Historically adoption has been marked by concerns about the need for an heir – or cementing social ties between families. What characterised 'Western' adoption was the ideology of the child's interests being central – and a tradition of total severance of previous links – and of secrecy. The focus on the best interests of the child is apparent in Britain in official reports from the 1950s. For instance, the 1954 Hurst Committee wrote that:

The primary object at which all should aim is the arrangement of adoption in the welfare of the child . . . adoption should, therefore, be approached as a means of finding the right home for the child rather than satisfying would-be adopters.

Eighteen years later the Houghton Committee stressed that: 'the long-term welfare of the child should be the first and paramount consideration', and in 1974 Raissa Page, deputy director of the Association of British Adoption Agencies (ABAA, the precursor of BAAF, British Agencies for Adoption and Fostering) argued that: 'no couple has the right to have a child, but every child has the right to have parents . . . our first duty must be to the child. We cannot accept responsibility for the problems of infertility' (*Sunday Times*, May 19, 1974)

Adoption was seen as offering more security than fostering in providing for children whose parents could (or would) not care for them (Goldstein *et al.* 1973). Such a belief continues to inform legislation and policy about adoption both nationally and internationally, but throughout this period there have been doubts raised about the primacy of the interests of the child in reality and a growing awareness that the rights of the birth parent(s) continue to be largely ignored.

In an influential book in the 1970s Mandell (1975: 28) argued that:

the main function of 'child welfare' adoption is to provide children for childless middle class and upper class couples . . . interest in finding homes for older, handicapped and coloured children has grown only because of a dramatic decline in the availability of young white babies to meet their needs.

Similar points are frequently made by critics of intercountry adoption as practised in America and Europe (Gailey 1999; Triseliotis 2000), despite the clear recognition in the UN Convention on the Rights of the Child (Article 21) that:

The primary aim of adoption is to provide for the child who cannot be cared for by his or her own parents with a permanent family. If that child cannot be . . . cared for in any suitable manner in the country of origin, intercountry adoption may be considered as an alternative.

Benet talks about the needs of 'children without families' and the purest form of adoption is arguably that of an orphan (or of an abandoned child whose parents cannot be found) – but this is something of a myth as in the West few adopted children are 'orphans', whether in domestic or intercountry adoption, and increasingly the wishes of birth parents are ignored or overruled (Ryburn 1994; Mason and Selman 1997). US statistics on intercountry adoption (which numbered over 20,000 in 2002) still refer to 'immigrant visas issued to orphans coming to the US' (http://state.gov/orphan_numbers.html), which Gailey (1999) argues may reassure American adoptive parents that there will be no threat from the child's birth family.

Involuntary childlessness: the best interests of the parents

In his book *The Hostage Seekers*, Michael Humphrey (1969: 130) writes that 'although adoption may be undertaken for a wide variety of reasons, reproductive failure is statistically the commonest and emotionally the most compelling'. In Britain in the 1960s involuntary childlessness was a characteristic of most adopters and social work departments usually required that prospective adopters undergo infertility tests before assessment. Adoption had become a cure for the ills of biological infertility, albeit one sought by only a minority of the involuntary childless. Prospective parents sought a child not because they wanted an heir but in order to enjoy all aspects of parenthood – hence the preference for a young baby and the 'rejection of difference' noted by Kirk (1964). Adoption was not of course a 'cure' for infertility – although there was a widespread belief that after adopting a couple were more likely to have a child of their own.

Adoption agencies sought in adopters 'ideal' parents, who had to be married and replicate natural parenthood in terms of age (not too old, but certainly not as young as the typical birth mother!). In 1952 Margaret Kornitzer noted that agencies would 'always inquire if the wife is working and will not place a baby with her unless she promises to give up her job' (cited in Mandell 1975: 85). Childlessness was seen as acceptable motivation where altruism or a choice not to have children of their own was not – unless the parents were prepared to take a child deemed unsuitable for childless adopters. As the availability of 'babies' declined and placement of special needs children increased, infertility ceased to be a prerequisite for adoption and even came to be seen as a disadvantage.

The growth of intercountry adoption renewed interest from the childless in the possibility of a baby, although the rejection of difference became more difficult to maintain, and the arrival of the new reproductive technologies and recourse to surrogacy encouraged a belief in 'the right to a child'. In most Western societies only a married couple may adopt jointly, but increasingly single parent adoptions are permitted – or even encouraged – enabling 'cohabiting' couples whether heterosexual or gay/lesbian to adopt, albeit at the cost of nominating one partner as the adoptive parent.

Birth mothers: the 'hidden dimension'

I have looked at examples of adoption as a cure for the ills of the child without a family and a couple without children. But what about the birth parent(s)? The language of 'orphans' and relinquishment make it easy to see why birth mothers have been what Hughes and Logan (1993) called 'the hidden dimension' in adoption. But it was also assumed that adoption is of benefit to the birth mother – in providing a socially acceptable means of shedding responsibility for the care of a child. In late Victorian England, 'adoption' was often an indirect form of infanticide as 'baby farmers' allowed their charges to die having received payment for taking them in.

Later in debates about legal adoption one finds a recurrent anxiety lest adoption be seen as the 'right' of the unmarried mother. To quote Kornitzer (1952: 46–47) again: 'The mother of an illegitimate child does not have the *right* to get it adopted. Adoption must not be seen as an easy means to get rid of the results of sin.' Such words seem strange a half century later, when such concerns have either lapsed or refocused on abortion as the 'easy way out' and adoption is encouraged by pro-Life groups.

A common characteristic of children adopted by non-relatives in the 1960s was that they were illegitimate, and approximately a quarter were placed for adoption with non-relatives, while a further proportion were adopted by their mother following marriage or re-marriage. Adoption was seen as resolving the child's status – as well as providing a secure home – and offering an escape from the stigma of unmarried parenthood for the mother. But within a decade the stigma had lifted and the alternative of legal abortion was available. The consequent decline in availability of babies for domestic adoption reflects social changes in West – but the issue remains in countries like South Korea, where single parenthood is unacceptable and 'illegitimate' children are offered for both domestic and intercountry adoption.

Before we see adoption as a successful cure for the ills of both child and mother in a birth outside marriage in the 1960s, we must recall the accumulating evidence that many birth mothers have regretted their decisions to relinquish, feeling that they were given no real choice, and that for some this has had a devastating impact on their mental health; and note that the undoubted 'success' of most non-relative adoptions has not removed the desire of most adoptees to learn more about their origins and increasingly to trace and meet with their birth relatives.

Changing patterns of adoption

The decline in adoption as a cure for illegitimacy can be seen in Table 17.1, which shows the pattern of adoption in England and Wales between 1959 and 1984, a period during which data were collected and presented in a standardised format by the General Register Office (and later the Office for Population Censuses and Surveys, OPCS).

The total number of adoptions peaked in 1968 at 24,831, of which 14,461 (58 per cent) involved the placement of 'illegitimate' children with non-parents. Sixteen years later the number had fallen by more than 40 per cent to 8,648, of which only 2,910 (34 per cent) were illegitimate children placed with strangers. By 1999 the total had fallen to 4,317, although since then numbers have been rising as a result of government encouragement of adoption of 'cared for' children. Similar declines in the number of white babies of unmarried mothers placed for adoption are found in most other countries, particularly the Netherlands and Scandinavia, where such placements are very rare and non-relative adoption is dominated by intercountry adoption.

Table 17.1 Children adopted in England and Wales under orders registered 1959–1984

Year	All	Legitimate/ Parent	Legitimate/ Non-parent	Illegitimate/ Parent	Illegitimate/ Non-parent
1959	14,109	1,541	1,289	3,105	7,887
1964	20,412	2,291	1,569	2,951	13,408
1968	24,831	4,038	1,390	4,479	14,461
1972	21,599	6,792	1,097	5,441	8,114
1975	21,299	9,262	806	5,305	5,774
1980	10,609	3,668	835	2,482	3,529
1983	9,029	2,872	1,000	2,067	3,008
1984	8,648	2,650	1,177	1,809	2,910

Sources: The Registrar General's Statistical Review of England and Wales for the years 1959 to 1973; adoptions in England and Wales 1975 to 1984 (OPCS Monitors FM3, 1976–1986); see also Selman (1976).

The overall decline is largely accounted for by the decline in placements of illegitimate children, despite the fact that the number of such children rose during this period. From 1959 to 1968 over one in five children born outside marriage were placed for adoption. By 1984 the proportion had fallen to one in twenty. The decline in adoption coincides with the liberalisation of abortion laws in 1967, but the increasing reluctance of unmarried mothers to relinquish their children also reflects greater support for single parents and an increase in non-marital cohabitation – a growing proportion of extra-marital pregnancies were planned or accepted and those which were unwanted tended to end in a termination. Some prospective adopters saw the Abortion Act as killing the babies that might have been theirs.

Custody issues in reconstituted families

The other significant feature of Table 17.1 is the rise in the adoption of *legitimate* children by their own parent, the so-called 'step-parent' adoptions, where one parent (usually the mother) adopts her own child together with a new partner following divorce and re-marriage. Here adoption is seen as a solution to the insecure position of the step-parent and a means of resolving issues of responsibility and custody.

In 1975 there were over 9,000 'step-parent' adoptions – amounting to 43 per cent of all adoptions – and a further 5,000 parental adoptions of illegitimate children. Over the next ten years the number declined but parental adoptions continued to account for about half of all adoptions. Most concern has arisen over parental adoption of 'legitimate' children in that it involved one birth parent becoming an adoptive parent and cut out the other from the life of their child. Such adoptions were rarely contested by the non-custodial parent (usually the father), but this did not mean that for many the decision was not a bitter blow (Clapton 2002).

The Houghton Committee saw both types of parental adoption as unnecessary and undesirable but stopped short of recommending a ban, preferring that courts should look first to alternatives, such as a variation of custody order by the court which granted the divorce, or 'custodianship' orders which could provide security for the children without excluding the other birth parent.

Thirty years later step-parent adoptions still account for about a half of all adoptions in Britain and the United States, suggesting that they remain an attractive solution for many re-married couples. They continue to be seen as unproblematic by most courts, although still subject to a requirement of welfare supervision. At first sight they seem to be closer to the patterns of relative adoption found in traditional societies, but the legal processes of adoption have meant that the arrangements are irreversible and usually involve excluding one birth parent. In England and Wales the Adoption and Children Act will now make it possible for a step-parent alone to adopt, ending the anomaly of a mother adopting her own birth child.

The high number of children in public care

From the 1970s – as the number of 'illegitimate' babies placed for adoption declined – there was growing interest in the USA and in Britain in the possibility of a 'permanent placement' for 'hard to place' (Goldstein *et al.* 1973) or 'special needs' (Avery 1997) children, including those with disabilities. It was argued that 'No child is unadoptable!' and the rejection of children for minor disabilities such as cleft palate, so common in the 1960s, became a thing of the past. Recent debates in both countries have focused on the continuing high number (and cost) of children in public care and former US president Bill Clinton and British Prime Minister Tony Blair have issued calls for a substantial increase in the adoption of 'looked after' children.

This has led to an increase in 'subsidised' adoption to widen the potential range of adopters but also to more contested adoptions where birth parent(s) do not consent. Both developments raise issues of the failure of 'preventive' child care policies – why money is available to support adopters with 'high cost' children but not birth parents and how we justify the overriding of parental rights in the absence of clear evidence of cruelty or neglect by birth parents? Permanency planning has not been a feature of adoption in mainland Europe where the needs of the childless are met rather by intercountry adoption and where there is strong opposition to any policies which might involve overriding the rights of birth parents (Warman and Roberts 2003) and a belief that more generous welfare support and more effective policies for prevention and rehabilitation make such steps unnecessary.

In England and Wales the adoption of older children in public care was encouraged by the 1975 Children Act in the aftermath of the Maria Colwell case (Howells 1974) and revelations of children drifting in care (Rowe and Lambert 1973). The Act gave rights to foster parents who had cared for a child for five or more years to apply for adoption, even if the birth parents and/or local authority were opposed. Permanency planning has been a feature of child care policy in Britain and the United

States for the last thirty years (Maluccio 1986), but the number of children adopted from care remained limited, despite the introduction of adoption allowances and an increase in the number of orders made without parental consent. More recently political leaders in both countries have made adoption a personal crusade, believing strongly that the number of adoptions can – and should – be increased and that the barrier has been bureaucratic inefficiency and a lack of will and commitment by local social services departments, rather than any shortage of suitable parents for even the most disturbed children. This is reflected in recent legislation such as the 1997 Adoption and Safe Families Act in the USA and the Adoption and Children Act 2002 in England and Wales.

It is in this area of domestic adoption today that the issues implicit in the title of this chapter are most apparent. Here surely we must see adoption at its best – an underutilised resource which reflects a truly child-centred approach approximating to the ideal of a true 'gift relationship'. Research on families adopting children with Down's Syndrome (Mason *et al.* 1999) has convinced me of the enormous potential of adoption for children with special needs who would have languished in institutions barely two decades ago. But we have also talked to mothers whose children have been taken away by the courts (Mason and Selman 1997) and found that many have paid a high a price for the new lives offered to their children.

Adoption breakdowns increase with age and the most needy children also have the lowest prospect of success. The costs of failure are great for both child (facing rejection) and parents (who may have entered the adoption with little real understanding of the difficulties involved). But the evidence of society's failure in respect of 'looked after children' is compelling. Commendable plans to rescue children from institutional care have led to renewed calls for a wider use of adoption as a cure for social ills – including the problem of teenage pregnancy which looms large on the agenda of both governments. However, any return to the pattern of the 1960s – even if Bill Clinton's 'second-chance homes' or Tony Blair's 'hostels' are less oppressive than the mother and baby homes of that decade – would demonstrate how little we have learned from history.

Problems of ethnic minorities

From the mid-1960s an increasing number of black and Native American children were adopted by white couples. Such children were overrepresented in public care but the reasons for this were often ignored in seeking substitute homes with white couples. By the mid-1970s a reaction had set in and transracial adoption became relatively rare – with stress placed on same-race placements as a priority. Arguments against transracial adoption stressed the importance of racial identity – but also the political issues of what was seen by some opponents as a form of 'genocide'. Special concern was raised over the adoption of children from minorities such as Native Americans in North America, Aboriginals in Australia and Gypsies (e.g. in Switzerland). One in three Native American children were being adopted by white Americans until such placements were made virtually impossible by the Indian Child Welfare Act of 1978. A similar pattern is observable in Britain, in contrast to mainland Europe where transracial adoption means intercountry adoption.

More recently there have been strong attacks on this opposition to transracial placements (Bartholet 1993; Dale 1987; Hayes 1993 and 1995; Simon and Altstein 1994) arguing that research evidence demonstrates the success of such placements and its rejection disadvantages black and mixed race children in the care systems of both countries. In the USA this has led to new legislation, notably the 1994 Multi-Ethnic Placement Act, which forbids the use of race alone as a criterion for rejecting adoptive parents. As a means of avoiding unnecessary drift of black children in institutions the case for limited use of transracial adoption is convincing – claims that it will lead to a more tolerant and less racist society are less so.

The growth of intercountry adoption: a cure for the ills of poor countries?

The last decade of the twentieth century saw a significant increase in the number of intercountry adoptions (Selman 2002). By 1998 the number of intercountry adoptions was approaching 35,000 – an increase of over 60 per cent on Kane's (1993) estimate for the late 1980s. The United States accounted for nearly half the total, but the incidence of intercountry adoption was higher in other countries such as Norway and Sweden (see Table 17.2). This number seems destined to grow further in the new millennium – the number of overseas adoptions in the United States alone has risen from 15,774 in 1998 to 20,099 in 2002.

In 1998 the largest number of children came from Russia, China and Vietnam, ahead of South Korea, which for so long dominated the world of intercountry adoption (see Table 17.3), but it is Russia and other countries of the former Communist Eastern Europe, such as Bulgaria and Romania, which have the highest *incidence*. Since 1998 the number

Table 17.2 Numbers and rates (per 1,000 births) of intercountry adoptions to selected receiving countries 1998 and 1989

Country	1998	Adoptions per 1,000 births	1989	Adoptions per 1,000 births
United States	15,774	4.2	7,948	2.0
France	3,777	5.3	2,383	3.0
Italy	2,263	4.4	2,332	3.8
Sweden	928	*10.8*	1,074	*9.4*
Germany	922	1.2	875	1.6
Netherlands	825	4.6	509	6.2
Switzerland	686	8.6	642	3.7
Norway	643	*11.8*	578	*11.0*
Denmark	624	9.9	468	*9.4*
Total for 9 countries	27,339		16,831	
Estimated total for 14 countries*	31,763		18,195	

Sources: Kane (1993); Lehland (2002); Selman (2002).

Note
* including Spain, Belgium, Canada, Australia and Finland – where Kane's data are incomplete.

of children adopted from the Ukraine has risen sharply, especially to Italy and the United States, where 1,246 children were granted visas in 2001.

This raises the issue of whether the rise reflects an increase in supply or demand and of the impact of intercountry adoption on the sending countries. Whose needs are served by the growing numbers – the childless couples of rich countries or children without a family? (Ngabonziza 1988; Triseliotis 2000).

The consequences of war and famine

Following the Second World War, many children orphaned by the war were adopted from Germany, Greece and Japan – mainly to the United States. Later a similar pattern developed in the aftermath of the Korean and Vietnam wars. Initially most adoptions from Korea involved not orphans but mixed race children rejected by Korean society, but today most are the children of young single mothers, who face social rejection

Table 17.3 Major sources of intercountry adoptions to selected Western countries, 1998 and 1980–1989

Country	No. of adoptions 1998[a]	Adoptions per 1,000 births 1998	Country	Annual adoptions 1980–1989[b]	Adoptions per 1,000 births 1989
Russia	5,064	5.4	South Korea	6,123	5.4
China	4,855	0.24	India	1,532	<0.1
Vietnam	2,375	1.4	Colombia	1,484	2.5
South Korea	2,294	3.4	Brazil	753	0.5
Colombia	1,162	1.2	Sri Lanka	682	1.0
Guatemala	1,143	2.9	Chile	524	3.0
India	1,048[c]	0.04	Philippines	517	0.4
Romania	891	4.4	Guatemala	224	0.8
Brazil	443[c]	0.13	Peru	220	0.9
Ethiopia	438	0.17	El Salvador	220	1.0

Notes
a Adoptions to 10 receiving countries (USA, France, Germany, Sweden, Netherlands, Norway, Denmark, Australia, UK and Ireland) = c. 75–80 per cent of intercountry adoptions. (see Selman 2002 for more details).
b Kane (1993): adoptions to 13 receiving countries.
c Total numbers recorded in official statistics for India and Brazil are significantly higher –1,406 and 637 respectively – due to omission of Italy and Spain from the 10 countries listed.

and shame and have no means of financial support and few are of mixed race. Intercountry adoption from Vietnam increased dramatically in the 1990s as a means of meeting the needs of poor or abandoned children, but there are reports of many abuses which led France to suspend adoptions from Vietnam, which had become the main source of children from overseas (Selman 1999). In both cases the 'ills' which intercounry adoption purports to cure have changed but the phenomenon continues in the face of the continuing high social and financial costs of maintaining rejected children and the sustained and rising demand for children by childless couples in richer countries.

The consequences of overpopulation

One of the justifications of intercountry adoption has been that it solves the 'Malthusian' problem of overpopulation in poor countries and meets the need for children by individuals in countries with sub-replacement fertility. But today a majority of children come from states of origin where

Table 17.4 Economic and demographic indicators for selected countries sending and receiving children for intercountry adoption, 1998

	Adoptions	Income	Fertility	Mortality
Countries of origin	Children sent for adoption to 10 countries	Per capita GNP (US$)	Total fertility rate	Infant mortality rate
Russia	5,064	2,680	1.3	21
China	4,855	860	1.8	38
Vietnam	2,375	310	2.6	31
Korea	2,294	10,550	1.7	5
India	1,406	370	3.1	69
Colombia	1,162	2,180	2.8	25
Guatemala	1,143	1,580	4.9	41
Romania	891	1,410	1.2	21
Receiving countries	Children adopted from abroad in 1998	Per capita GNP (US$)	Total fertility rate	Infant mortality rate
United States	15,774	29,080	2.0	7
France	3,777	26,200	1.7	5
Italy	2,263	20,170	1.2	6
Sweden	928	26,200	1.6	4
Germany	922	28,250	1.3	5
Netherlands	825	25,830	1.5	5
Switzerland	686	43,060	1.5	5
Norway	531	36,100	1.9	4

Source: Selman (2002).

the fertility level is also sub-replacement and population growth is slowing (see Table 17.4).

Furthermore, although intercountry adoption is clearly dominated by the movement of children from poorer countries to rich developed countries, those states of origin sending most children are not the poorest countries of the world nor those most evidently afflicted by famine or disease. Most such countries are now to be found in sub-Saharan Africa and of these countries only Ethiopia has featured as a major source of children.

A cure for other ills?

So why do countries which are not producing enough children to replace their population continue to send children to other countries – often, as in the case of Russia and other parts of the former Eastern Europe, in ever increasing numbers? The 1993 Hague Convention on the Protection of Children and Co-operation in respect of Intercountry Adoption sees intercountry adoption as a resource for individual children deprived of a normal family life and justified only where no substitute family can be found in the child's own country. In some countries the answer seems to lie in the characteristics of the children – so that virtually all adoptions from China involve baby girls abandoned in orphanages, largely as a consequence of the one-child policy and its impact on a society where son preference still exists.

But new issues arise with the awareness that intercountry adoption not only removes the cost of maintaining such children in institutions (which themselves have been a cause of much adverse publicity) but has also become a source of income (Duncan 2000) with prospective adopters from China paying $3,000 to the home from which the child is taken – a sum several times higher than the per capita GNP in the country! In some cases the prime beneficiaries of intercountry adoption are individuals involved in arranging adoptions and here we are witnessing a market in children (Freundlich 2000), in which both birth parents and adopters are exploited by intermediaries. However rare such cases may be, they show how essential it is to monitor intercountry adoption and restrict mediation arrangements to authorised agencies with high ethical standards. Yet there are still many children in institutions in poor countries, especially those with special needs, who desperately need a family and for some of these intercountry adoptions can offer new hope. However, we are also hearing the voices of adults who were adopted from abroad many years ago, articulating concerns about issues of identity.

Whatever views one may hold about the ethics of intercountry adoption, one thing remains clear – that it can at best provide help for some individual children, never a solution to wider issues of poverty. Even allowing for the increasing support which many agencies offer, through sponsorship or other funding, for those children not adopted, the amount of money spent by prospective parents in the process of overseas adoption would amount to a huge sum if invested in the improvement of child care services in the states of origin.

Summary and conclusion

The theme of this chapter has been the variety of 'justifications' of the practice of legal adoption in Britain and the USA. The earlier chapters in this volume show how narrow a view of adoption this is and the extent to which I may seem to reflect the Euro-American assumption that adoption is somehow less 'normal' as a family structure – in contrast to many of the societies considered in those chapters. I would rather characterise my position as similar to that of sociologist David Kirk in his seminal work *Shared Fate* (1964) where he articulated the importance of acknowledging – but not exaggerating – the difference between adoption and birth parenthood, and as sharing a concern that all members of the so-called 'adoption triangle' should be respected. My interest in adoption in Western countries today has increasingly been with the perspective of governments and policy-makers. I am aware of the lack of understanding by governments – and professionals – of the good will and motivation of adoptive parents, but also of the needs and rights of birth families.

Throughout its history, legal adoption in the UK and the United States has been marked by a fear of openness, seen initially in the sealing of birth records (which still continues in many states in America) and more recently by a reluctance to extend the right to information to birth relatives. But now we have a new development in which adoption has become a priority in both countries, a development which reflects the attraction of adoption as an assertion of family values, an acknowledgement of the limitations of state intervention and a means of reducing public costs, as well as the impact of effective lobbying by a number of organisations – from parents' groups to pro-Life supporters.

My use of the phrase '(too) many ills' arises from a belief that often the 'cure' has involved the creation of new ills; that legal adoption has sometimes been inappropriate and unnecessary and that great caution should be exercised before calling for increases in the number of adoptions – with an assumption that this is an indisputably good idea, opposed only by those who portray adoption as being 'anti-child, anti-woman, and anti-black, redistributing children from the poor to the middle class' (Morgan 1998).

Looking back over its brief history, we can see examples of this in the pressures brought on birth mothers to relinquish children in the 1950s and 1960s and the reluctance to allow adopted persons to gain information about their origins, even when they had reached adulthood. We have 'learned' from these lessons and would claim that adoption today is more open, acknowledges the rights of birth parents and adoptees and is more child-centred than ever before. And yet I fear that many politicians still see adoption as a cost-effective solution to all the problems of child neglect or abuse; that in thirty years time people will look back with horror at the extent of recourse to judicial overriding of parental consent and wonder how we could have failed to consider how adopted persons might feel when they discover that they were not given up by birth mothers who felt they had no choice and were doing the best for their child, but had been taken away by the state despite their mother's desire to keep them. We may also find that there are feelings about the failure of the world community to address the problems of poverty and inequality that lie behind much intercountry adoption and at the slow progress towards eliminating abuses, while affording more support to the use of incountry adoption and fostering to prevent the need for children to spend a lifetime in institutional care.

References

Avery, R. (ed.) (1997) *Adoption Policy and Special Needs Children*, Westport, CT: Auburn House.

Bartholet, M. (1993) *Family Bonds*, Boston: Houghton Mifflin.

Benet, M. K. (1976) *The Character of Adoption*, London: Jonathan Cape.

Clapton, G. (2002) *Birth Fathers and their Adoption Experience*, London: Jessica Kingsley.

Dale, D. (1987) *Denying Homes to Black Children*, London: Social Affairs Unit Research Report 6.

Duncan, W. (2000) 'The Hague Convention on the protection of children and co-operation in respect of inter-country adoption; its birth and prospects', in P. Selman (ed.) *Intercountry Adoption*. London: BAAF.

Freundlich, M. (2000) *Adoption and Ethics*, Washington, DC: Child Welfare League of America.

Gailey, C. (1999) 'Seeking "Baby Right": race, class and gender in US international adoption', in A. Rygvold, M. Dalen and B. Sætersdal (eds) *Mine, Yours, Ours and Theirs*, Oslo: University of Oslo Press.

Goldstein, J., Freud A., and Solnit, A. (1973) *Beyond the Best Interests of the Child*, New York: Free Press.

Hayes, P. (1993) 'Transracial adoption: politics and ideology', *Child Welfare*, 72(3)

Hayes, P. (1995) 'The ideological attack on transracial adoption in the USA and Britain', *International Journal of Law and the Family*, 9: 1–22.

Howells, J. (1974) *Remember Maria*, London: Butterworth.

Hughes, B. and Logan, J. (1993) *Birth Parents*, Manchester: University of Manchester, Department of Social Policy and Social Work.

Humphrey, M. (1969) *The Hostage Seekers: A Study of Childless and Adoptive Couples*, London: Longman.

Kane, S. (1993) 'The movement of children for international adoption: an epidemiological perspective', *The Social Science Journal*, 30(4): 323–339.

Kirk, H. D. (1964) *Shared Fate*, New York: Free Press.

Kornitzer, M. (1952) *Child Adoption in the Modern World*, London: Putnam.

Lehland, K. (2002) *Crude Adoption Rates for Receiving Countries*, Olso: Adopsjonsforum.

Maluccio, A. (1986) *Permanency Planning for Children*, London: Tavistock.

Mandell, B. R. (1975) *Where are the Children?* Lexington, MA: Lexington Books.

Mason, K. and Selman, P. (1997) 'Birth parents' experiences of contested adoptions', *Adoption and Fostering*, 21(1): 21–28.

Mason, K., Selman, P. and Hughes, M. (1999) 'Permanency planning for children with Down's Syndrome', *Adoption and Fostering*, 23(1): 21–28.

Morgan, P. (1998) *Adoption and the Care of Children*, London: Institute for Economic Affairs.

Ngabonziza, D. (1988) 'Inter-country adoption: in whose best interest', *Adoption and Fostering*, 12(1).

Potts, M. and Selman, P. (1979) *Society and Fertility*, Plymouth: Macdonald & Evans.

Rowe, J. and Lambert, L. (1973) *Children who Wait*, London: BAAF.

Ryburn, M. (1994) *Contested Adoptions*, Aldershot: Arena.

Selman, P. (1976) 'Patterns of adoption in England and Wales since 1959', *Social Work Today*, 7(7): 194–197.

Selman, P. (1999) 'The demography of intercountry adoption', in A. Ryvgold, M. Dalen and B. Sætersdal (eds) *Mine, Yours, Ours and Theirs*, Olso: University of Oslo Press.

Selman, P. (2002) 'Intercountry adoption in the new millennium; the "quiet migration" revisited', *Population Policy and Research Review* 21(3): 205–225.

Simon, R. J. and Altstein, H. (1994) *The Case for Transracial Adoption*, New York: American University Press.

Tizard, B. (1977) *Adoption*, London: Open Books.

Triseliotis, J. (2000) 'Intercountry adoption: global trade or global gift', *Adoption and Fostering*, 24(2): 45–54.

Warman, A. and Roberts, C. (2003) *Adoption and Looked After Children*, Oxford: Centre for Family Law and Policy.

Government reports

Report of the Committee of Inquiry into the Care and Supervision Provided in Relation to Maria Colwell, London: HMSO, 1974.

Report of Departmental Committee on the Adoption of Children (Hurst Committee), London: HMSO, 1954, Cmnd 9258.

Report of Departmental Committee on the Adoption of Children (Houghton Committee), London: HMSO, 1972 , Cmnd 5107.

Index

Index 275

Index

275